THE NATIONAL INSTITUTE OF
ECONOMIC AND SOCIAL RESEARCH

Economic and Social Studies

XX

A STUDY OF UNITED KINGDOM IMPORTS

The National Institute of Economic and Social Research is an independent, non-profit-making body, founded in 1938. It has as its aim the promotion of realistic research, particularly in the field of economics. It conducts research by its own research staff and in co-operation with the universities and other academic bodies. The results of the work done under the Institute's auspices are published in several series, and a list of its publications up to the present time will be found at the end of this volume.

A STUDY OF
UNITED KINGDOM
IMPORTS

BY

M. FG. SCOTT

CAMBRIDGE

AT THE UNIVERSITY PRESS

1963

PUBLISHED BY
THE SYNDICS OF THE CAMBRIDGE UNIVERSITY PRESS
Bentley House, 200 Euston Road, London, N.W. 1
American Branch: 32 East 57th Street, New York 22, N.Y.

©

THE NATIONAL INSTITUTE OF ECONOMIC AND SOCIAL RESEARCH
1963

Printed in Great Britain at The Whitefriars Press, Tonbridge, Kent

CONTENTS

PART I

A GENERAL SURVEY AND THE MAIN CONCLUSIONS

PART II

THE BEHAVIOUR OF IMPORTS OF FOOD, MATERIALS AND MANUFACTURES

LIST OF TABLES

LIST OF CHARTS

SYMBOLS AND CONVENTIONS IN THE TABLES

— means 'nil' or 'negligible'

.. means 'not available' or 'not estimated'

× means 'not applicable'

In all tables, detail may not add to totals because of rounding.

PREFACE

This book is an outcome of a programme of research into the post-war economic experience of the United Kingdom which began in the National Institute in 1954. It was financed in the main by a grant from the Rockefeller Foundation.

I have worked for the best part of three full years and for varying periods during the subsequent four years to produce it. During this time I have learned something not only about the behaviour of United Kingdom imports, but also about empirical research in economics. The book displays the former, and it may be worth touching upon the latter in this preface.

Perhaps my chief lesson has been the sheer difficulty of finding convincing evidence for any quantitative proposition about cause and effect in this field. A second lesson has been the importance of having a clear set of concepts and a theoretical framework *before* amassing a lot of facts. A third has been the value of existing economic theory and econometrics in providing these concepts and this framework. I wasted a great deal of time by plunging straight into the statistics, hoping that common sense would guide me to some worthwhile conclusions. I eschewed the usual econometric approach because I thought it involved too gross a simplification of reality. Perhaps it does, but I am now more keenly aware of the difficulties of improving upon it.

My failure to appreciate these facts partly explains why it has taken so long to write this book. But it was inevitable that much time should be spent in finding the statistics and then adjusting them in numerous ways so as to make them better measures of the concepts which seemed most relevant. The process of drafting and re-drafting in the light of criticism was also very time consuming, but not, I hope, time wasting.

Criticism is sometimes said to be a thankless task. When it is received, it must be admitted, it is not always welcome. It is painful to see one's bright ideas being dimmed in the light of the truth. I have had sufficient time now, however, to appreciate the value of the criticism I have received, and I must thank all those who gave it. I will not, I am afraid, have satisfied them on a good many points; but this book is immeasurably the better for their efforts.

My leading critic, and the supervisor of my part in the research programme, was Christopher Dow. He has read virtually every draft I have produced and, as a result, a great deal of dead wood has been cut out, obscure passages have been clarified, and the number of unsup-

ported assertions has been reduced. He has also given me many fruitful ideas.

I have learned much of what I know about economics from Sir
Donald MacDougall, first as a pupil and then as an assistant. My
education has been continued by his many constructive criticisms of
the earlier drafts of this book.

I was fortunate in being able to use the resources of two research
institutes. From the staff of the National Institute, and in particular
from its two Directors in my time, W. A. B. Hopkin and C. T. Saunders,
and from Mrs M. F. W. Hemming, I have received much helpful
criticism and assistance in other ways. For the first three years of my
work I was in Cambridge, where the Department of Applied Economics
made me free of its many facilities, and where its Director, W. B.
Reddaway, and some other members of the staff, gave me criticisms and
suggestions which were of great use to me.

On those parts of the book concerned with the output of British
agriculture I have benefited from suggestions made by J. R. Bellerby,
G. T. Jones and J. R. Raeburn.

There are many officials in the Board of Trade, the Ministry of
Agriculture, Fisheries and Food, the Ministry of Power and the Central
Statistical Office who have helped me in my search for data. For their
time and effort I am most grateful.

The hard work of typing and computing was mostly done by two
assistants, Mrs Mary Edwards and Mrs Bridget Noone. I very much
appreciate the pains they took to maintain accuracy and speed, and the
willing spirit in which they tackled the rather dreary columns of figures
with which I confronted them.

Finally, I must thank Miss A. A. Clarke for preparing the book for
the press and Mrs A. K. Jackson for getting it through.

M. FG. SCOTT

CHRIST CHURCH
OXFORD
September 1961

PART I

A GENERAL SURVEY AND THE MAIN CONCLUSIONS

CHAPTER I

INTRODUCTION

I. AIMS OF THE BOOK

The chief aim of this study is to derive some conclusions about the behaviour of United Kingdom imports which will be useful for economic policy. It is an attempt to combine econometrics and economic history.

Econometric studies are often too inflexible. Their aim sometimes seems to be to apply a single, often complex, method of analysis to the data of a single period, the interest lying in the method rather than the results. Yet it is the results which are of chief interest for policy, so that it would seem better to adapt the method to the data, constantly searching for the particular period in which the effects of some particular causal factor can be most easily measured, and drawing on any evidence which seems relevant.

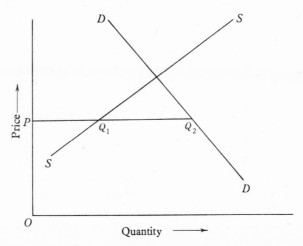

The economic historian has this readiness to search anywhere for evidence. He also brings a larger number of causal factors into a much more complex causal system than can the econometrician. But his conclusions are seldom quantitative, and it is the quantitative aspect which is often of crucial importance for economic policy. It is not enough, therefore, to catalogue past events, nor even to single out the principal causal factors at work. One should also try to assess their effects.

This is no easy task. The patterns of causation in human affairs are exceedingly complex and are not fully understood, so that one cannot hope to give a complete or a precise explanation of the past. What is done here is to set out a series of hypotheses, and to show that they are consistent with the events they seek to explain. Different hypotheses would also be consistent, but the ones chosen here seem to be the simplest which are also fairly plausible. Very complicated and more realistic hypotheses would not serve the purpose on hand. They would not be useful to the policy maker, and they have therefore been rejected.

2. ASSUMPTIONS AND LIMITATIONS OF THE ANALYSIS

The simplest of the hypotheses taken here is illustrated in the diagram. We regard the imports of any particular commodity as the difference between home consumption and home production of that commodity. DD is the demand curve for the commodity, and shows how much consumers in this country would like to buy at various prices. SS is the home supply curve, and shows how much producers in this country would like to produce at various prices. OP is the price set by conditions in the world market. Consequently, PQ_2 of the commodity is consumed in this country, PQ_1 is produced here, and the difference, Q_1Q_2, is imported.

The factors influencing the quantity of imports may be divided into those tending to shift the demand curve (for example, a rise in incomes in this country), those tending to shift the home supply curve (for example, a rise in wage costs) and those tending to raise or lower the price of imports. Our aim is to isolate and measure the effects of the most important factors.

This suggests ways of subdividing imports by commodity groups. In general, we want to group together commodities subject to similar causal influences. We therefore distinguish imports of food, for example, from other imports, since home food consumption is determined by different factors from those determining, say, the consumption of raw materials for industry. Similarly, home food supply and the level of food prices are determined by different factors from the home supply and level of prices of raw materials.

Another type of distinction is between those imports for which home supply provides a large part of home consumption and those for which home supply is insignificant. This distinction happens to coincide fairly well with that made in the official trade accounts between 'manufactures' and 'basic materials'. By far the greater part of our supplies of such goods as raw cotton, raw wool, timber, woodpulp, etc. come from abroad. A study of the imports of these goods therefore becomes a study, for the most part, of the consumption of these materials. For manufactures the situation is very different, since home output is large in relation to total consumption, and this leads to marked differences in the behaviour of imports. Imports of fuels are more complex. As a source of heat and light they are marginal, since most of our demands are met by home-produced coal, coke, gas and electricity; but imported oil is the principal source of power for transport.

Table 1. *United Kingdom retained imports in 1957*

	£ million, c.i.f.	Percentage of total
Food	1,472	37
Materials	1,185	30
Fuels	463	12
Manufactures	689	17
Alcoholic beverages	28	1
Tobacco	85	2
Postal packages	8	—
Live animals not for food	7	—
Total	3,937	100

Note: For details of the classification see pp. 210 ff.
Source: Board of Trade, *Accounts relating to Trade and Navigation of the United Kingdom*, December 1957.

Table 1 shows imports in 1957 subdivided into the four major groups considered in this study (food, materials, fuels and manufactures), together with four minor groups which are not examined in such detail. The major groups account for all but 3 % of the total. The divisions correspond closely with those used in the official trade returns (which is one reason why they were chosen), the main differences being that animal and vegetable oils, fats, nuts, oilseeds, etc. are included in 'food' (instead of in materials), and non-ferrous metals are included in materials instead of in manufactures, since most of our supplies of these metals are imported. Steel, however, remains in manufactures, since our imports are marginal.

Besides this four-fold division, some subdivisions are also considered. For example, there are three subdivisions of materials: textile materials and leather, metals and ores, and all other materials. The demand for textile materials depends chiefly on the output of the textile industries, and that for metals and ores on the output of the metals and engineering industries. In the past, these two groups of industries have expanded at very different rates, and there are other differences which make it desirable to consider them separately. But why should one not, for similar reasons, proceed to further subdivisions—cotton, wool and synthetic fibres, for example? The degree of subdivision in this study is admittedly rather arbitrary, being determined largely by the time available in which to complete the work. It is possible that some further refinement would have improved matters; but at some point the increase in complexity would have outweighed the gains on other heads. The interests of the economic policy-maker lie mainly in the behaviour of total imports, and possibly in the behaviour of large groups, and it is impractical to attempt to explain that behaviour in terms of the behaviour of numerous subdivisions. To do so involves not merely an increase in the number of groups which have to be examined, but also a study of the inter-relations between these groups. If livestock products and grains are lumped together one ignores, perforce, the inter-relations between their relative prices and the relative quantities demanded or supplied. One's conclusions may become less certain, but they are simpler and probably more useful. Grouping certainly raises some difficult problems of interpretation, since one cannot avoid classing very dissimilar things together. These problems are studied more fully in Appendix I. For the reasons given both there and above, the present study of the behaviour of rather large groups is thought to be more useful than a very detailed study.

The choice between a more realistic but more complex analysis and a simpler and possibly more uncertain one has to be made again and again. The simple hypothesis described on page 4 had to be modified in several respects. In the first place, changes in stocks and exports of the commodity were taken into account wherever possible. The consumption and home production of the commodity may not change and yet imports may increase or decrease because stocks are being built up or run down. Changes in exports from home production may have similar effects, and it is surprising how many commodities we import, produce at home and export. There is little information available about changes in stocks before the last war. To eliminate their erratic effects, imports in four or five successive years were grouped together on the assumption that over such long periods the net changes in stocks were small.

Secondly, the assumption made in the diagram that there is a single price for the imported and home-produced commodity was not always retained. Tariffs or subsidies must be brought into account, but, even apart from these, differences may arise simply because the imported commodity is not exactly the same as the home-produced one, or because the markets in which they are sold are imperfect. Since the 'commodity' is always a rather large group of commodities, it is clear that the average prices of the imported and home-produced groups may diverge appreciably, even if for the individual commodities of which they are composed the imported and domestic products are identical and sold in perfect markets. This divergence may occur if the prices of the different commodities change in different proportions, and if the composition of imports differs from that of home production. One might take the view that such divergent price movements are likely to be haphazard, or at least to bear no relation to changes in the demands or supplies of the groups considered as groups. To explain them it would be necessary to make the detailed commodity analysis which has already been rejected. There is some truth in this contention, but there are also reasons for believing that the behaviour of the average prices and quantities of the groups is to some extent analogous to the behaviour of the prices and quantities of individual commodities which are imperfect substitutes for each other. These reasons are discussed in Appendix I and cannot easily be summarized. In any case, the conclusion is partly a matter of faith. If one accepts it, one can treat a group of imports and of home-produced goods as if they were two goods, one imported and one home-produced, which are imperfect substitutes for each other; but this means that the hypothesis described on p. 4 must be modified.

If the imported and home-produced commodities (or commodity groups) are not identical, we need two demand curves and two supply curves, one pair for imports and one pair for home production. The demand curves are related to each other in the following way. The demand for imports, for example, is influenced not only by the price of imports and by various factors (such as incomes in this country) which tend to shift the curve one way or another, but also by the price of the home-produced substitute. If the latter increases, for example, it will tend to increase the demand for imports. Buyers in this country will switch from the home to the imported product. The amount of switching depends on the extent of the price rise and on the similarity of the two products, that is, on the size of the elasticity of substitution between them. For identical products sold in a perfect market the switching would be complete for even the smallest price rise, so that in fact no divergence of price could occur. But the products are usually not identical, and so the amount of switching and the extent of the price divergence are related to each other in a systematic fashion (the larger is the former, the larger is the latter).

All this modifies but does not radically change the hypothesis described on p. 4. An expansion of home supply or a contraction of home demand still leads to a fall in the demand for imports, although the chain of causation takes a little longer to describe. An expansion of home supply drives down the price of the home product, and so buyers switch from imports to the home product. A contraction of home demand due, say, to a fall in incomes, has both direct and indirect effects on the demand for imports. The direct effect needs no elaboration. The indirect effect is via the drop in the price of the home product. This price falls on account of the fall in demand for the home product, and consequently buyers switch towards it and away from imports. But although the *direction* of the change in the demand for imports caused by shifts in home supply or demand is the same, the size is not, and this is one reason why it is worth adding this extra complication. A given shift in the home supply curve to the right, for example, will cause a smaller reduction in the demand for imports if the imported and home-produced goods are not very similar than if they are exactly similar— that is, if they are imperfect rather than perfect substitutes. This can readily be seen if we take the extreme case of the two goods being completely different from each other and totally unrelated in demand, for in that case the expansion of home supply will not reduce imports at all. At the opposite extreme, if the goods are perfect substitutes, the shift in home supply will cause an equal reduction in the demand for imports. In between we have the more general case of imperfect substitutes, where the reduction in the demand for imports is finite, but smaller than the shift in home supply. Just how closely substitutable imported and home-produced goods are is therefore a matter of some importance.

Assumptions have to be made about the precise way in which the different causal factors combine. The assumptions made are: that the different factors act independently; that their effects are usually multiplicative rather than additive; and that these effects are constant for given changes in the factors and vary directly with the latter. The meaning of these assumptions is most easily seen from an example. The demand for food is assumed to depend upon, *inter alia*, the population, its real income per head, the price of food and the price of all other consumer goods. If the population doubles and the other determining factors are unchanged, then we assume that the demand for food doubles (this is an additional assumption, which is commonly made). Furthermore, we assume that a doubling of the population will cause the demand for food to be double what it otherwise would have been even if one or more of the other determining factors happen to change as well. The effect of a change in population on the demand for food is to double it *quite independently* of the level of or changes in the other factors. Suppose now that in addition to the doubling of the population there is an increase in real income per head which, by itself, would lead to a trebling of the demand for food. The combined effect of the increase in population and in its real income per head will be to multiply the demand for food six times. Their combined effect is *multiplicative* and not additive. This follows from the assumptions that their individual effects are multiplicative and independent. Next, we assume that a doubling of the population always causes a doubling in the demand for food—in 1900 as much as in 1955—and that likewise a given proportionate increase in real income per head, or in the price of food, or in the price of all other consumer goods, always causes a *constant* proportionate change in the demand for food. Finally, we assume that if you double, say, the proportionate change in real income per head you will double the resulting proportionate change in the demand for food. In technical language, we assume that the income and price elasticities of demand are constant, the elasticities being the (small) proportionate changes in quantities demanded divided by the (small) proportionate changes in the corresponding causal factors (for large changes we must divide the corresponding *logarithmic* changes).

Assumptions similar to these are frequently made by econometricians, and so have acquired some of the sanctity of tradition. Their justification is the same as that of the other assumptions already described: they lead to relatively simple and fairly plausible hypotheses. An additional justification is that there are so few data that the use of more complicated hypotheses is unnecessary. Again, an example may serve to clarify the point. There is only one occasion in the past half-century which enables us to measure with any confidence the effect of relative price changes on the demand for imports of manufactures, and that is when this country abandoned the gold standard and imposed tariffs on a wide range of imports in 1931–2. On this occasion there was a large drop in the volume of imports of manufactures which could fairly certainly be attributed to relative price changes. From this one can discover that a 10 % rise in the price of imports relative to the price of home products seems to have caused a 50 % drop in the relative quantity of imports demanded. Taking the assumptions mentioned above, one would say that an $X\%$ relative price rise or fall would, in general, be expected to cause approximately a $5X\%$ fall or rise in relative quantities demanded. (This is not quite accurate since the assumption of constant elasticities requires this calculation to be done using logarithmic rather than percentage changes, but this point may be ignored here.) One can then show that this simple hypothesis is consistent with the experience of other years, but it clearly *might* be wrong. A price rise might have a different effect from a price fall, and the relation might not be the same when X was small as when X was large. Unfortunately there are no other periods for which one can clearly mark out the effects of relative price changes on relative quantities demanded, and hence one might as well take the simplest hypothesis.

Lack of data and the virtues of simplicity are also the reasons why certain other *a priori* assumptions were made about the form of the demand and supply relations, even though these other assumptions are not so commonly made by econometricians. An example is the assumption that equal proportionate changes in all relevant prices leave demand or supply unaffected, so that only relative price changes matter. Some econometricians might be reluctant to make such an assumption and instead would determine the magnitude of the effect of all price changes on the demand for food by the usual statistical techniques. Yet the data are so inadequate that it seems preferable to make the assumption. It is at least as plausible as any estimate would be, and it is simpler. Rather arbitrary assumptions are also made about the way in which the effects of price changes are lagged. There are not enough data to determine just how the effects are distributed through time, and a few experiments with apparently plausible distributions suggested that one's general conclusions were not much different whether one took three, six or ten years as the period during which the effects were assumed to work themselves out. These and other similar assumptions are discussed in Part II.

To plead lack of data as an excuse may surprise some readers, since many of the statistical series given here stretch back for fifty years or more. At one time it was customary in the statistical analysis of time series to treat the data for each year as an independent observation, but this is now generally held to be unsatisfactory. We can probably learn something about the magnitudes of the effects of different causal factors only when they change by large amounts and when these changes are not quickly reversed. Uncertainty about the way in which effects are lagged, together with possible errors of measurement (of which more below) are alone sufficient to make this so. Hence we have effectively very few observations, and our conclusions are correspondingly uncertain. This shows how desirable it would be to support the conclusions reached here by studies of the behaviour of imports of other countries. Econometricians have various techniques for calculating the degree of uncertainty of their estimates, but they have not been used here. They seem plausible only when there is a fairly large number of independent observations. Furthermore, they do not make any allowance for errors in measuring the causal factors, and these can be important. Instead, some crude *ad hoc* methods have been adopted here for setting upper and lower limits to the various estimates. From what has been said it can be seen that these limits must be wide. They are given and explained in Part II.

A most serious limitation of much of this study is that it is confined to the more immediate factors influencing imports and that the interactions of these factors are largely ignored. To return to the diagram on p. 3, we study the effects of, say, changes in home income on the demand curve DD, and hence on the demand for imports, Q_1Q_2. We also study the effects of a change in the price of imports, OP, on the quantity of imports demanded. But we usually ignore any effects which a change in the price of imports might have on home income. Our 'effects' assume 'other things' are held constant, although in fact these 'other things' may very likely change as a direct consequence of a change in the causal factor considered. In the example just given, a rise in the price of imports could, in the short run, lead to a fall in home real income. In the long run, via the wage-price spiral, it could lead to a rise in home money income. Yet all this we ignore. The study of these other interactions must be left to other workers and other times.

The limits of this study are, indeed, well illustrated by the diagram. We consider the effects of shifts in each of the three lines (demand curve DD, supply curve SS, and price PQ_1Q_2) on the demand for imports, and we also consider the main factors directly influencing each of these lines with the exception of the price of imports. We consider the factors directly influencing home demand and home supply, but we attempt no explanation of the price of imports. Since only a partial analysis of this kind is attempted, one must be careful about drawing conclusions for economic policy. We only bring together some of the pieces of the jig-saw puzzle, and the picture is far from complete.

3. STATISTICS

Much of the labour that went into this study was devoted to estimating the basic statistics. A great many series were computed, of which the most important are given in Appendix II. The sources and methods used are described there in sufficient detail, it is hoped, for those who may wish to employ the figures for other purposes and who have an interest in these matters. For the general reader it may be sufficient to give here an indication of what was done, and a warning of the possible errors and uncertainties involved.

The main series computed were: index numbers of the quantity and price of retained imports for peace-time years 1900 to 1955, distinguishing the four groups mentioned above—food, materials, fuels and manufactures—and subdividing materials into three groups—metal, textile and other materials; industrial production of the metals and metal-using industries and of the textiles, leather and clothing industries for peace-time years 1900–55 (the index of total industrial production used was that computed by Ridley, see p. 218); an index of the price of the national product, 1900–55; an index of the quantity and price of agricultural output, net only of imported feeding-stuffs, seeds and livestock, for groups of years 1870–1955; the value of production,

retained imports, exports, change in stocks and consumption of food
and of raw materials, 1935–8 and 1946–55, with similar estimates for
coal and oil (but only for certain groups of years) and for manufactures
(omitting stock changes); index numbers of expenditure on fuels at
constant prices by three groups of consumers (domestic and commercial, manufacturing and transport) for 1924–38 and 1946–55; index
numbers of the quantity of sales and imports of five groups of manufactures, 1924–38 and 1946–55; and index numbers of the quantity
and price of retained imports from foreign countries (i.e. excluding the
Commonwealth, roughly speaking) and of sales from other sources
(mainly home production) on the home market of fifteen individual
manufactures for various census of production years 1907–54.

The basic data were mostly official estimates (of trade, production,
prices, etc.) published in the *Board of Trade Journal*, the Central
Statistical Office's *Annual Abstract of Statistics* and Blue Book on *National
Income and Expenditure* and other official periodicals. These were supplemented by unofficial estimates published in the learned journals and
elsewhere.

On the whole, these data needed to be processed in two different
ways. First, series relating to different commodities, trades, or sectors of
the economy had to be combined or recombined in various ways. Thus
figures of stock changes for thirty-eight materials were combined to
form a series for stock changes of materials. Again, non-ferrous metals
were shifted out of the import category 'manufactures' and into 'raw
materials'. Secondly, series relating to different periods were linked
together to obtain continuous series for the whole period under review.
The series for the quantity of imports since 1900, for instance, is the
result of linking together series for eleven sub-periods.

The problems involved in making these computations were the usual
ones associated with the construction of index numbers: the choice of
formula for weighting and of base period. If the weights were chosen
differently (and it is hard to defend any particular choice) the series
would be different. So far as was practicable, similar base years and
weighting formulae were used for series whose relative movements were
being studied (for example, quantity of imports of materials and
industrial production), but no more than a rough approximation to
this aim could be made.

The index numbers of quantity were the Laspeyres type, that is,
weighted by the prices of a base year, this base year generally remaining
the same for a period of years and then changing when the index was
linked to a new series with a later base year. The index numbers of
price were of the Paasche type, that is, weighted by the prices of the
(changing) current year. They were obtained by dividing index numbers

of current value by index numbers of quantity, and are sometimes known as 'average value' index numbers.

Very often the series in their final form are not precisely what is wanted. They have included those things which they ought not to include, and they have left out those things which they ought to have included. The coverage of the estimates for changes in stocks of food and materials, for production of materials and expenditure on fuels is particularly inadequate or uncertain.

Generally speaking, the reliability of a series diminishes the further back in time one goes and the smaller the number of items included in it. Thus the index numbers of production of the metals and metal-using industries are much less reliable for the years 1900–13 than for 1946–55, and they are less reliable for all years than the index of total industrial production since, amongst other reasons, the inclusion of many more industries allows more scope for the cancellation of errors. A more volatile series is also generally less reliable than a less volatile one, so that for example the possible (absolute) error in the percentage change in the index of metals and metal-using industries production over a given period is larger than that for the index of total industrial production. Since thousands of computations were involved, some arithmetical errors must remain, although naturally every effort was made to avoid them. For all these reasons one cannot attach much significance to small changes in the series of the order of one or two per cent over, say, five years or less, or of the order of 5 % over ten or twenty years. These percentages should be increased for series for the earlier years, or for the subdivisions of the main groups, or for particularly volatile series.

4. PLAN OF THE BOOK

The rest of Part I contains the main results of the study. It is designed for the less specialized reader, so that mathematical symbols have been avoided and references and footnotes kept to the minimum.

Chapter II is a description and attempted explanation of the behaviour of imports since 1935–8. There are several reasons for starting with a rather detailed account of this particular period which, as may be seen from Chart 1, is after all only a small part of the period covered by the series for this study. It has more and better statistics than earlier periods. It is probably the most interesting for most readers since it is recent, and since in it there occurred such a remarkable downward displacement of imports in relation to industrial production (Chart 1). To explain this behaviour we draw on the experience of earlier years and, to a lesser extent, of other countries. Hence Chapter II is more than an account of imports in one period, it is also a summary of the conclusions reached about the main determinants of imports, together with the principal reasons for these conclusions (the full explanation being given in Part II). It is hoped that this way of setting them out makes the results more 'live', and also prevents one underrating the importance of 'special factors', such as import controls.

Chapter II is concerned with the behaviour of imports in the past. In Chapter III attention is given to their likely behaviour in the future, both to trends in the demand for imports and to year-to-year fluctuations in imports. Estimates are given of the probable change in the demand for imports over the next five or ten years on certain assumptions about the behaviour of industrial production, consumers' real expenditure per head, the population and various other factors. The effects on the demand for imports of altering some of these assumptions are also estimated. Details of the estimates are given at the end of the chapter. The discussion of fluctuations in imports is largely concerned with estimates of the short-term effects of changes in the level of domestic economic activity on the demand for imports.

Chapter IV starts with the outlook for the balance of payments on various assumptions. There is then a review of the various measures which might be taken to influence imports (changes in the exchange rate, measures to influence the general level of demand, import controls, subsidies to agriculture and tariffs on imported manufactures), together with some estimates of their likely effects. This chapter draws on the estimates made and conclusions reached elsewhere in the book.

Part II contains the evidence for some of the statements made in Part I. It consists of a preliminary chapter (V) which gives the system of notation used in the mathematical parts of the discussion, and also a mathematical formulation of the main assumptions made in estimating the various elasticities. Chapters VI, VII and VIII deal with food, materials and manufactures respectively. They contain details of estimates of various elasticities which are only briefly described in Chapter II. Some of the estimates are obtained by the usual least-squares procedure, but others are not. A variety of evidence is considered and an attempt is made where possible to set upper and lower limits to the estimates, which are wide enough to make it very unlikely that the true values of the elasticities could lie outside them. Chapter VI contains a brief discussion of imports of tobacco and alcoholic beverages, as well as food, but there is no chapter in Part II on fuels. An attempt was made to measure the effects of relative price changes and other factors on the demand for fuels, but it was unsuccessful.

Appendix I considers the problem of grouping, known to some as 'the aggregation problem'. In the rest of the book it is groups of imports rather than imports of individual commodities which are

considered, yet the economic theory which is used is based on the
behaviour of the demand and supply of individual commodities. It is
not clear whether this theory can be profitably applied to the behaviour
of groups of commodities, but in Appendix I a justification for such an
application is attempted.

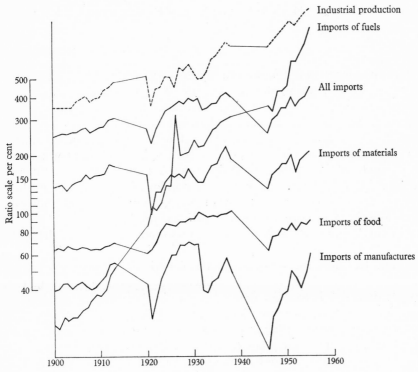

Chart 1. Volume of imports and industrial production, 1900–55

CHAPTER II

THE BEHAVIOUR OF IMPORTS SINCE BEFORE THE WAR

1. INTRODUCTION

The last war saw what was probably the largest drop in the volume of British imports during the last two hundred years (Chart 1). From 1935–8 to 1946–9 it fell by about a quarter to a level rather lower than in 1913. This fall, unlike that in the First World War, was unaccompanied by a fall in the general level of production or by heavy unemployment. On the contrary, the real national product was about 10% greater in 1946–9 than in 1935–8 and unemployment was extremely low. The drop in imports was followed by a rapid rise which did not, however, at least up to 1960, fully restore the pre-war relationship of imports to the real national product.

In this chapter we seek to explain these movements—the drop, the rise and the seemingly permanent reduction in the ratio of imports to output. In doing so, we draw on the experience of earlier years, for without this guide it would be difficult to explain very much. Our wider objective is to draw general conclusions about the way imports behave, and this is a convenient framework in which to display some of our conclusions. So far as possible we try to give the main reasons for them, but the full explanation is left to Part II. Detailed reference forward is, however, avoided, along with all other footnotes.

We take the four main groups of imports in turn: food, materials, fuels and manufactures. Imports of alcoholic drink and tobacco are also considered briefly. For the most part, we compare imports in three periods, 1935–8, 1946–9 and 1954–5, grouping years together so as to eliminate chance factors and unrecorded stock movements. Only two years are taken together in the last period because most of the statistical work was completed before data for 1956 and later years were available, and because it was desirable to choose a period which was relatively free of the influence of direct controls on imports or consumption (which ruled out 1953 and earlier years). Some comments are also given on developments since 1955.

Table 2 summarizes the changes in imports, distinguishing the main groups which are separately examined in the following pages. Chart 1 shows the same changes in a longer perspective.

Table 2. *Total retained imports, pre-war and post-war*

Annual rates, £ million (1948 c.i.f. prices)

		1935–8	1946–9	1954–5
1	Food	1,180	890	1,080
2	Alcoholic drink and tobacco	60	70	70
3	Materials	730	580	750
4	Fuels	110	140	310
5	Manufactures	430	250	460
6	Total retained imports	2,530	1,940	2,660
		(Index numbers)		
7	Gross domestic product	100	110	140
8	Total retained imports	100	77	105

Sources: See pp. 209 ff. and pp. 220 ff., S 2, 4, 6, 8, 10 and 24.

2. FOOD

From 1935–8 to 1946–9 imports of food fell by about a quarter, under the double impact of a drop in consumption (if measured at the farm gate—see below) and a rise in home production. Thereafter, consumption, production and imports all rose—imports rather faster than the others.

Table 3. *Consumption, production and imports of food, pre-war and post-war*

Annual rates, £ million (constant 1948 market prices)

		1935–8	1946–9	1954–5
1	Consumption	1,420	1,350	1,620
2	Production	490	650	760
3	Exports	40	30	60
4	Change in stocks	..	—	−40
5	Imports (1−2+3+4)	970	730	880

Note: The items in this table are measured at farm or dock gate prices *less* any subsidy (or plus any import duty). Imports differ in this table from their value in Table 2, since there they are measured at c.i.f. prices (i.e. before subsidies are paid or taxes levied).

Sources: See pp. 221 ff., S 30–4.

Our explanation of these changes in imports of food consists, first, of an explanation of the changes in food consumption by reference to consumers' real incomes or expenditure, the population, the price of food in relation to the price of other consumer goods and some other factors mentioned below; we next explain home food production mainly in terms of the prices paid to farmers, in relation to an index of the general price level, and 'trend' factors; finally, there are the changes in exports and stocks of food. Estimates are given for the separate effects of each of these factors on imports (Table 4 below).

Food consumption may be measured at retail or 'at the farm gate', and the distinction is an important one since the two totals behave rather differently. Most imports consist of food which has undergone little or no further processing after leaving the farm—such things as grains, meat, fish, fruit and vegetables. Imported oils, butter, cheese, sugar, tea, coffee and cocoa have only been processed to a small extent. For this reason it seems best to measure food consumption by adding imports to the production of food by British farms and fisheries, and thus to secure a total which corresponds approximately to food 'at the farm gate'. Food consumption at retail is roughly twice as great in value as food consumption measured 'at the farm gate', the difference being the value added by further processing and distribution. In what follows we treat the whole of food imports as if they were unprocessed. Some slight error is involved, and the element of manufactured food is likely to behave more like imports of manufactures than like the bulk of food imports.

Econometric studies of the demand for food suggest that when real income per head increases it is the demand for the processing and distributive services which increases most, while the demand for food at the farm gate increases very little. A rise of 1 % in real income per head might be expected to raise the demand for food at retail by something like 0·5 % but to raise the demand for food at the farm gate by only about 0·25 % (that is, the income elasticities of demand are respectively 0·5 and 0·25). The effect of a change in total real consumers' expenditure (which is used in the following analysis in preference to real income for various reasons) would be similar, if perhaps slightly greater.

The same econometric studies suggest that the demand for food is not very responsive to changes in the price of food relative to the prices of other consumer goods. A relative increase in the price of food at the farm gate of 1 % would probably reduce the volume demanded only by about 0·25 %. As might be expected, the demand for food at retail is somewhat more responsive to changes in relative prices and the corresponding effect is thought to be around 0·5 % (that is, the price elasticities of demand for food at the farm gate and at retail are respectively −0·25 and −0·5).

One can use these results to try to explain the change in the demand for food from pre-war to post-war. It is convenient to take the change from 1935–8 to 1954–5 first, since food rationing was unimportant in both these periods, and then to consider demand in 1946–9, when food was rationed. Between 1935–8 and 1954–5 consumers' total real expenditure per head rose by about 7 % and the population by about 8 %. Taken together these changes may have increased the demand for food at the farm gate by rather less than 10 %. Food at the farm gate

became about 30 % dearer in relation to other consumer goods, however, and this may have reduced demand by rather more than 6 %, so
that the net increase in demand should have been roughly 3 %. In fact,
consumption of food measured at the farm gate rose by almost 14 %.
The discrepancy may be due to statistical errors, to errors in our
estimates of the effects of the various factors mentioned above, or to
the operation of some other factors which we have failed to bring
into our analysis. The last explanation seems the most plausible one.
If the same exercise is performed using the statistics of food consumption and prices at retail, the result is much the same: changes in
consumers' total expenditure, in population and in food prices relative
to other consumer prices suggest a rise in the demand for food at retail
of about 8 %, whereas the actual increase in food consumption was
nearly 20 %. The discrepancy is much the same. One factor omitted
from our analysis is the marked levelling of incomes which occurred.
The relative rise in the incomes of the poor would have increased their
demand for food without leading to much of a drop in the demand for
food by the rich. Another stimulant to food consumption was provided
by the welfare food schemes, cheap school meals, and cheap canteen
meals supplied at the firm's expense. Finally, the propaganda for
better nutrition may have had some effect. All these factors are omitted
from the calculations given above and they might well account for the
10 % or so extra demand for food. Changes in the age composition of the
population were not significant in this context.

In 1946–9 the factors just mentioned were all operating (except that
some of the levelling of incomes took place after 1949) and in addition
the shortages of other consumer goods must have tended to increase the
demand for food. Changes in consumers' real expenditure, in population and in relative prices should have led to a *fall* in the demand for
food, as compared with 1935–8, of about 2 %, but if we allow for the
other factors the demand should have increased by, say, 8 %. In fact,
food consumption measured at the farm gate seems to have fallen by
5 %, which suggests that food rationing may have held consumption
12 % or so below free demand. This estimate is, however, statis-
tically suspect, since the figures of food consumption measured at the
farm gate are inconsistent with those of food consumption measured
at retail in 1946–9. The gap between consumption and demand may
therefore have been smaller than 12 %. On the other hand, similar
calculations for food at retail suggest that rationing cut demand by
16 %, and allowance for the inconsistency just mentioned would tend
to increase this figure.

In any case, these are substantial effects, both on food consumption
and on imports. If, for example, extra food imports could have been

obtained in sufficient quantities to satisfy demand, and without having to pay higher prices for them, the absence of rationing and import controls would have led to an increase of something like 12 % in consumption and hence about one-quarter in our imports of food during 1946–9. At current prices this would have cost us over £200 million a year. In fact, the extra imports could probably not have been bought— certainly not in 1946 or 1947 when the world food shortage was particularly acute. Also, the attempt to buy them might have led to a rise in food prices which would have choked off demand (at least initially) and which would have had further repercussions on wages and other incomes and expenditure which cannot be considered here. Food prices were instead kept down by subsidies, which thus accounted for part of the gap between supply and demand.

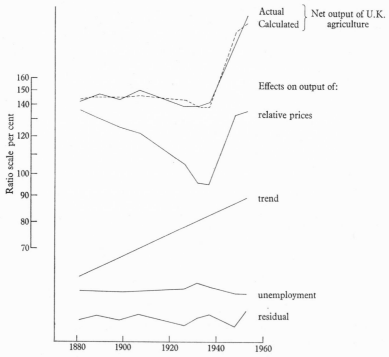

Chart 2. Regression analysis of volume of United Kingdom agricultural output

British agricultural production, which is mostly food, rose by over 50 % from 1935–8 to 1954–5, thus bringing to an end a period of stagnant or gently falling output which had lasted since the 1870's. This rise was accompanied by the first large increase in farm prices, relative to the general level of prices, that has occurred since the

1870's (see Chart 2). It seems plausible, therefore, to explain much of the first development in terms of the second: one main reason why output rose was probably because farming became so much more profitable. It was not the only reason, however. Even if farm prices do not change relatively to the general level of prices, farm output may be expected to increase because of the continual improvement in farming techniques. It was this which prevented output falling more in the long period following the 1870's when relative price movements were generally adverse to farmers. Both improvements and output were stimulated after 1939 by various acts of the Government. So-called 'production grants' were made—such as grants for drainage, subsidies to fertilizers, grants for tuberculosis-free herds, etc., none of which enters into our calculations of the prices received by farmers. Free technical advice was increased. The farmers were given long-term assurances about prices or markets, and capital improvements were encouraged in various ways. Another factor influencing agricultural output was the great fall in industrial unemployment, which made work in industry more attractive and so made it more difficult for farmers to get or keep labour. This would therefore have tended to reduce agricultural output, but it is not thought that the effect was substantial.

The writer's best guess at the quantitative importance of some of these factors influencing output is as follows. A rise of 1 % in farm prices relative to prices in general probably leads to an *eventual* increase in farm output of about 0·5 %. The increase in relative farm prices from 1935–8 to 1954–5, allowing for some lag in its effect on output, would then account for rather less than half of the rise in output in the same period. Rather more than half the rise is thus attributable to the normal improvements in techniques and to the other special factors already mentioned, and the latter were probably important since the upward trend in output not attributable to price movements was appreciably greater than in the years before 1935 (about $1\frac{1}{3}$ % per annum compared with about $\frac{1}{2}$ %).

We must now bring the threads of our analysis together and show how each of the factors, whose influence on home consumption or production of food we have been discussing, affected imports of food. The rise in the market price of food at the farm or dock gate from 1935–8 to 1954–5 clearly tended to reduce food consumption and so food imports. This price rise may be further analysed into a rise in the price of imported food at factor cost and a change in *net* indirect taxes on imports. Since food subsidies increased, until they were far in excess of indirect taxes, the change in *net* indirect taxes tended to increase consumption and imports of food. The rise in the prices of other consumer goods also tended to raise food consumption and imports.

On balance, however, since food became relatively dearer, the net effect of all these price movements was to reduce consumption and imports of food. These price effects on consumption were outweighed by the other factors tending to increase it, namely an increase in population, the rise in its real expenditure per head, and the various other factors (such as the levelling of incomes) which were mentioned on p. 19. So the total effect was to raise food consumption and imports of food. Both relative price movements and other factors (such as changes in techniques and direct grants by the Government) tended to raise home food production and so to reduce imports, and their combined effects outweighed the effects on imports via changing food consumption. After making a small allowance for changes in stocks and exports of food, we are thus left with a drop in imports of food from 1935–8 to 1954–5.

Table 4. *Causes of the change in the volume of imports of food, 1935–8 to 1954–5*

Annual rates, £ million (1948 market prices)

Factor	Effect on imports of food assuming substitutability	
	Perfect	Imperfect
A. Effects via changing consumption of food		
1 Price of imports of food	−520	−460
2 Net indirect taxes on imports of food	30	30
3 Residual food price (see p. 112)	50	×
4 Price of consumer goods, non-food	340	310
5 Population	110	100
6 Real expenditure per head	30	30
7 Other (distribution of income, etc.)	150	110
Sub-total	200	110
B. Effects via changing home output of food		
8 Price paid to farmers relative to general price level	−120	−80
9 Other (techniques, direct grants, etc.)	−140	−100
Sub-total	−270	−180
C. Effects via changing stocks and exports of food		
10 Stocks	−40	−30
11 Exports	20	10
Total actual change in imports of food	−90	−90
Total of 'price factors' (lines 1, 2, 4, 8)	−260	−210

Note: Imports of food in 1935–8 averaged £970 million a year at 1948 market prices. The above figures can therefore be transformed into approximate percentage effects by dividing by 10.

For further details see pp. 109 ff.

In Table 4 estimates of all these separate effects are given. It is a complicated table, and some further explanation of it is given below. The estimates are the writer's 'best guesses', and are subject to wide margins of error, for which some limiting values are given in Part II. Taking the figures as they stand, however, it seems that the main factors influencing imports were (i) the changes in relative prices (which, taking consumption and production together, probably reduced imports by 20–25 %); (ii) the rise in population and the residual group of other factors influencing consumption (each responsible for an increase of 10–15 % in imports); and (iii) the expansion in home food output due to government aid of various kinds (other than direct price subsidies, which are included amongst the relative price changes) and technical improvements, etc. (which may have caused a fall of 10–15 % on imports). The change in net indirect taxes on food, in consumers' total real expenditure per head and in exports and stocks of food were all minor factors.

There are several aspects of these estimates which require comment. Similar estimates are given for other groups of imports, and what follows is relevant to them as well.

The effect of any factor influencing the demand for imported food depends, for reasons discussed in Chapter I, on how closely substitutable imported food is for home-produced food. The evidence on this is uncertain. On the one hand, it seems that the changeover in consumption from imported to home-produced food, between the pre-war years and 1954–5, was accompanied by quite a substantial cheapening in home-produced food as compared with imported. This suggests that the two groups are not very closely substitutable for each other. On the other hand, if comparisons are made over a longer period, the relative price situation in the 1930's appears abnormal—imports seem to have been abnormally cheap relative to home-produced food. It is possible, therefore, that the two groups are more closely substitutable than the pre-war to post-war comparison suggests. To meet this difficulty two sets of assumptions were taken, one with perfect substitutability (the left-hand column of estimates in Table 4) and one with the degree of imperfect substitutability suggested by the pre-war/post-war comparison. The estimated effects of the various factors in the right-hand column (assuming imperfect substitutability) are arithmetically smaller than those in the left-hand column, for reasons mentioned in Chapter I, but the relative importance of the different effects is similar for either column.

Each entry in Table 4 shows the effect on the volume of imports of food of the change which took place between 1935–8 and 1954–5 in the factors listed in the left-hand column. These effects are calculated under a set of assumptions the most important of which were discussed in Chapter I. The effect of any particular factor, for example the change in the price of imports of food, is approximately the change in imports which would have occurred if that factor had changed and if the other factors listed in the table had remained constant. Thus, if the factors listed in lines 2 to 7 had remained constant, and if home food output, food stocks and food exports had remained constant, the rise in the price of food imports would have resulted in a fall of approximately £520 million in food imports at 1948 market prices, assuming perfect substitutability of imports and home food output.

The word 'approximately' is used here because, even if the assumptions and calculations were all exactly right, imports would not have fallen by *exactly* £520 million if the *only* factor to change had been the import price of food. This is because one assumption which is made is that the effects of the various factors are *multiplicative*. Hence the calculations on which Table 4 is based threw up answers in terms of *proportionate* effects on food imports or consumption. There is no uniquely correct way of expressing these proportionate effects in terms of absolute effects on the value of imports at constant prices, and yet it is desirable to do so. For otherwise, the table would have to show one factor having such-and-such a proportionate effect on consumption of food, and another having such-and-such a proportionate effect on the home supply of food, and it would be difficult to compare the two effects or to relate them to imports. To overcome this difficulty a method has been adopted which satisfies two requirements: first, the calculations show the *relative* importance of the different effects correctly, and, secondly, the sum of the effects equals the actual change in imports. Using this method does, however, lead to the effects being different (though only slightly so) from the changes in imports which would result if *only* the factor in question changed, the other factors remaining at their 1935–8 levels. Instead, the effects are nearer to the changes in imports which would result if the factor in question changed as it did and if the other factors remained unchanged but at levels *intermediate* between 1935–8 and 1954–5, rather than at the levels ruling in 1935–8. (Some readers may find the arithmetical example on p. 91 helpful.)

An unsatisfactory feature of the table is the failure to allow for a fuller interaction of supply and demand. For example, the rise in the price of food imports is only shown as reducing the demand for imports by reducing food consumption. Its effect on imports via a stimulation of the home supply of food is concealed in line 8. Again, the only effect of the increase in population on imports which is shown is that which worked by increasing food consumption and on the assumption that home food supply was constant. In fact, the increase in the demand for food would have tended to raise the price of home-produced food above what it otherwise would have been (assuming imports and home produce were imperfect substitutes—if they were perfect substitutes the price would have been determined by the import price and by taxes and subsidies). This in turn would have stimulated home food supply and so would have reduced the demand for imported food. In short, if we were to allow for these further interactions, the fall in imports attributed to the rise in their price would be greater (in either column of the table) and (in the right-hand column only) most of the other factors would be shown as having smaller effects on imports, since the further interactions lead to offsetting effects on imports. The reason why these interactions are not allowed for in the table and a discussion of their probable magnitude are reserved for Part II (p. 115). Very briefly, the calculations would have been invalidated by the absence of a free market in food prior to 1954.

The same reason makes it difficult, if not impossible, to give a similar causal analysis of the change in imports over the post-war period. It may suffice to say that the volume of food imports rose about 20 % from 1946–9 to 1954–5 (Table 3) and that we have already estimated that the removal of rationing and import controls would have raised the effective demand for imported food by about the same percentage. It is clear that this was probably the most important single factor tending to increase the effective demand for food imports in this period, and that the other factors (rise in population and real expenditure per head, rise in price of food relative to other prices, further expansion of home food output) must have largely cancelled each other out.

This also suggests that the rate of increase in the volume of imports of food from 1946–9 to 1954–5 (some 2·7 % per annum) was abnormally high, and it is interesting to inquire into the behaviour of imports since 1954–5 to see whether they have risen less rapidly. The estimates on which this study is based were not carried beyond 1955. Mr G. F. Ray, in an unpublished study referred to on p. 224, gives estimates of imports of food adjusted for changes in stocks of food. He also excludes some commodities which are materials for industry (e.g. certain oilseeds) or are used for making alcoholic drink (e.g. some barley). With these adjustments, the increase in imports from 1955 to 1958 becomes only $1\frac{1}{4}$ % per annum, which is appreciably smaller than the rate of increase from 1946–9 to 1954–5. Furthermore, the estimates of food consumption measured at farm or dock gate prices given by Mr Ray show a rate of increase from 1955 to 1958 which is only about $\frac{1}{4}$ % per annum in excess of that to be expected on account of the accompanying fall in the relative price of food and the increases in consumers' total real expenditure and population. The tendency for food consumption to grow much faster than could be explained by these factors, which was very noticeable in the years from 1946–9 to 1954–5, had virtually disappeared. The behaviour of food consumption measured at retail also bears this out.

3. MATERIALS

Imports of materials, as defined here, consist for the most part of goods such as raw cotton, wool, timber, rubber and metallic ores, which are used by industry and of which most of our supplies are imported. Such home production as there is consists largely of scrap and waste products (cotton waste, shoddy, scrap rubber, scrap metal, etc.) and hence depends to a considerable extent on the level of imports of the primary materials. One would normally expect the volume of imports of materials to change in much the same proportion as the total consumption of materials by industry, and hence in much the same proportion as industrial production.

Table 5. *Imports and consumption of materials, pre-war and post-war*

Annual rates, £ million (1948 c.i.f. prices)

		1935–8	1946–9	1954–5
1	Consumption	800	720	900
2	Production	130	180	210
3	Exports (crude and crude content of semi-manufactures)	120	70	80
4	Imports (crude content of semi-manufactures)	—	10	10
5	Change in stocks	..	−20	—
6	Imports (mainly crude) (1−2+3−4+5)	780	580	750
		(Index numbers)		
7	Industrial production	100	108	149
8	Consumption of materials	100	90	112
9	Imports of materials	100	74	96

Note: Imports and industrial production in 1935–8 adjusted for weighting bias as described on pp. 219, 234. The figures therefore differ from those in Table 2, in which no such adjustment is made.

Sources: See pp. 227 ff. and p. 218, S 41–6.

A glance at Table 5 shows that this simple relation between imports and industrial production can be modified by several important factors. From 1935–8 to 1954–5 industrial production increased by a half, while the volume of imports of materials hardly changed. Part of the divergence was due to the difference between the consumption of materials and imports of them, and we may consider this first. The difference consists of home production of materials, less exports and less any increase (or plus any decrease) in stocks of materials. In addition, we have allowed in the table for exports and imports of materials embodied in semi-processed goods which have a high material content (it is only this material content which is included)—for example, raw cotton in cotton yarns. The behaviour of these items led to a sharp drop in imports relative to the consumption of materials, all of which occurred between 1935–8 and 1946–9. By increasing our home production of materials, by cutting down our exports of them and of goods with a high material content, and by importing more semi-finished goods with a high material content, we were able to supply industry with an extra £100 million or so per annum of materials in 1946–9, equal to one-sixth of our imports. In 1946–9 a further £20 million a year was taken from stocks.

The sharp increase in home production of materials is the more remarkable in that much of it consisted of scrap and waste products whose supply was increased despite the fall in the total rate of consumption of materials. To some extent, especially for metals, the increase in supply came from the destruction of war material. The same happened after the 1914–18 war. Another explanation must have been the very great increase in the price of materials relative to the general level of prices, which made it more profitable to collect

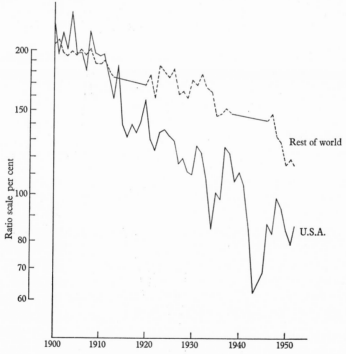

Chart 3. Apparent consumption of materials per unit of manufacturing output: United States and rest of world

waste products and to develop substitutes such as rayon for cotton. The
expansion of home production of materials was as rapid as that of home
agricultural production, while the rise in material import prices was
rather greater than in food import prices. Finally, the shortage of some
imported materials, the habits of economy developed during the war
and various government measures all stimulated the supply of scrap,
waste products and other substitutes. The reduction in exports of
materials was partly due to controls, and the drawing down of stocks
in 1946–9 was made possible by the large stocks of some materials
(especially wool and cotton) built up at the end of the war.

We must next consider the divergence between the changes in consumption of materials and in industrial production. The latter increased
faster than the former both from 1935–8 to 1946–9 and from 1946–9
to 1954–5. The same phenomenon is to be found in other times and
places. The consumption of roughly the same materials per unit of
manufacturing output has fallen more or less persistently since 1900 in
the United States and in the rest of the world (Chart 3). In the United
Kingdom, imports of materials (probably a fair guide to consumption
of these materials in most periods) per unit of output fell between the
wars and also from 1913 to 1920, though not, apparently, from 1900 to
1913 (Chart 4). It must be admitted that, to judge by Chart 4, the

Chart 4. Relative quantity and price of imported materials: United Kingdom

fall in the ratio of imports of materials to industrial output in the United Kingdom seems to have taken place mainly during the two world wars. There is little evidence in the chart of the strong downward trend in the ratio in peacetime which occurred in the United States or the rest of the world. Nevertheless, there are reasons (discussed in Part II) for believing that this trend is a peacetime phenomenon in the United Kingdom as well, and there are several factors which account for it.

In the first place, the consumption of materials per unit of industrial output (measured in terms of money values) is by no means uniform throughout industry. In this study we only distinguish between three broad groups of materials: metals, textiles and 'other'. Metals (metallic ores and non-ferrous metals) are mainly consumed by the metals, engineering and vehicle industries, and are small in relation to the output of those industries. Textile materials (to which are added hides and skins) undergo much less processing by the textile, leather and clothing industries. Other materials are widely used throughout industry and are intermediate between metals and textiles so far as the degree of further processing is concerned. Since 1913, the output of the metal industries has expanded considerably faster than the output of the textile industries (as we shall call them for short). Indeed, the latter have never recovered the level of output they achieved in 1913, whereas the former now produce about five times as much as they did then. This change in the composition of output has appreciably reduced the consumption of materials per unit of total industrial output, since more and more of total output has consisted of metal goods with a low material content, and less and less of textiles with a high material content. An estimate of the effects is given on p. 132. About a third of the fall in the ratio of imports of materials to industrial production from 1900 to 1955 was due to this shift in composition, and it tended to reduce imports by roughly 0·5 % per annum.

Besides this switch from textiles to metals, there were large reductions in materials consumption per unit of industrial production due to what we may call 'trend' factors. After 1935–8, and in earlier periods as well, there was a reduction in consumption per unit of output *within* the metals and textiles industries and the consumption of other materials also rose more slowly than total industrial output (since these materials are so widely used, it seems best to relate them to total output rather than to the output of any particular group of industries). To some extent this was due to changes in the composition of output within the metals and textiles industries, to a substitution of more complex goods requiring more manufacturing processes, for simpler goods. Indeed, it is arbitrary what we call a change in composition, and what we call a pure case of economy in materials consumption per unit of output. Economies have been achieved both in physical terms (for example, less tin is now needed because of the change from hot-dip to electrolytic tin-plating) and in value terms (for example, the substitution of aluminium for copper as the former became cheaper per cubic foot than the latter). It must also be remembered that many important materials are not included in the group we are considering just now, since they are produced for the most part in this country and only to a small extent imported. Amongst these are steel and cement, the consumption of which has risen faster than total industrial production since 1935–8, and which have been substituted for some mainly imported materials (for example, non-ferrous metals and timber). Petroleum is also excluded here (and considered in the next section) and has provided much of the material for plastics and other chemical products. Finally, we must note that the rate of fall in materials consumption per unit of industrial output is measured by comparing two index numbers and that different systems of weighting would show different rates of fall. This raises difficult problems of interpretation, which are discussed in Chapter VII. The same type of problem is encountered throughout this study (see Chapter I and Appendix I).

Apart from changes in stocks and exports of materials, we have distinguished four groups of factors which influence the level of imports of materials: the level of industrial production, the price of imported materials relative to prices in this country, the composition of industrial production as between the metals and textiles industries, and trend factors. In Chapter VII we attempt to estimate the quantitative importance of these factors. The chief difficulty in making the estimates is that industrial production generally rose through time, so that it is not easy to separate its effect on the demand for imports from the effects of the trend factors. The fact that imports rose more slowly than production might have been due either to the production elasticity of demand being less than one (so that any given increase in production tended, by itself, to lead to a less than proportionate increase in the demand for imports) or to trend factors.

The conclusion reached in Chapter VII is that the production elasticity of demand for imports of materials was probably about one. In other words, excluding the effects of changes in the composition of production as between metals and textiles, and excluding the effects of trend factors and relative price changes, it is estimated that a 1 % rise or fall in industrial output caused a 1 % rise or fall in the demand for imports of materials. Consistently with this estimate of the production elasticity, it is estimated that trend factors tended to reduce the demand for imports of materials by about 1 % per annum. For the reason mentioned these are uncertain estimates, and a higher or lower value for the production elasticity would be quite plausible provided it was combined with a bigger or smaller downward trend factor. What is reasonably certain is that the combined effect of increases in production and of the trend factor was to increase the demand for imports of materials more slowly than the increase in industrial production.

There is strong evidence that the effect of changes in the price of imported raw materials relative to the general level of prices in this country on the demand for imports of materials was small in relation to the size of the price changes. There were very large changes in these relative prices which did not have any very marked effect on imports of materials per unit of industrial output. In the United States and in the rest of the world the downward trend of consumption of materials per unit of manufacturing production was not greatly influenced by relative price movements. While it is reasonably certain that the changes in demand caused by changes in prices were relatively small, any estimate of their size is uncertain. The 'best guess' given in Chapter VII is that a 1 % rise in the price of imported materials relative to the general price level in this country eventually led in itself to a fall of about 0·2 % in the demand for them (i.e. the long-run price elasticity of demand was −0·2). This estimate includes the effects which such a price change would have by stimulating home production of materials as well as by reducing total consumption of materials per unit of industrial production.

Table 6. *Causes of the change in the volume of imports of materials, 1935–8 to 1954–5*

Annual rates, £ million (1948 c.i.f. prices)

	Factor	Effect on imports of materials
1	Changes in stocks, exports and imports (semi-processed)	−50
2	Industrial production	270
3	Ratio of metals and textiles output to total	−70
4	Trend	−120
5	Relative prices of imports and internal prices	−110
6	Residual unexplained	50
	Total = Actual change in imports of materials	−30

Note: In making the calculations for this table, imports and industrial production in 1935–8 were adjusted for weighting bias as described on pp. 219, 234. The change in imports therefore differs from that in Table 2, in which no such adjustment is made.

The above estimates can be used to give an explanation of the change in the demand for imports of materials from 1935–8 to 1954–5. The resulting best guesses of the effects of the various factors are given in Table 6. This is similar to Table 4, and there is no need to repeat the explanation and warnings given there. The main difference is that here we have estimated the effects after allowing for interactions between demand and supply, so that we do not separately show effects via changes in consumption and effects via changes in home output.

The rise in industrial production tended to increase imports, but the other factors we have mentioned all tended to reduce them with the result that there was little net change. The effects of the rise in material prices were probably quite large, despite the small price elasticity of demand, because the rise was so big.

In Chapter VII there is a more detailed analysis of the above changes in which the behaviour of imports of metals, textiles and other materials are considered separately. The changes from 1946–9 to 1954–5 are also examined.

It seems likely that in 1946–9 import controls held down the demand for imports of other materials (for example timber and pulp for paper) for these imports fell especially severely from 1935–8 to 1946–9 and then rose sharply as controls were relaxed. At a rough guess the controls may have reduced demand by about £40 million a year at 1948 prices (or by 6 %) during 1946–9, but this is a very uncertain estimate. There is no clear evidence that controls reduced the demand for metal or textile materials by significant amounts, but in so far as they restricted exports of these materials they saved imports indirectly, as we have seen. They may also have influenced import prices, and caused short-term fluctuations in stocks of materials.

From 1946–9 to 1954–5 the quantity of imports of materials rose rather more slowly than industrial production (Table 5). Metals production continued to outstrip textiles production, the relative price of materials continued to rise and the trend factor continued to reduce consumption per unit of industrial output. The relaxation of controls and the end of the withdrawals from stocks were the main factors working the other way.

From 1955 to 1959 imports of materials, taking a classification which roughly corresponds to that used for the earlier years, decreased in quantity by about 3·4 %, whereas industrial production increased by 7 %. The shift in the pattern of industrial production as between metals and textiles probably reduced imports by about 2·8 %. Changes in recorded stocks of imported materials accounted for a further fall of about 1·6 % in imports. If we remove the effects of changes in the pattern of industrial production and of changes in recorded stocks we are left with an increase of about 1 % in imports compared with the 7 % increase in industrial production. The residual fall in imports relative to production therefore amounted to about 1·5 % per annum, appreciably faster than the 1 % per annum in earlier years. However, one cannot safely draw conclusions about a possible change in trend from so short a period.

4. FUELS

Imports of fuels consist of coal and mineral oil. The latter is now mainly crude oil for refining in this country, but imports of refined products are still important. The analysis is confined to crude oil and to those refined products which are mainly used as fuels (imports of lubricating oil, paraffin wax and some other minor items being excluded). As may be seen from Table 7, these excluded items are small.

Imports of fuels were only 12 % of total imports in 1957, but are increasing very rapidly. They more than doubled from 1946–9 to 1954–5 and, unlike any other major category of imports, they were then far above their pre-war level.

Table 7. *Imports and consumption of fuels, pre-war and post-war*

Annual rates, £ million (1948 c.i.f. import prices)*

		1935–8	1946–9	1954–5
Coal				
1	Inland consumption	860	910	1,050
2	Production	1,110	980	1,090
3	Exports and bunkers	250	60	80
4	Change in stocks, etc.	—	—	—
5	Imports $(1-2+3+4)$	—	—	40
Crude oil				
6	Inland consumption and stock change	10	30	190
7	Production	—	—	—
8	Exports	—	—	—
9	Imports $(6-7+8)$	10	30	190
Refined oil for fuel				
10	Inland consumption	70	100	170
11	Production	10	20	210
12	Exports and bunkers	10	10	80
13	Change in stocks, etc.	10	10	20
14	Imports $(10-11+12+13)$	80	100	70
15	Other oil imports	10	10	10
16	Total coal and oil imports $(5+9+14+15)$	110	140	310

* The average value of imported coal in 1948, used in this table, was about £5 per ton, which was double the price of British coal at the pit-head.

Sources: See p. 235.

During most of the period from before the war to 1954–5, there was a shortage of coal. Coal production could not be expanded sufficiently to meet demand, and was inelastic in the short run, so that any rise in inland coal consumption had to be met either by reducing coal exports or by increasing coal imports. Changes in inland consumption of refined

oil also impinged fairly directly on imports or exports. It is true that
home production of refined oil could be (and was) substantially
increased but, as home output of crude oil was negligible, this increase
in home refining necessitated an increase in imports of crude oil.

In seeking to explain the rise in imports of fuels from before the war
to some years afterwards, one must therefore concentrate primarily on
the changes in inland consumption of coal and refined oil. As may be
seen from Table 7, inland coal consumption rose by £190 million per
annum from 1935–8 to 1954–5, if valued at 1948 c.i.f. import prices.
Imports of coal rose by only £40 million per annum, mainly because
exports and bunkers were cut by £170 million. Inland consumption of
refined oil rose by £100 million. Imports actually fell slightly. The
expansion in consumption, together with an increase of £70 million in
exports and bunkers, was met by the increased output of home refineries
which consumed an extra £180 million per annum of imported crude
oil.

To explain the rise in inland fuel consumption we divide it into
consumption by three 'final' sectors—domestic and commercial consumers, industry (which is almost entirely manufacturing industry) and
transport—and consumption by the 'intermediate' sectors—the electricity, gas and coke industries. Coal and oil are consumed by all these
sectors, but the 'intermediate' sectors turn them into other fuels which
compete directly with them for the demand of the 'final' sectors. Table 8
shows how coal and oil were distributed between these sectors in 1954
and also how electricity, gas and coke were distributed (the coal and
oil refining industries are shown as intermediate sectors since they

Table 8. *Inland distribution of fuels in 1954*

(Percentage of total inland consumption of each fuel)

Consuming sector	Coal	Refined oil	Electri-city	Gas	Coke
'Final'					
1 Domestic and commercial	24	7	45	62	36
2 Manufacturing industry	23	30	45	38	64
3 Transport	7	57	3	—	—
'Intermediate'					
4 Coal	—	—	5	—	—
5 Oil refining	—	—	1	—	—
6 Electricity	19	1	—	—	—
7 Gas and coke	27	3	1	—	—
8 Total inland consumption	100	100	100	100	100

Note: The consumption by 'intermediate' sectors of their own fuels is subtracted
in each case from their output, and so is excluded from the table. Electricity privately
generated (except by railways) is not included. The coal or oil used to generate it
is shown as going to the sector which converted it into electricity.

Sources: See p. 236.

consumed small quantities of electricity). The table is to be read vertically.

About half of the inland consumption of coal is channelled to the 'final' consumers through the electricity, gas and coke industries. Little coal goes to transport. The bulk of oil, however, goes to transport (and the proportion was even higher, about three-quarters of the total, before the war). Manufacturing industry takes most of the rest, so that very little oil goes to the 'intermediate' sectors.

The percentages in Table 8 are calculated from data expressed in tons. In Table 9, the original data are expenditures at prices paid by the purchaser. This table shows the relative importance of the different fuels in the total fuel bill of each sector in 1954. The table is to be read horizontally. Coal, either directly or indirectly, is easily the most important fuel purchased by each sector except transport, where oil accounts for nine-tenths of expenditure on fuels. It is to be noted, however, that domestic and commercial consumers and manufacturing industry spend more on 'indirect' coal, in the form of electricity, gas and coke, than they do on direct coal. Before the war, the reverse was true.

Table 9. *Purchases of fuels in 1954*

(Percentages of total purchases by each sector)

Consuming sector	Coal	Refined oil	Electricity	Gas	Coke	Total
'Final'						
1 Domestic and commercial	44	4	20	23	9	100
2 Manufacturing industry	33	10	26	11	20	100
3 Transport	9	89	2	—	—	100
'Intermediate'						
4 Electricity	99	1	—	—	—	100
5 Gas and coke	96	3	1	—	—	100

Note: See note to Table 8. Purchases of fuels by the coal and oil refining industries are not shown. They consisted almost entirely of electricity or crude oil.

Sources: See p. 236.

We are now in a position to trace the changes in inland consumption of fuels, from the pre-war to the post-war period, which were responsible for the large increase in fuel imports and the drop in coal exports. We consider each of the three 'final' sectors in turn. Chart 5 shows the development of their expenditure on all fuels taken together at constant prices from 1924 to 1955. Chart 6 shows how the pattern of fuel expenditure changed between 1935–8 and 1954–5 in two of the sectors: domestic and commercial, and manufacturing industry. Finally, Table

10 sets out the estimated effects on inland consumption of coal and refined oil of the changes in fuel consumption in each sector which occurred over the same period. These estimates include both the increase in coal or refined oil consumed as such in each sector and the increases resulting from higher consumption of electricity, gas or coke. The changes in quantities are valued at 1948 import prices, and so are directly comparable with the figures in Table 7.

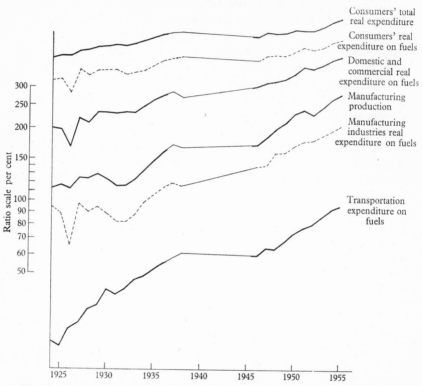

Chart 5. Domestic, commercial, manufacturing industries and transportation expenditure on fuels

Domestic consumers' expenditure on all fuels at constant prices changed in approximately the same proportion as their expenditure on all goods and services at constant prices from 1924 to 1938 and again from 1938 to 1946–7 (Chart 5). It then appears to have risen slightly in relation to expenditure on all goods and services, and then to have more or less maintained the same relative position. As fuel rationing was probably more severe immediately after the war, this suggests a slight rise in the demand for fuel relative to total demand from pre-war to post-war, but the figures are too unreliable to place much reliance on the relative movement involved (which was only about 5 % or less). Domestic *and commercial* expenditure on fuels increased more rapidly than domestic consumers' expenditure, presumably because of the more rapid growth of commercial expenditure—in shops, offices, hospitals, street lighting, etc. (the two series in Chart 5 are derived from different sources, and may not be exactly comparable). Coal consumption fell from 1935–8 to 1954–5, but consumption of all other fuels increased, the rise in electricity consumption being especially striking (Chart 6). The shift away from coal and towards electricity was

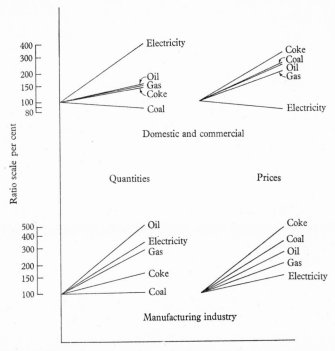

Chart 6. Changes in quantities and prices of fuels, 1935–8 to 1954–5

a continuation of a long-standing trend, and was associated with a relative cheapening of electricity in terms of coal. The increase in coal consumed indirectly in the form of electricity, gas and coke outweighed the fall in direct coal consumption by an estimated £90 million at 1948 import prices (Table 10, line 1). The rise in oil consumption amounted to only a few million pounds sterling—too small to feature in Table 10.

Manufacturing industry's expenditure on all fuels at constant prices increased rather more slowly than manufacturing production from 1924 to 1938 and again from 1946 to 1955 (Chart 5), the relative drop being of the order of 1 % per annum. From pre-war to post-war, however, expenditure on fuels increased by about 17 % more than manufacturing production. There seems to have been no obvious shift in the composition of manufacturing production which would explain this increase in fuel consumption per unit of output. Iron and steel and building materials are two industries with a relatively high level of fuel consumption per unit of output, but from 1935–8 to 1946–9 the output of the former increased by about the same amount as, and the output of the latter by much less than, the output of all manufacturing industry. Yet in the inter-war period both iron and steel and building materials production rose faster than manufacturing production. Part of the explanation may lie in the shift in the composition of fuel consumption. From 1935–8 to 1954–5 consumption of coal barely changed, while consumption of oil, electricity and gas all rose very substantially (Chart 6). The last three fuels cost more per ton of coal equivalent than does coal, so that the rise in fuel consumption per unit of manufacturing output when the former is measured in value terms would be greater than the rise when it is measured in terms of coal (or calorific) equivalent. On the other hand, the more expensive fuels can often be more efficiently used and there were similar (though perhaps less marked) shifts in the composition of fuel consumption from 1946 to 1955, a period in which fuel expenditure per unit of manufacturing output fell. The increase from 1935–8 to 1954–5 in coal consumed by manufacturing industry (nearly all indirectly as electricity, gas or coke) is estimated to have cost £140 million at 1948 import prices, and the increase in refined oil consumption amounted to a further £30 million (Table 10, line 2).

Expenditure on fuel for transport (which includes motor spirit consumed by private motorists) rose very rapidly from 1924 to 1938 and again from 1946 to 1955 (Chart 5), but barely changed from 1938 to 1946. The increases were almost all due to the increased consumption of refined oil. Coal consumption by railways and coastwise shipping declined slowly, except between the pre-war and post-war periods when the shortage of oil and motor vehicles stimulated the demand for railway transport. Electricity consumption for transport, after increasing in the 'twenties and 'thirties, stagnated in the 'forties and fell in the 'fifties. Oil consumption roughly doubled from 1924 to 1930, increased by another two-thirds from 1930 to 1938, then fell to 1946 and from 1946 to 1955 increased at a rate sufficient to double itself in ten years. The rise in refined oil consumption for transport from 1935–8 to 1954–5 cost about £60 million at 1948 import prices (Table 10, line 3) and there was a small fall in the cost of coal consumed.

In Table 10 the estimates of the costs of the changes from 1935–8 to 1954–5 in the three 'final' sectors' consumption of coal and refined oil are brought together. They accounted for most of the change in inland fuel consumption of £290 million. The change in manufacturing industry's consumption was the most important in total, but the increase in consumption of refined oil for transport accounted for most of the change in inland consumption of refined oil.

Three other items explain the rest of the change in inland consumption. Firstly, there was a reduction in coal inputs per unit of electricity and gas and coke output, and a small increase in refined oil input per unit of output which altogether reduced inland consumption by £30 million (line 4 of Table 10). The estimates of the cost of the changes in the consumption of the three 'final' sectors were made on the assumption of constant input-output ratios, so the improvement in efficiency is shown here separately. Secondly, there was an increase in fuel consumption by the coal and oil refining industries, which cost £10 million (Table 10, line 5 and footnote *). Finally, the fall in exports of coke and manufactured fuel reduced inland coal consumption (line 6 of Table 10).

Table 10. *Causes of the change in inland consumption of coal and refined oil, 1935–8 to 1954–5*

Annual rates, £ million (1948 c.i.f. prices)

	Item	Effect on consumption		
		Coal	Oil	Total
1	Domestic and commercial consumption	90	—	90
2	Manufacturing industry consumption	140	30	180
3	Transport consumption	—	60	50
4	Fuel input per unit of output—electricity, gas and coke	−40	—	−30
5	Fuel used by coal and oil refining*	10	—	10
6	Exports of coke and manufactured fuel†	−10	—	−10
	Total above = change in inland consumption of coal and refined oil	190	100	290

* Change in consumption of coal in the form of electricity used by the coal or oil refining industries plus change in coal consumption by the oil refining industry. Changes in the coal industry's consumption of coal as such, or in oil refiners' consumption of refined oil, are excluded, since they are deducted from gross output to arrive at the net output figures in Table 7.

† Reduction in inland coal consumption due to fall in exports of coke and manufactured fuel.

The coal shortage had almost disappeared by 1957, and in 1958 and 1959 stocks of coal in this country rose to very high levels. Exports of coal were limited by demand rather than (as before) by supply and imported coal became much cheaper in relation to home-produced coal, partly because the fall in Atlantic freight rates reduced the landed cost of American coal. Imports were, however, restricted in order to maintain the demand for home-produced coal, and so fell to a negligible quantity.

In this situation, changes in inland coal consumption no longer impinged directly on imports or exports of coal, since the changes could be met by reducing or increasing stocks of coal or coal production. Fuel imports consisted almost entirely of oil, either crude or refined, and an explanation of their changes required, in the first place, an explanation of the changes in inland consumption of refined oil.

In this respect the situation was similar to that which existed between the wars when, apart from the years affected by strikes (1921, 1926 and 1927), coal imports were negligible. But there were differences. About two-thirds of retained imports of fuels in 1930 consisted of motor and aviation spirit. About four-fifths of the increase in retained imports of fuels from 1924 to 1938 was in the same products. An explanation of the expansion of imports of fuels and an explanation of the expansion of road and air transport (including private motoring) are much the same thing for this period. There were two main differences in the post-war situation. First, the growth in home refining meant that most imports consisted of crude and not refined oil. Second, there was the growth in oil consumption outside the field of transportation. In 1954 transport accounted for only 57 % of inland consumption of refined oil (Table 8, p. 34), compared with about 75 % in 1938. We have already seen that transport only accounted for 60 % of the growth in inland consumption of refined oil from 1935–8 to 1954–5 (Table 10, line 3). Much of the rapid continuing increase in oil imports was due to the switch away from coal to oil, especially fuel oil, in manufacturing industry, and there was also a rapid growth in oil consumption for space-heating by domestic and commercial consumers.

From 1955 to 1959 inland consumption of petroleum products from refineries, measured in tons, rose by rather more than 12 % per annum, or somewhat faster than in the years 1946 to 1955 when the rate of growth was nearly 11 % per annum. The value of retained imports of oil at constant prices increased by about 9 % per annum from 1955 to 1959. It was mainly the slower rate of growth of exports that accounted for the faster increase in consumption than in imports.

5. MANUFACTURES

Imports of manufactures in general represent only a small part of the total sales of similar manufactures on the home market. This is the characteristic which distinguishes them most sharply from the other groups of imports. In many other respects they are similar to imports of materials. In 1954 about two-thirds consisted of intermediate goods (or semi-manufactures), that is, they were 'materials' for some further manufacturing process. Chemicals, leather, plywood, paper, textile yarns and fabrics and iron and steel are typical. The rest consisted of finished capital goods and finished consumer goods (respectively about a quarter and an eighth of the total).

Table 11. *Imports and sales of manufactures, pre-war and post-war*

Annual rate, £ million (1948 c.i.f. or factory prices)

		1935–8	1946–9	1954–5
1	Sales on the home market	5,870	6,680	9,780
2	Production (gross)	6,380	7,540	10,940
3	Exports	950	1,110	1,610
4	Imports (1−2+3)	430	250	460
			(Index numbers)	
5	Manufacturing production (net)	100	120	172
6	Sales of manufactures on the home market	100	114	167
7	Imports of manufactures	100	57	106

Note: Production and sales of manufactures in lines 1, 2 and 6 are measured gross of duplication. For example, production and sales of yarn are included as well as production and sales of cloth and clothes. Food, drink and tobacco manufactures, mineral oils and non-ferrous metals and manufactures are excluded from all lines except line 5, which refers to manufacturing industry as conventionally defined.

Sources: Similar to those used for S 72–7, see p. 231.

The marginal nature of imports of manufactures lends itself to large fluctuations in their volume. Of our four main groups of imports, manufactures fell proportionately the most from 1935–8 to 1946–9, and only fuels showed a faster increase from 1946–9 to 1954–5. Hence, although manufactures were only about 17 % of total imports at 1948 prices in 1954–5, they accounted for about 30 % of the fall and subsequent rise in the total volume.

Despite their rapid recovery, imports of manufactures in 1954–5 were barely greater than before the war, while manufacturing production and total sales of manufactures on the home market were each about 70 % up. There were still some controls which restricted imports in 1954–5, particularly imports of paper and board and imports from the dollar area. A higher proportion of imports than of home production may also have consisted of those goods for which sales on the home market were increasing the slowest. The main reason why imports fell behind, however, was probably that they became relatively more expensive than home-produced manufactures. The extent to which they did so is uncertain, but, for the reasons discussed below, a moderate relative increase in price (10 to 20 %) would have been quite enough to explain the whole of the relative fall in quantity, and the available data suggest that there was an increase of this order.

There are several reasons for supposing that the demand for imported manufactures is sensitive to changes in their prices relative to the prices of manufactures in this country (that is, that the price elasticity of demand for manufactures is high). The most persuasive evidence relates to the experience of 1932. At the end of 1931 and the beginning of 1932 the pound depreciated relatively to the currencies of our main foreign suppliers of manufactures, and we imposed tariffs on most

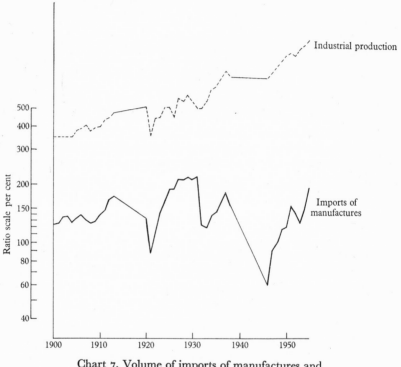

Chart 7. Volume of imports of manufactures and
industrial production

imports of manufactures. There was a large and rapid fall in these imports (see Charts 7 and 18). From 1931 to 1932 they fell by more than 40% in volume. The timing of this fall, the fact that it was un-accompanied by any significant drop in total sales of manufactures on the home market, and its permanent nature—imports of manu-factures remaining at roughly the same (lower) proportion of sales on the home market until 1938—all suggest that it was due to the relative price changes accompanying the changes in exchange rates and tariffs. Yet, to judge from the statistics available, the average price of imports, including tariffs, only rose by about 10 % relatively to the average price of home-produced manufactures. From these changes one can calculate a price elasticity of demand for imported manufactures of about -7, on certain assumptions. This is considerably larger than previous estimates have suggested.

The fact that the relative price of imported manufactures increased by only about 10 % in 1932 might be attributed to some freak of the index numbers. An examination of some individual imported commodities does not bear this out. For standardized semi-manufactures like yarn, cloth, steel, leather and newsprint, the prices of imports and home products moved closely in line with each other. This was true both for the years 1930 to 1935 and for other pre-war years for which the data are available (see Chart 20 and pp. 176 ff.). For these goods (and it must be remembered that most imports of manufactures are semi-manufactures, and probably have similar characteristics) the implication seems to be that imports and home products are very close substitutes for each other, so that any significant divergence in price will usually lead to a marked switch from one source of supply to another. For imports like cars, toilet soap, carpets and cycle-tubes, the relative price movements were larger, though still small compared with the accompanying changes in relative quantities (Chart 20). For these goods the price data are less reliable and all one can say is that the evidence is consistent with the view that the demand for imports is sensitive to relative price changes.

It is significant, too, that the price index of imported manufactures moved closely in line with the price index of exported manufactures both from 1900 to 1913 and from 1920 to 1938 (Chart 19). If we can take the export price index as an indication of changes in the prices of home-produced manufactures sold in the home market (and no better index seems available for all these years), this supports the view that imported and home-produced manufactures are close substitutes for each other. In the early 1920's there was a very rapid increase in the volume of imports of manufactures (Chart 7), and yet they did not become noticeably cheaper in relation to our exports.

The fact that the relative prices of imported and home-produced manufactures changed little in peace-time before the last war also explains why previous econometric studies of the demand for imports of manufactures often found that relative price changes were not closely related to changes in the quantity of imports. Such relative price changes as occurred were small, and are best regarded as merely chance fluctuations such as one expects to find in index numbers. One cannot conclude from this that the price-elasticity of demand for imports is low. Instead one should ask *why* the relative price movements were so small, and the most plausible explanation seems to be that the price-elasticity of demand was high.

In the post-war years we no longer find such a close correspondence between the prices of imported and home-produced manufactures. This is true both for the average prices of all imports (see Chart 19 for a comparison with export prices) and for the prices of individual commodities—even semi-manufactures like steel and superphosphate of lime (see Chart 20). The main explanation probably is that in those years home-produced manufactures were not always easy to get. Home steel producers, for example, were working at full capacity for much of the period. Their steel was much cheaper than imported steel, so that steel consumers usually bought it when they could. But whenever there was a sharp increase in the demand for steel it could only be satisfied by imports, for which steel consumers were then prepared to pay (either individually or collectively) very large premiums. As a result of this situation, steel imports were extremely volatile. Instead of rising or falling in roughly the same proportions as total sales of steel on the home market, as they had done before the war, they multiplied several times in years of shortage and in other years sank to almost nothing. The same was true, though to a lesser extent, of other manufactures for which home production was at or near maximum capacity. The greater volatility of imports in the post-war years was also due to import controls, which were alternately tightened and relaxed in response to changes in the balance of payments situation.

The rapid increase in imports of manufactures from 1946-9 to 1954-5 (over 9 % per annum) may be attributed to the general expansion of the home market, to the recovery of our continental suppliers, and to the relaxation of import controls. There is no evidence of any marked cheapening in imports relative to home-produced manufactures over this period.

If the proportion of total sales of manufactures on the home market that consisted of imports had been the same in 1946-9 as in 1954-5, imports would have been some £70 million a year higher in the earlier period in terms of 1948 prices. This is equivalent to a rise of about 25 %, and is a minimum estimate of the increase which would have taken place in the absence of import controls and if foreign supplies had been available. The increase would almost certainly have been larger in view of the shortage of many manufactures on the home market at that time. One cannot easily separate the effects of the import restrictions and of the shortage of foreign supplies. After the 1914-18 war, imports of manufactures were also low in relation to total sales on the home market, and they increased rapidly in the 1920's as we have seen. Yet there were no import controls on the scale of those in

1946–9. This suggests that the effect of the controls in 1946–9 was small. Yet the two situations were not exactly the same. There was no general shortage of manufactures on the home market after 1920. Unemployment then was 10 to 15 % instead of $1\frac{1}{2}$ to 3 % as in 1946–9. Consequently, imports from countries relatively unaffected by the war (for example, the United States and Canada) did not flood in so much as they might have done in 1948 or 1949 if import controls had been removed.

From 1955 to 1959 imports of manufactures increased by about $5\frac{1}{2}$ % per annum. The slower rate of growth was due to the slackening in demand for such products, which led to a more than proportionate slowing down in the rate of growth of imports of manufactures. As the steel shortage disappeared, and became replaced by a surplus, imports of steel fell by nearly two-thirds. Other imports of manufactures, while much less volatile than steel, behaved similarly. The behaviour of imports in this period is analysed in greater detail on pp. 54–7. It seems likely that the underlying upward trend in imports was considerably more than $5\frac{1}{2}$ % per annum, but that it was masked by the effects of the changes in the pressure of demand. This upward trend owed something to a continued relaxation of import restrictions, and also to a lowering of labour costs and a faster rate of expansion of supplies of manufactures abroad compared with this country. The relaxation of import restrictions may also have partly accounted for the much more rapid growth of imports of finished than semi-finished manufactures over this period.

6. SUMMARY

From 1935–8 to 1954–5 national output rose about 40 % while imports barely increased in volume. Probably the main reason for the failure of imports to rise by more than a small percentage was the increase in their price in relation to the prices of goods produced in this country. This chiefly affected the demand for imports of food and manufactures, but the effect on imports of materials may also have been quite substantial. The writer's best guess is that total imports, but for the relative increase in their price, might have risen by something like a third in volume between 1935–8 and 1954–5.

There were, however, other important factors which tended to reduce the demand for imports. Much of the expansion in agricultural production was unrelated to the rise in the price of food. The change in the pattern of industrial production as between the metals and textiles industries and the continuing trend towards economy in consumption of materials both reduced the demand for imported materials. Each of these factors may have reduced imports by something of the order of

4 %, and the cut in coal exports, given the levels of coal consumption and production, saved extra coal imports which would have increased the total import bill by something like 6 %.

The level of imports in 1946–9 was substantially below the level of free demand for them. Had supplies been available abroad, the removal of all controls might have increased them by perhaps something like £300 million a year (but the effect might have been much larger or smaller—it is most uncertain). It was largely because of the removal of these controls that the effective demand for imports rose faster than the national product in the post-war years up to 1955. Similar factors to those mentioned above were damping down demand—the rise in import prices (less important in this period), the expansion of agriculture, the change in the pattern of industrial production as between the metals and textiles industries, and economy in materials. The cushion of coal exports had gone, however, and there was a rapid growth in oil consumption and exports which increased the demand for imports of oil.

From 1955 to 1959 the national product rose by nearly 7 % and the quantity of imports by about 9 %. The ending of the coal and steel shortages caused a sharp drop in the imports of these commodities. Apart from these, imports grew by over 13 %, appreciably faster than the national product. The main reasons for this were probably the fall in import prices, which stimulated demand for imports of food and manufactures, the increasingly rapid growth of inland consumption of oil and the further relaxation of restrictions on imports of manufactures.

CHAPTER III

TRENDS AND FLUCTUATIONS IN IMPORTS

I. INTRODUCTION

In this chapter we are no longer concerned only with the past effects of various factors on the demand for imports, but also with their probable future effects, both in the long and the short run.

It is convenient to discuss the long-run effects in terms of the probable trend in imports over the next five years or so. The estimates are based on certain assumptions about the way in which the various determinants of the demand for imports are going to change, and this is christened for short the 'normal trend'. This is not, however, meant to be a forecast of the way in which imports actually will change, and it is followed by estimates of the effects on imports of altering some of the assumptions so that any number of forecasts could be made by choosing different sets of assumptions. Details of the estimates are given in a note at the end of the chapter.

The discussion of year-to-year fluctuations in imports deals, first, with some of the differences between annual changes in the volume of retained imports, which form the main subject of this study, and annual changes in the value of imports as they appear in the balance of payments accounts. There is then an attempt to estimate the short-run marginal propensity to import, that is, the change in the volume of imports which is likely to accompany a given change in the real national product in the short run.

The estimates in this chapter are of some relevance both for forecasting imports and for deciding economic policy. The latter is discussed in Chapter IV.

2. TRENDS

The estimates of the long-term effects of various factors on the demand for imports are mostly those described in Chapter II and Part II, but in order to obtain as complete a picture as possible some additional estimates and guesses were made. While all are very uncertain, it is hoped that bias has been avoided in the estimates for the separate commodity groups, so that the estimates for the total may be more accurate owing to the cancelling of errors.

The main influences taken into account are industrial production, consumers' real current expenditure per head, the population, and import prices in relation to prices in this country. It was thought useful to estimate the likely rate of growth in the demand for imports on certain fairly plausible assumptions about the behaviour of the first three factors assuming no change in tariffs, subsidies or in the level of import prices relative to prices in this country. For short, we may call this the 'normal' increase in imports. It does not depend *solely* on the behaviour of these key factors. Assumptions have also to be made, for example, about the increase in home agricultural output, the rate of switching from coal to oil, and so on. Other plausible assumptions about all these factors could be made, but since we must start somewhere we have chosen a particular combination of them and christened them 'normal'. In what follows, every attempt is made to help the reader to see how he should adjust the 'normal' increase to allow for variations in the assumptions.

As a start, then, we assume that industrial production grows at 3·3 % per annum, consumers' expenditure per head at 2·4 % per annum, and the population at 0·4 % per annum. These are all the rates of growth of these factors from 1953 to 1957. The reasons for choosing them are given in the notes on p. 58. Very briefly, it is thought that the relation of output to the amount of capital and labour available was 'normal' in both years, so that the rates of growth from one to the other were due to long-run rather than cyclical factors. The rate of population growth of 0·4 % per annum is also that officially forecast for the years 1957 to 1963.

Besides these, the other principal assumptions made were that home food production would rise by 1⅓ % per annum, which is the same rate of increase as that achieved from 1935–9 to 1951–5 after eliminating the effects of the relative increase in the price of food (assuming a price elasticity of supply of 0·5); that imports of materials would rise by 1·4 % per annum less than industrial production; that there would be a continued rapid switch in demand from coal to oil, the estimated increase in inland oil consumption being based on a recent forecast for 1965 made for the National Coal Board[1]; that imports of coal would be negligible; and that imports of manufactures, in the absence of relative price changes and changes in import restrictions, would rise at the same rate as sales of manufactures on the home market. For further details of these and other assumptions, together with estimates of the effects on imports of varying some of them, see pp. 58–63.

Given all these assumptions, the 'normal' increase works out at 2·4 % per annum. This is probably rather less than the increase in the gross domestic product which would follow from our assumptions, since from 1953 to 1957 it rose by 2·7 % per annum.

[1] See below, p. 60, n. 1.

Table 12. *Long-term effects of some factors on the volume of retained imports*
£ million 1957 (c.i.f. prices) and percentages of imports in 1957

Item	Retained imports in 1957 (£m.) (1)	'Normal'* annual increase		Effects on imports of 1% changes in							
				Industrial production		Consumers' expenditure per head		Population		Price of imports	
		(%) (2)	(£m.) (3)	(%) (4)	(£m.) (5)	(%) (6)	(£m.) (7)	(%) (8)	(£m.) (9)	(%) (10)	(£m.) (11)
Food	1,472	0·9	14	—	—	0·4	6	1·4	21	0·6	9
Alcoholic beverages	28	2·5	0·7	—	—	0·9	0·3	1·0	0·3	..	..
Tobacco	85	3·6	3·1	—	—	0·3	0·3	1·0	0·9	..	..
Materials	1,185	1·9	23	1·0	12	—	—	—	—	0·2	2
Coal†	25	—	—	×	12	×	3	×	9	..	..
Oil†	437	×	27	×	2	×	1	×	1	..	..
Manufactures	704	4·0	28	1·0	7	—	—	—	—	7·0	49
Total (excluding coal)	3,912	2·4	96	0·5	21	0·2	8	0·6	23	1·5	60
Total (including coal)	3,937	2·4	96	0·8	32	0·3	11	0·8	32	1·5	60

Note: $\times$ = not applicable, since for coal and oil the various changes in imports were estimated in absolute terms, rather than as percentage changes of imports in 1957.
    .. = not estimated, and assumed zero in obtaining the total.
  * Assuming, *inter alia*, the following annual percentage increases:

industrial production	3·3
consumers' expenditure per head	2·4
population	0·4
price of imports relative to prices in this country	nil

† For coal and oil the effects of the changes in cols. (5), (7) and (9) show the cost of the resulting changes in consumption at import prices. These would only be the effects on imports if home production of coal or refined oil, and exports and investment in stocks, were unaffected.

The estimated effects of changes in the assumed rates of growth of industrial production, consumers' expenditure per head, population and import prices relative to internal prices are shown in columns (4) to (11) of Table 12. These effects are independently additive. To take a simple arithmetical example, a 1% faster growth in population coupled with a 1% faster growth in industrial production and a 1% slower growth in consumers' expenditure per head would increase the rate of growth from 2·4% per annum to 2·4 + 0·6 + 0·5 − 0·2 = 3·3% per annum (excluding coal throughout). Two totals are given, one excluding and one including coal. The latter would only be relevant in the event of a renewed shortage of coal. It shows the effect on imports of changes in the various factors, assuming that the whole of any increase in coal consumption leads to an equal increase in imports of coal.

The most striking effect shown is that of a change in import prices in columns (10) and (11). It is estimated that a drop of 1% in the price of each group of imports would, in the long run, increase the demand for imports by about $1\frac{1}{2}$%. This is a particularly uncertain estimate, but it is not thought to be biased. The true increase might be greater or smaller. Most of the increase would probably occur in imports of manufactures, and the reasons for believing that the change here could be large are mentioned in Chapter II (pp. 42 to 44) and are set out at length in Chapter VIII.[1] The assumptions on which these price effects are estimated must be briefly mentioned here. First, for food and raw materials, it is assumed that the change in import prices is accompanied by no change in the general price level in this country (as measured by the average value of the gross domestic product at factor cost). Second, for manufactures it is assumed that the fall (say) in import prices is accompanied by a fall in the quantity of United Kingdom exports of manufactures, due to the fall in manufacturing costs abroad relative to costs in this country, and that the government keeps the level of employment constant in this country so that, in order to offset the fall in exports, the price level of home-produced manufactures for sale on the home market at least does not fall. No allowance is made for any increase in the demand for imports of tobacco, alcoholic beverages or oil as a result of a drop in their price. Because of the high specific duties, the effects on the demand for the first two of these groups of imports would be small, and for the same reason the demand for motor spirit would be little affected. The demand for other grades of oil might, however, increase somewhat. Chart 6 suggests *some* responsiveness of *relative* fuel demands to *relative* fuel prices, so that, unless coal prices fell, oil might be substituted for coal to some extent.

Some readers may find the effect of a 1 % change in population on imports surprisingly large, and that of a change in consumers' expenditure per head surprisingly small. It must be remembered that the change in population assumes consumers' expenditure *per head* is constant, so that a 1 % increase in population is accompanied by a 1 % increase in consumers' expenditure. This leads to an equal proportionate increase in food consumption and to a more than proportionate increase in food imports, since home food output is little affected. On the other hand, the increase in consumers' expenditure per head (which excludes any effect this would have through increasing industrial production) leads to a much less than proportionate increase in food consumption, and so to a smaller increase in food imports.

If it is assumed—the rate of growth in the population and relative import prices being unchanged—that an extra 1 % per annum in the rate of growth of the real gross domestic product is accompanied

---

[1] See p. 161 for the estimate of −7 for the elasticity of substitution; and pp. 167–8 for the reasons why, and the assumptions on which, the elasticity of demand approximately equals the elasticity of substitution.

by an extra 1 % per annum in the rate of growth of consumers' real expenditure and $1\frac{1}{4}$ % per annum in industrial production (these being the approximate relative rates of growth in 1953–7), then the extra imports demanded would be about 0·9 % per annum taking the estimates in the penultimate line of Table 12 (i.e. excluding coal). The long-run marginal propensity to import would thus be rather less than the average propensity to import, and the ratio of imports to the gross domestic product would tend to fall provided the rate of growth of the latter exceeded a minimum level of about 1·2 % per annum. Imports at constant prices would tend to grow faster than the gross domestic product if import prices fell sufficiently fast, and generally speaking a small fall would be sufficient. Thus, taking the 'normal' increases in industrial production, etc., a fall of little more than 0·1 % per annum in import prices would be enough to make imports grow faster than the gross domestic product, on the estimates given here. Changes in some of the other assumptions, described in the note at the end of this chapter, could also bring this about.

3. FLUCTUATIONS

Our main concern is with changes in the quantity of imports as recorded in the official trade returns, but for analysing or forecasting the balance of payments it is changes in the current value of imports as recorded for balance of payments purposes which is relevant. Year-to-year changes in these two magnitudes may differ, both because of differences between the value of imports on a trade and payments basis, and because of changes in the price of imports.

We consider first the difference between imports in the official trade returns and imports as recorded in the official estimates of the balance of payments. The former are on a c.i.f. basis (that is, their value includes the insurance and freight costs of bringing them to this country) while the latter are f.o.b. (that is, their value 'free on board' at their port of departure overseas). This is the main difference, but there are other differences of timing and coverage. For various reasons it was not easy to account for the whole of these differences in the past, let alone forecast them in the future.[1] One might have assumed that the

---

[1] For a full account of the sources and methods used in earlier years, see the Treasury's *United Kingdom Balance of Payments 1946–57* (H.M.S.O. 1959) and *United Kingdom Balance of Payments 1956 to 1959*, Cmnd. 861 (H.M.S.O. 1959); and Anne Romanis, 'The Shipping Bill for British Imports', *Bulletin of the Oxford University Institute of Statistics*, vol. 16, nos. 9–10, September–October 1954, p. 329. More recently, however, the use of the Exchange Control records as the main source for the estimates of imports from non-sterling countries in the balance of payments

value of imports on the payments basis was going to change in the same proportion from year to year as the value on the trade basis, but this could have led to sizeable errors. For example, if one had proceeded on this assumption in the years 1952 to 1958, then, with a correct forecast of imports on a trade basis, one would on average have been some £50 million out with imports on a payments basis. The range of error would have been —£60 million to +£100 million.

Year-to-year changes in the price of imports have been an important component of the changes in their value. From 1952 to 1958 the average year-to-year change in the average value of imports (that is, the price index obtained by dividing an index of current value by an index of volume) accounted for a change (plus or minus) of about £150 million in the value of imports. This was about the same as the average change in value due to changes in the volume of imports. The range of year-to-year changes on account of price was —£400 million (in 1952–3) to +£110 million (in 1954–5), which is greater than that on account of volume, —£30 million to +£380 million. In the earlier post-war years the changes in both price and quantity were greater but, since these were somewhat exceptional, the following analysis will be confined on the whole to the more recent years.

Annual changes in the rate of investment in stocks of mainly imported commodities may also be substantial in relation to annual changes in the value of imports. From 1952 to 1958 the average annual change (plus or minus) in the current value of the rate of investment in these stocks was about £80 million and the range was from —£110 million to £150 million.[1] It is difficult to explain these changes in investment in stocks. In the earlier post-war years there were occasions on which some stocks were run down so as to save imports, and other occasions when shortages of supplies led to unwanted reductions in stocks. Stocks of strategic foodstuffs and materials were built up, mainly in 1951 but also in 1952–5, following the Korean War in 1950; some of these were liquidated in 1956–8. At the end of the war large stocks of certain textile materials had been accumulated, and these were reduced in the ensuing years. There is no clear relationship between the rate of investment in stocks of mainly imported commodities and the rate of investment in all stocks and work in progress in the economy. Nor is there

accounts has been abandoned, and the Trade Accounts are now being used, after adjustment, for all imports. This means that the differences between imports in the official trade returns and in the official estimates of the balance of payments are all statistical adjustments made by the authorities themselves. See *Economic Trends* (H.M.S.O.), March 1961.

[1] Based on estimates given in the *National Institute Economic Review*, no. 6, November 1959, p. 54.

any clear tendency for investment in stocks of imported industrial materials to vary systematically with the level of industrial activity. Fluctuations in manufacturing production in the United States and in the rest of the world appear to have been greater than fluctuations in their apparent consumption[1] of materials, which suggests that stocks of these materials are built up in a recession and run down in a boom. As production of materials cannot easily be adjusted immediately in response to changes in industrial demand, this result is not surprising. Imports of materials into the United Kingdom can, however, be more easily adjusted, and there is no similar tendency for United Kingdom production to fluctuate more (or less) than imports (see Chart 11). Finally, in this catalogue of negative conclusions, there is no obvious systematic relationship between the rate of investment in stocks of imported commodities and changes in import prices. It is possible that the variety of influences playing upon investment in stocks is such as to obscure the effects of any one. For example, the fact that price changes are not related in any obvious way to investment in stocks does not mean that they are not related at all. But since there are no adequate data for pre-war, and since in the years immediately following the war there were important special factors such as import controls, it is doubtful whether there is yet enough data available to make a study of these relationships fruitful.[2]

It is clear from the foregoing that the various causal factors, whose effects on the quantity of imports demanded are described briefly in Chapter II and more fully in Part II, account for only a modest part of the year-to-year changes in the value of imports as they appear in the balance of payments. Somebody charged with the task of forecasting this value would need much more than a series of forecasts of these causal factors. The results of this study are not very useful for making short-term forecasts even of the volume of imports, since there are many factors, such as stock changes and the weather, which behave erratically and whose influence in the short run can be important. For some questions of economic policy, however, these erratic influences may be ignored. What is needed is a rough idea of the effect of making a change in some economic magnitude *ceteris paribus*. We therefore conclude this section with a discussion of the probable size of the short-run marginal propensity to import, that is, of the effect on the demand for imports of a change in the gross domestic product. The relevance

[1] That is, production plus imports and less exports of materials, which would differ from true consumption by the amount of investment in stocks of materials.

[2] For some further comments see the writer's 'Changes in Stocks of mainly Imported Goods in the United Kingdom', *Bulletin of the Oxford University Institute of Statistics*, vol. 20, no. 1, February 1958, p. 53.

of our estimates to questions of economic policy is discussed in the next chapter.

As a first approximation to what we are seeking, we may take the estimates in Table 12. In order to use them, we first need to know what changes in industrial production and consumers' expenditure per head are associated in the short run with a given change in the gross domestic product. We cannot assume that the long-run relationships taken in the previous section (a 1 % change in the gross domestic product being accompanied by a 1 % change in consumers' expenditure and a $1\frac{1}{4}$ % change in industrial production) also apply in the short run. For here we are concerned with deviations from trends, rather than with the trends themselves. We want to know how much higher above their respective trends consumers' expenditure or industrial production will be in any year in which the gross domestic product is x % above *its* trend. To judge from the experience of recent years, a 1 % deviation in the gross domestic product is accompanied by about the same deviation in consumers' expenditure and by about a $1\frac{1}{2}$ % deviation in industrial production. In particular circumstances the deviations could be different, and in fact there is no unique short-run marginal propensity to import. It is useful, all the same, to estimate its value in circumstances which may be regarded as typical.

Applying these changes in industrial production and consumers' expenditure to the estimates in the penultimate line of Table 12 (i.e. excluding coal), we find that a 1 % deviation in the gross domestic product would be accompanied by about the same percentage deviation in the quantity of imports. The marginal and average propensities to import would thus be the same. The latter equalled 0·20 in 1957,[1] so that the estimate implies that for every £5 deviation in the gross domestic product the deviation in imports would be £1.

This estimate may be applicable when there is a fair amount of slack in the economy, as there was before the war. In post-war conditions of full or over-full employment, however, there is evidence that imports of manufactures changed by more than the same proportion as sales of manufactures on the home market. Mention of this was made in Chapter II (p. 44). Although changes in import controls undoubtedly accounted for much of the volatility of imports, there were other important factors at work. Steel imports are easily the most volatile group distinguished in Chart 17, and here the explanation lies in the relative cheapness of home-produced steel and the fact that home producers were operating for most of the period at their maximum

---

[1] This figure is the result of dividing the value of retained imports as recorded in the Trade and Navigation Accounts by the value of the gross domestic product at factor cost.

capacity, so that fluctuations in demand led to exaggerated fluctuations in imports. Steel was probably an extreme example of a situation which existed for several groups of manufactures. In general, foreign manufacturers followed a more flexible pricing policy than British manufacturers. Import prices of manufactures rose more sharply during the boom of 1951 and also fell more rapidly when the boom subsided. A sudden increase in home demand for manufactures no longer led to roughly equal proportionate increases in imports and home-produced sales as it did before the war. Instead, it led to a much more than proportionate increase in imports. The latter were more expensive than the home products, but they were more readily available.

The rise in imports of engineering products in 1952 (Chart 17) was partly the result of this phenomenon. Rearmament led to increased demands being placed on the engineering industry just at the time the steel shortage was hampering its efforts to increase output. Large orders were accordingly placed abroad, and imports increased very sharply since the shortages there were less acute. After defence orders had subsided, imports of engineering products fell although total sales on the home market continued to expand (Chart 17).[1]

In conditions of full employment, therefore, we may expect that each 1% deviation in industrial production above its trend value will lead to a deviation in imports of manufactures of *more* than 1% above their trend value. In order to get some rough idea of how much more, we may examine the behaviour of imports of manufactures since 1953. It is unsafe to conclude anything from the previous years, since the effects of changes in import controls cannot be eliminated. Their relaxation after 1953 is included in our trend for imports—an unsatisfactory procedure, since we assume a uniform trend whereas the relaxations may have taken place unevenly. But at least the direction of their effect was the same throughout the period.

We assume that the trend rates of increase for both industrial production and the quantity of imports of manufactures are given by their

[1] Probably one reason encouraging the Government to place orders in Europe was the large surplus in the European Payments Union which was accumulated by the sterling area up to the middle of 1951. But private orders were influenced by availability:

'Considerable orders for machine tools have been placed by private firms, as well as by the Government, in Germany, France, Belgium and Italy. As a rule the reason is not that the machine tools are not made in this country but that delivery dates are much shorter abroad.' (*Manchester Guardian Review of Industry, Commerce and Finance*, 1952, pp. 11 and 12.) Later the reverse happened. 'In many industries the flow of new orders has been increasing for six months or more . . . it seems to have been the shortening of order books that made deliveries more reasonable and induced customers at home and abroad to place more orders in this country.' (*Manchester Guardian Survey of Industry, Trade and Finance*, 1955, p. 18.)

average annual rates of increase from 1953 to 1957. The reasons for selecting this period for industrial production, and for regarding the levels of production in 1953 and 1957 as being equal to their trend values, are given in the notes to this chapter on p. 58. The trend rate of growth of production was then 3·3 % per annum and that of imports of manufactures 10·8 % per annum. The 'trend' of imports here is meant to show the effects on imports of all factors other than those associated with short-run changes in the pressure of demand. The reasons why these led to such a rapid growth of imports were, first, the relaxations in controls already mentioned, second, the relative reduction in labour costs and, third, the faster expansion of supplies of manufactures abroad as compared with the United Kingdom.[1] After eliminating these trends we obtain a comparison of deviations from trend in production and imports which is given in columns (5) and (6) of Table 13.

Table 13. *Analysis of changes in imports of manufactures, 1953–9*

(Index numbers, 1953 = 100)

	Industrial production		Quantity of imports of manufactures		Percentage deviations from trend		
					Production	Imports	Imports excluding steel
	Actual	Trend	Actual	Trend			
	(1)	(2)	(3)	(4)	(5)	(6)	(7)
1953	100	100	100	100	0	0	0
1954	106	103	111	111	3	0	6
1955	112	107	146	123	5	19	12
1956	112	110	149	136	2	9	1
1957	114	114	151	151	0	0	0
1958	113	118	150	167	−4	−10	−8
1959	119	121	180	185	−2	−3	0

Sources: Official statistical publications. Imports of manufactures were adjusted to obtain a series with roughly the same coverage as S 10 (see p. 211).

According to the calculation, 1955 was the year in which output was most in excess of 'normal', and also the year in which imports of manufactures rose furthest above their normal level. Although the behaviour of steel imports accounts for much of this 'hump' in imports, it does not account for all of it. The figures in column (7) were obtained in the same way as those for column (6), except that imports of steel were excluded throughout the calculation. As can be seen, the deviations from trend in imports excluding steel were still much greater than the deviations in industrial production.

[1] For further details, see p. 66.

The average relationship between columns (5) and (6) suggests that for every 1 % in the industrial production index above or below trend, the quantity of imports was about 3 % above or below trend. Naturally this figure is only a very rough guide to similar behaviour in the future. It seems likely that the relationship would not be uniform. The higher production was above trend, the greater would be the percentage excess of imports accompanying each 1 % increase in production. The lower was production below trend, the nearer would the percentage change in imports accompanying a 1 % change in production itself approach 1 %. There is evidence to support this second proposition from the behaviour of imports of manufactures before the war, referred to above. The first proposition seems *a priori* plausible, and the figures in Table 13 are broadly consistent with it, but clearly more evidence is required than that provided by the table —particularly in view of the very large upward trend in imports there assumed, whose exact size is most uncertain.

If, despite these uncertainties, we take the ratio of 1 to 3 for the changes in industrial production and imports of manufactures as giving at least a better approximation to the likely behaviour of imports in current conditions than the 1 to 1 ratio assumed in our first estimate of 0·20 for the short-run marginal propensity to import (which assumed there was a fair amount of slack in the economy, see p. 54), we obtain a second estimate of 0·31. This implies that a 1 % deviation in the gross domestic product is accompanied by a 1·5 % deviation in imports, and that a change of £3·2 in the gross domestic product would be required to change imports by £1.

A still higher value for the short-run marginal propensity to import would rule in conditions of coal shortage. Assuming, as in the last line of Table 12, that changes in coal consumption lead to equal changes in coal imports, and making the same assumptions about the behaviour of imports of manufactures as in the last paragraph, the marginal propensity to import becomes 0·42. This implies that a 1 % deviation in the gross domestic product is accompanied by a 2 % deviation in imports, and that a change of £2·4 in the gross domestic product would be required to change imports by £1.

None of the estimates of the short-run marginal propensity to import given above makes allowances for changes in stocks of imported goods, or the effects of changes in import or domestic prices, induced by changes in the gross domestic product.[1] As explained above, no systematic behaviour in stocks could be discovered; and in the short run, changes

[1] Except to the extent that such changes affected imports of manufactures in the years from 1953 to 1958, in which case their effects are included in the estimate of the change in imported manufactures.

in relative prices would probably have little effect on the quantity of imports demanded. They might, however, significantly affect the *value* of imports.

It would seem, then, that there are three different values for the short-run marginal propensity to import, 0·20, 0·31 and 0·42, depending on how highly the economy is employed, and what 'bottlenecks' appear. In reality, the marginal propensity at any particular moment of time would depend on a variety of factors, only one of which is the degree of full employment; and it would be a continuous rather than a discontinuous function of the latter. There are not just three values for the marginal propensity, but an infinite number. Yet the three given here are, it is hoped, sufficiently typical of certain situations to be useful guides to future possibilities.

4. NOTES TO THE ESTIMATES IN TABLE 12

We discuss, first, the basis for the assumed 'normal' or trend rates of growth of industrial production, consumers' expenditure per head and population; then we discuss the estimates relating to each of the groups of imports distinguished in Table 12. These notes may be omitted by the non-specialist reader.

(a) Trends in production, consumption and population

The trend rates of growth in industrial production and consumers' expenditure are their average rates of growth between 1953 and 1957. The rate of growth in the population is the official forecast for the period 1957 to 1963[1] and is approximately the same as the actual rate of growth from 1953 to 1957.

The level of industrial production in 1953 and 1957 was thought to be about 'normal' (that is, on trend) so that the rate of growth between these years corresponded to the trend rate of growth, for three reasons. First, so far as can be judged from the statistics of unemployment and unfilled vacancies, the level of excess demand for labour throughout the economy was about zero in both years.[2] Second, the ratio of the fixed capital stock in manufacturing to the rate of manufacturing output was about the same in both years.[3] Third, it was estimated that, at the end of 1958, there was enough 'slack' to allow industrial production to

[1] *Annual Abstract of Statistics*, no. 96, 1959, tables 11 and 12.
[2] *National Institute Economic Review*, November 1959, p. 51. For an explanation of this measure of excess demand see J. C. R. Dow and L. A. Dicks-Mireaux, 'The Excess Demand for Labour: a Study of Conditions in Great Britain, 1946–56', *Oxford Economic Papers* (New Series), vol. 10, no. 1, February 1958, pp. 1–33.
[3] *National Institute Economic Review*, no. 1, January 1959, p. 9, table 6, col. (6).

rise by 10 to 15 % over two years before 'the normal, more gradual, upward trend in productivity was resumed', and this estimate seems consistent with the trend assumed here.[1]

Since the years 1953 and 1957 provided reasonable 'bench marks' for the trend in industrial production, it seemed both convenient and plausible to assume that they did so for the gross domestic product and for consumers' expenditure. It is true, of course, that in other periods different relative rates of growth have occurred, and they might equally occur in the future, but the rates taken here at least provide a plausible starting point for estimation.

(b) Food

Two sets of estimates were made for food imports, one assuming perfect substitutability between imported and home-produced food, and the other assuming the rather low degree of substitutability suggested by the changes in relative prices and quantities from pre-war to post-war (see p. 98). The average of these estimates is shown in the table. The upward trend in home food output (that is, the increase which would occur if price changes were neutral) was assumed to be $1\frac{1}{3}$ % per annum. This is the same increase as occurred from 1935–9 to 1951–5 after eliminating the effects of changes in relative prices, assuming an elasticity of supply of 0·5. It is lower than the 2 % per annum which appears[2] to have been achieved over the last ten years or so. A reduction of 1 % per annum in the assumed upward trend would increase the rate of growth of food imports by about 0·5 % per annum. Exports of food were assumed to be constant. For each 1 % per annum rise in exports assumed, imports of food would be increased by about 0·04 %. No changes in the average *ad valorem* rate of tax or subsidy on food imports or home food output are allowed for. The effects of changes in subsidies are briefly discussed in the next chapter. The effect of a 1 % rise in food import prices would be the same as that of a fall of 1 % in the prices of non-food consumer goods plus a fall of 1 % in the general price level (the latter being assumed to influence the level of home food output and the former the level of food consumption). The estimated effect of the change in import prices allows for the repercussions on home

---

[1] The estimate and quotation are from the *National Institute Economic Review*, January 1959, p. 12. The trend assumed here of 3·3% per annum in industrial production implies that, at the end of 1958, after making seasonal adjustment, actual production was about 5·3% below trend (it being 'on trend' in 1957). If this 'slack', plus the normal 3·3% per annum, were made up in two years, the total increase over the two years would be approximately 12%.

[2] The true rate of increase may have been less. See Appendix II, p. 224.

food supply. The 'normal' rate of increase of food imports, and the effects on them of changes in consumers' expenditure per head and in food import prices, may all be underestimated because of our treatment of the whole of food imports as equivalent to food 'at the farm gate'. The demand for imported manufactured foodstuffs is likely to increase faster, and to be more responsive to changes in consumers' expenditure and relative prices.

(c) Alcoholic beverages and tobacco

The estimates are based on Professor Stone's demand equations (see Part II, pp. 115 ff.). A continued upward trend in tobacco consumption is assumed ($2\frac{1}{2}$ % per annum, which is additional to any increases in consumption due to rising population or consumers' expenditure per head). This is based on past experience, but for various reasons the increase might well be lower, and the reader may reduce the estimated increase in imports accordingly. No trend is allowed for in the demand for imported alcoholic beverages, although recent experience suggests the possibility of an upward trend in imports of wine. Price elasticities of demand for imports were not estimated, but they would probably be small because of the large specific duties (see p. 119).

(d) Materials and fuels

The 'normal' trend assumes a decline in the ratio of imports to industrial production of 1·4 % per annum. About 1 % per annum is due to what we have called 'materials economy', and the rest to an assumed continued change in the composition of industrial output, with textiles production increasing more slowly and metals production more quickly than average. The effect of the latter will probably be rather smaller in the future than over the post-war period so far, simply because the relative importance of imports of textile materials is progressively diminishing. The effect on imports of a fall in import prices and of an equal proportionate rise in the general price level in this country would be the same.

No independent estimate of the growth of imports of *coal* or *oil* was made. In view of the importance of 'trend factors', it seemed preferable to use recent estimates made for the National Coal Board of the increase in the inland demand for fuels from 1959 to 1965.[1] Two such estimates

---

[1] The estimate was by Mr F. Wilkinson, Director-General of Marketing for the National Coal Board, and quoted in *The Financial Times*, 7 October 1959. Inland consumption of coal was estimated to be lower, and that of oil higher, than in previous official estimates. Consumption of oil in 1965, for example, was put at 67 to 69 million tons of coal equivalent, as compared with some 61 million tons in the forecast described by the Paymaster General, Mr Reginald Maudling, in April 1957 (*House*

were made, one assuming that manufacturing production grew by 4 % per annum and the other that it grew by 3 % per annum from 1959 to 1965. The estimate taken here was interpolated on the assumption of a 3·7 % per annum rate of growth, which was the average annual rate from 1953 to 1957.

It was assumed that coal imports would be negligible. After allowing for increased consumption of non-fuels (lubricating oil, paraffin wax, etc.), the rise in inland oil consumption from 1957 to 1965 worked out at about 2·4 million tons a year. This was multiplied by the average value of all imports of oil (crude and refined) in 1957 to give the figure of £27 million shown in Table 12. This assumes that there is no change in exports and bunkers, nor in the residual item (rate of investment in stocks and unrecorded consumption). It also assumes that the composition of imports remains unchanged, so that home refinery output is assumed to expand. If exports rose, imports would have to increase faster, but the balance of payments might, if anything, be improved. If home refinery output expanded more slowly than is assumed here, the value of imports would rise faster, since they would contain proportionately more refined products and less crude. A rough estimate suggests that, if there were no increase in home refining at all, the annual increase in oil imports would be £30 million instead of £27 million.

In estimating the effects of changes in industrial production, consumers' expenditure per head and population on coal and oil *consumption*, we made use of the 1954 fuel balance sheets described in Chapter II, Tables 8 and 9. Since no estimates of the effects of these factors based on past experience were made, some further assumptions were necessary. Industrial fuel consumption was assumed to vary in direct proportion to industrial production. Changes in domestic and commercial consumption were assumed to depend as to two-thirds on the level of consumers' expenditure, and as to one-third on the level of industrial production. Professor Stone's consumers' expenditure elasticity of demand of about 0·4 was taken for the first part, and changes in population were also assumed to lead to equal proportionate changes in consumer demand. Changes in transport demand for fuels were simply assumed to equal the average of the percentage changes in consumers' expenditure and industrial production, the former being again sub-

of Commons Debates, 30 April 1957, cols. 33–53). This latter forecast was closely related to the estimates given by Dr G. H. Daniel in 'Britain's Energy Prospects', *Institution of Production Engineers Journal*, vol. 36, no. 2, February 1956, p. 76. Forecasts made by Mr W. F. Luttrell were also very similar ('Realities of the National Fuel Position' and 'Britain's Fuel and Power Budget', I and II, *Times Review of Industry*, February, March and April 1958).

divided into changes in expenditure per head and changes in the population. These various assumptions made it possible to estimate the effects of changes in our first three key variables on the consumption of eight different fuels (coal, coke, gas, motor and aviation spirit, gas and diesel oil, fuel oil and electricity). The changes in coke, gas and electricity consumption were then converted into changes in coal and oil consumption using the data in Tables 8 and 9. Finally, the physical quantities of coal and the various oils were multiplied by the corresponding average values of imports in 1957.

The resulting estimated changes in *consumption* were taken as changes in imports, on the assumption that home output and exports are unaffected.[1] This might not always be a reasonable assumption to take. For oil it makes less difference, since an increase in home refinery output necessitates increased crude oil imports, and only the refining margin is saved. But for coal the actual effects would generally be appreciably smaller than those given here, since one might expect coal output to change in the same direction as coal consumption, which would reduce the impact on imports. In conditions of coal shortage, however, nearly all the impact may be on imports or exports of coal.

No estimates of the effects of changes in the import prices of coal or oil on the demand for imports were made. Present policy seems to be to exclude coal imports even when they are cheaper than home-produced coal. For oil, the effect would probably be fairly small. Transport's demand for oil is unlikely to be much affected by changes in the import price, both because of the absence of competitive fuels and because of the large specific duties. The demand for kerosene and fuel oil, however, might be fairly responsive to changes in import prices. Past experience suggests that changes in prices paid by the domestic or industrial consumer *have* had some effect (see Chart 6).

(e) Manufactures

The estimated 'normal' growth of 4·0 % per annum in imports of *manufactures* is nearly 0·8 % per annum faster than the assumed growth in industrial production. It is assumed that imports of manufactures would grow at the same rate as sales on the home market in the absence of relative price changes. From 1951 to 1955 sales of non-food manufactures on the home market increased by about 0·8 % per annum faster than industrial production, and this is the main basis of the estimate. If anything, this probably errs on the high side, since there was probably an abnormally large increase in sales of manufactures

[1] Except that home refinery output is assumed to increase so as to maintain the same composition of imports of oil as in 1957, see above.

on the home market from 1951 to 1955 in relation to the growth in industrial production which occurred at that time. There was hardly any increase in exports of manufactures, so that an increasing proportion of home output was sold on the home market.

The estimated effect of changes in the price of imported manufactures on the demand for them is based on the estimates described on pp. 42–4 and p. 50. It is an uncertain one. The percentage effect might be as low as 4 or as high as 14. It allows for repercussions on home supply and exports, but assumes that the United Kingdom Government maintains a constant level of employment.

CHAPTER IV

IMPORTS AND ECONOMIC POLICY

1. INTRODUCTION

Economic policy, like economic forecasting, is a hit and miss affair. Nobody knows the extent or timing of the effects of many measures which are taken, though it is usually possible to guess their direction. Even this may be uncertain where balance of payments policy is concerned. One can draw some conclusions from this study which, despite their great uncertainty, may be useful where so much is uncertain. One of their chief limitations, as we may remind the reader from time to time, is the failure to take proper account of the repercussions of various changes on factors which, throughout this study, we have for simplicity's sake assumed to be given independently of everything else (see Chapter I, p. 11). In the real world everything affects everything else, but it is extraordinarily difficult to allow adequately for this, and the conclusions in this chapter certainly do not.

Our first concern is with the outlook for the United Kingdom's current balance of payments, seen in the light of long-term trends.[1] We shall look at ways in which it might be affected by certain factors that are, for the most part, outside the control of the British Government. The combined effect of these factors might be to strengthen or weaken the balance. No attempt is made to decide which outcome is the more probable; the aim is simply to isolate those factors which are most likely to be important. We then turn to the different measures which might be used by the British Government to influence the current balance of payments and consider their probable effect on imports.

2. OUTLOOK FOR THE CURRENT BALANCE OF PAYMENTS

During most of the post-war period there has been a very rapid increase in world trade in manufactures. In the years 1953–7[2] the quantity increased by about 10 % per annum. If this rate of increase were to be

[1] As given in Chapter III.

[2] In what follows we take these years as the basis for our estimates since this makes comparison with the 'normal' increase in imports in Table 12, p. 49, easier. The 'normal' increase in the table was estimated on the assumption that industrial production, consumers' expenditure and population all increased at the same rate as from 1953 to 1957.

maintained in the future, and if prices of manufactures in this country rose no faster than prices abroad, United Kingdom exports of manufactures might increase at the same rate,[1] and, assuming constant prices, the gain to the current balance of payments from this would be about £270 million a year. If the rest of our exports grew as fast as in the years 1953–7, total United Kingdom exports would increase by some £290 million a year. Assuming no change in net invisible receipts[2] and taking the 'normal' annual increase in imports of nearly £100 million estimated in Table 12, the improvement in the current balance of payments would amount to roughly £200 million *each year*.[3]

On the assumption stated there would, it seems, be an extremely rapid improvement in the United Kingdom's current balance of payments. An increased outflow of long-term capital might reduce the resulting improvement in our short-term capital position, and, as long as our reserves remained low, fluctuations in our fortunes could still lead to crises. But if the current balance were to improve at something like this annual average rate for a few years, it seems probable that such crises would become things of the past. With different assumptions, however, the outlook can change completely, and as a start to the consideration of some possibilities we may look at what actually happened from 1953 to 1957.

Between these years a good number of our assumptions were fulfilled: those relating to the rates of growth of output, consumption and population in the United Kingdom, of world trade in manufactures, and of United Kingdom exports of non-manufactures. But the annual average improvement in the current balance was only some £20 million instead of £200 million. The whole of the difference can be accounted

---

[1] Assuming that the supply of exports were to expand fast enough, and apart from the effects of differences in the commodity or country of destination pattern of our exports compared with those of all exporting countries. These effects, and other factors likely to restrain the growth of our exports, are discussed below.

[2] Although there has been a serious reduction in our net invisible earnings over the past few years, at least part of this was a once-and-for-all loss and part was due to similar competitive weaknesses to those which affected our exports of manufactures (see below) and which are here being assumed away. It is possible that, after allowing for these factors, the residual downward trend (if any) was small.

[3] A necessary condition for the improvement in the current balance would be an increase in savings, or a cut in domestic investment, equal to the annual improvement in the balance. It might not always be easy to achieve this, especially with the very large improvement in the current balance assumed here. But the difficulties involved are likely, in the writer's view, to be minor compared with those of shifting resources from one use to another. The problem of securing an improvement in the current balance of payments is not primarily one of 'disabsorbing' sufficient home resources, but rather of ensuring that the resources freed produce for export or replace imports, and it is therefore the latter problem which is given the most attention in the text.

for by the slower rate of expansion of the quantity of our exports of manufactures and the faster rate of expansion of the quantity of our imports (especially of manufactures) than is assumed above. These, in turn, were probably due for the most part to two factors which together tended to make our exports relatively dearer overseas and our imports relatively cheaper at home. The two factors were, first, the more rapid increase in the cost of labour and, second, the slower expansion of supplies (at any given level of labour costs) in this country than abroad. In what follows, we consider only costs and supplies of manufactures, since it was our trade in these which was principally affected.

The rise in labour costs in manufacturing[1] tended to raise the prices of our manufactures in relation to those of our competitors both on home and foreign markets. Assuming that the elasticities of demand were as high as is suggested elsewhere in this book, the actual prices of British and foreign manufactures did not need to diverge very much[2] for there to have been a substantial drop in the share of our exports in world exports, and a substantial increase in the share of imports in sales on the home market.

But even if the cost of labour in manufacturing in this country had not diverged appreciably from that in other countries, the faster rate of increase of the supply of manufactures in those countries[3] must have tended to produce similar effects. It must have expanded the supply of manufactures imported by this country more rapidly than the supply

[1] Weighting the index numbers of hourly earnings (or rates) in manufacturing in Belgium-Luxembourg, Canada, France, Germany, Italy, Japan, the Netherlands, Sweden, Switzerland and the United States by the values of their exports of manufactures in 1955, one obtains an average increase of 24 % from 1953 to 1957. Over the same period the increase in hourly earnings in manufacturing in the United Kingdom was 31 %. This index omits social security payments, which are an important element in labour costs in some countries.

[2] From 1953 to 1957 the price index of United Kingdom exports of manufactures rose 8 %, while the United Nations' price index of world exports of manufactures (which includes exports by the United Kingdom) rose 7 %. The average value of United Kingdom imports of manufactures (Class D, excluding non-ferrous metals) rose 6 %, and the wholesale prices of all manufactures other than food, tobacco and fuel rose 11 %. The small divergences between these various index numbers has led some commentators to belittle the importance of relative price changes, but, for reasons given elsewhere in this book, the writer rejects this view.

[3] Weighting the index numbers of manufacturing output for the same countries (except Switzerland, for which no index is available) and with the same weights as in footnote 1 above, the average increase in output from 1953 to 1957 works out at 30 %. Over the same period, the increase in manufacturing output in the United Kingdom was 17 %. These index numbers of output do not, of course, necessarily show what the relative increases in supplies would have been at given levels of labour cost, but it seems likely that the increases in the countries mentioned would have been faster than in the United Kingdom.

of manufactures from home producers. This greater supply of imports could only have been sold if their prices had been lowered relatively to home products, but, again, the lowering did not need to be very great. Similarly, other countries' exports of manufactures expanded faster than our own, and their prices fell in relation to ours. No attempt is made here to gauge the relative importance of these two factors, lower labour costs and greater supplies, since that would require much further research.

To some extent the slower rate of growth of our exports was also due to the fact that we sent a higher than average proportion to countries whose markets expanded more slowly than average, and to the fact that the commodity composition of our exports was more heavily weighted with slower-expanding groups, such as textiles.[1] There was also a worsening of about £30 million a year in our net invisible receipts. On the other hand, the improvement in our terms of trade increased the current surplus by about the same amount each year.[2]

It is clear that a crucial assumption concerns the behaviour of prices in this country relative to those abroad. A rise in prices in this country would probably have its greatest effect on the balance of payments through the drop in export earnings it would cause. We cannot estimate the probable size of this effect here. But if United Kingdom imports of manufactures are as responsive to price changes as we have argued they are, it seems likely that United Kingdom exports of manufactures are also very responsive. Four-fifths of our exports consist of manufactures, so that even moderate changes in prices could, in the long run, have large effects on exports and the balance of payments.

The effect on imports would probably be smaller but still appreciable. The estimates in Table 12 suggest that for every 1 % rise in prices in this country relative to prices abroad the quantity of imports demanded would in the long run rise about $1\frac{1}{2}$ %: that is if we assume that import prices would be unaffected and the general level of employment kept constant, and if we make no allowances for the repercussions on the level of industrial production or consumers' real expenditure. It is hard to say what allowance should be made for these other effects. If import prices rose *evenly* as our demand increased, the value of imports demanded might be reduced on that account by about half the

[1] It has been estimated that, from 1951 to 1956, the adverse commodity and country composition of United Kingdom exports accounted for a decline of one point in their share in world trade in manufactures from 1951 to 1956. Since the share in 1951 was about one-fifth, the fall in exports of manufactures due to this was about 5 %, or about 1 % per annum. This would represent £20 to £30 million per annum. See the *Board of Trade Journal*, 8 August 1958, pp. 265–9.

[2] This is the beneficial aspect of the relative price changes which occurred. Their adverse effects in changing the quantities of exports and imports are discussed above.

proportionate increase in price (since the average elasticity of demand seems to be about 1·5). On the other hand, real incomes in this country would rise as a result of the improved terms of trade, and hence we should increase our estimates of the extra imports demanded on this count. Hence the estimate of an extra 1·5 % of imports might not be far out. In this case, purely on the import side of the account, for every extra 1 % a year by which prices increased in this country relative to prices abroad, the import bill would increase by about £50 million a year. The effects would take some time to show themselves fully, but after a few years the increase in imports alone would add up to a sizeable amount.

Other crucial assumptions concern the growth of world trade in manufactures and the behaviour of the terms of trade between manufactures and primary products. In the future, the quantity of world trade in manufactures might not expand so fast as from 1953 to 1957, and there might be a rise in world prices of primary products relative to those of manufactures, instead of the fall which occurred from 1953 to 1957. In the past, worsenings in the terms of trade have usually been accompanied by faster than average rates of growth in world trade, so that such a combination of unfavourable developments might seem unlikely. But the combination which occurred in the years 1953 to 1957 may have been unusually favourable,[1] so that a simultaneous worsening on both counts is possible.

It might be thought that a worsening in the terms of trade, which implies a drop in export prices relative to import prices, would tend to improve our balance of payments, quite apart from any expansion in world trade in manufactures which might accompany it. It would improve it because of the reduction in the quantity of imports demanded and the increase in the quantity of exports demanded, these quantity changes being proportionately greater than the proportionate changes in prices. However, this is not so, for we are not here considering a *general* increase in prices abroad relative to prices at home (i.e. the reverse of the case considered on p. 67), but an increase which is *confined to primary products*.

Suppose, for example, that world prices of primary products were to rise by 1 %, prices of manufactures remaining constant. Excluding the effects of this on the quantity of world trade in manufactures, the demand for United Kingdom exports would not change. For we are not

[1] See W. A. Lewis, 'World Production, Prices and Trade, 1870–1960', *Manchester School of Economic and Social Studies*, vol. 20, no. 2, May 1952, p. 105, and the present writer's 'The Problem of Living within our Foreign Earnings', *Three Banks Review*, no. 26, June 1955, p. 3; and Austin Robinson, 'The Problem of Living within our Foreign Earnings further Considered', *Three Banks Review*, no. 38, June 1958.

assuming any change in manufacturing costs in this country relative to those abroad. The United Kingdom's demand for imports would fall, but because the increases in import prices were confined to those products for which the demand is inelastic the fall in the quantity demanded would not offset the whole of the rise in price, and so the *value* of imports would increase. If we take the estimates in column (10) of Table 12 and assume a rise of 1 % in the price of imports of food and materials, the increase in the value of imports demanded works out at about £15 million.

Thus far we have considered the main factors which could strengthen or weaken the current balance of payments in the long run, and which are partly or wholly outside the control of the British Government. Some of these factors (such as changes in the terms of trade) could also produce large short-run fluctuations in the current balance. We next review the various measures by which the Government might seek to improve the current balance of payments: devaluation of the pound, deflation, import controls, subsidies to home agriculture and tariffs. We consider both short-run and long-run effects on imports.

3. DEVALUATION

Devaluation may be regarded as a method of offsetting the effects of too rapidly rising prices in this country. We are not concerned here with the many arguments for and against such a measure, but only with its probable effects on imports. In itself, the devaluation is likely to cause an appreciable fall in the quantity of imports eventually demanded, partially offset by a rise in import prices, so that in the long run the (sterling) value of imports is likely to be somewhat reduced. The size of these effects depends on the elasticity of supply of imports as well as on the elasticity of demand, and only the latter has been estimated here. If we assume that the foreign currency price of imports does not change following devaluation (which implies an infinitely elastic supply, and also that no other countries devalue when we do), then a 1 % devaluation would raise the sterling price of imports by 1 %; this would in the long run reduce the demand by 1·5 % (taking the estimate in Table 12, p. 49) and so lower the sterling value of imports by about 0·5 %. In the short run the value of imports may rise, since (apart from speculative movements) the volume may not fall much immediately, while import prices are likely to rise. The most important consideration which this analysis leaves out of account is the effect of the rise in import prices on prices in this country. Unless these effects are kept reasonably small, the devaluation will not have served its purpose. Devaluation would also have to be accompanied by measures to increase domestic saving or to cut domestic investment if the full improvement in the current balance were to be secured. For otherwise the initial improvement would tend to stimulate domestic incomes and demand and so reduce the extent of the final improvement in the current balance.

4. DEFLATION

A policy of deflation (or disinflation as some prefer to call it as practised in this country) aims at reducing the general level of demand for goods and services whether by fiscal or monetary means. If this policy is used principally as a means of improving the balance of payments, a crucial question is the extent to which a given improvement must be accompanied by a fall (below what it otherwise would have been—there may be no *absolute* fall) in home production, incomes and expenditure. The policy works both by stimulating exports and reducing imports, and we are concerned with the latter effect. The estimates in Chapter III may be used as a guide to the extent of the likely fall in home production which would have to accompany a given fall in imports. It was shown there (pp. 53–8) that in the short run the extent of the reduction in the real gross domestic product necessary to secure a given reduction in imports was less the higher the initial level of economic activity. If the general level of activity were low, the national product might have to be reduced in the same proportion as imports, but at high levels of activity a smaller proportionate reduction in the national product would suffice, especially in conditions of steel and coal shortage. Thus the amount of home output sacrificed to reduce imports by £1 varied, according to these estimates, from as much as £5 to as little as £2½.[1] It seems likely that the stimulus given to exports would vary in a similar fashion with the level of activity. The moral is clear. As a short-term method of improving the balance of payments, deflation is more efficient the higher the initial level of economic activity at which it is applied.

In the long run deflation might in principle reduce imports in two different ways. It might reduce the rate of growth of the whole economy,[2] and so the rate of growth of demand for imports; and it might reduce the rate of growth of the domestic price level, which would have a similar effect. As regards the first of these ways, it was

[1] The reader is reminded that these estimates allow nothing for changes in import prices or in stocks of imported goods induced by the changes in the national product. The saving in the import bill might be bigger if import prices fell as a result of the fall in the demand for imports, and if there were reductions in the rate of investment in stocks of imported goods.

[2] Some might argue that, up to a certain point, deflation could increase the rate of growth of the economy. Whether this is true or not, the argument in the text applies to *some* degree of deflation.

estimated in Chapter III (p. 51) that a given change in the long-term percentage rate of growth of the real gross domestic product would lead to the same change in the percentage rate of growth of the demand for imports, assuming no changes in the relative prices of imported and home-produced goods. The latter assumption would be approximately fulfilled if the long-term elasticity of supply of imports were high, as is quite probable. A reduction in the demand for imports achieved in this way would therefore be costly in terms of national product foregone. The position may be different for import-saving induced by a slowing down of the rate of growth of the domestic price level, but before any estimate can be made one needs to know what difference to the rate of growth of the price level results from a given reduction in the rate of growth of the national product, and this is a controversial matter.[1]

5. IMPORT CONTROLS

Until 1952, import controls were often used in the post-war period as a means of reducing imports in a crisis.[2] In the 1947 and 1949 crises the cuts in imports fell principally on those from the dollar area. In 1952 imports from Western Europe were severely cut. Since then, controls have been relaxed fairly swiftly and at the end of 1959 few of importance remained. Such evidence as we have examined suggests that controls (including rationing) can reduce the *effective demand* for particular groups of imports by substantial amounts. Our rough estimates for the years 1946–9 were that the annual rate of imports of food might have been greater by over £200 million at 1948 prices, imports of materials greater by £40 million and imports of manufactures greater by more than £70 million, had all controls been removed and supplies been freely available abroad. No estimate was made for fuels, but the

---

[1] It is possible that no reduction in the rate of growth of the national product is needed, but only a reduction in the degree of full employment at which the given rate of growth occurs. It is also possible that, at high levels of employment, a small reduction in employment may secure a relatively large reduction in the rate of growth of the price level at the cost of a relatively small reduction in the rate of growth of the national product. For an excellent discussion of this and related questions see Sir Donald MacDougall, *The World Dollar Problem* (London, Macmillan, 1957), especially appendix XVIIA, pp. 596–8.

[2] For detailed studies of the nature and effects of these controls, see M. F. W. Hemming, C. M. Miles and G. F. Ray, 'A Statistical Summary of the Extent of Import Control in the United Kingdom since the War', *Review of Economic Studies*, vol. 26, no. 70, February 1959, p. 75 and W. M. Corden, 'The Control of Imports: a Case Study', *Manchester School of Economic and Social Studies*, vol. 26, no. 3, September 1958, p. 181. For a discussion of the theoretical aspects of controls see M. F. W. Hemming and W. M. Corden, 'Import Restriction as an Instrument of Balance-of-Payments Policy', *Economic Journal*, vol. 68, no. 271, September 1958, p. 483.

rationed consumption of coal and oil was certainly well below the level of free demand. The effective demand for imports from a particular area could probably be cut even more drastically.

The administrative machine required to impose these controls was formidable; they were imposed in a period in which supplies were not freely available abroad and they were accompanied by price control and extensive consumer rationing. Whether the same restrictions would be feasible in present circumstances is a more doubtful matter. Given the administrative machine and the co-operation of consumers of imports, however, controls can be used as a short-term method of regulating imports. The effects on consumption can also be cushioned for a time by changes in the rate of investment of stocks of imported goods.[1] If controls are to be used to restrict the level of imports in the long run, they must be accompanied by measures to increase domestic saving or reduce domestic investment, for otherwise the initial improvement in the balance of payments will be at least partially offset by the effects on exports (or on any uncontrolled imports) of the induced rise in domestic demand.

6. SUBSIDIES TO HOME AGRICULTURE

Subsidies to home agriculture and tariffs on imports are not at present used in this country as short-term regulators of imports to correct a balance of payments deficit. In what follows we discuss only the long-term effects of these policies on imports.

First, we may consider the probable effect on imports of a change in the subsidies paid to farmers in this country.[2] An increase in subsidies would tend to raise home output of food and so depress imports of food. Assuming that the long-term price elasticity of supply of home-produced food is $0 \cdot 5$,[3] that home-produced food is a perfect substitute for imported food and that there is no change in import prices, it can

---

[1] Stock changes in the years 1946 to 1951, however, tended in general to aggravate rather than mitigate the severity of the balance of payments crises. Instead of reducing stocks in a crisis and building them up when the situation was more favourable, the reverse often occurred. See the writer's 'Changes in Stocks of mainly Imported Goods in the United Kingdom', *Bulletin of the Oxford University Institute of Statistics*, February 1958, p. 59.

[2] For a discussion of this and other aspects of the policy of subsidizing home agriculture so as to save imports of food, see E. A. G. Robinson and R. L. Marris, 'The Use of Home Resources to save Imports', *Economic Journal*, vol. 60, no. 237, March 1950, p. 177; and a comment by Sir Donald MacDougall, *Economic Journal*, vol. 60, no. 239, September 1950, p. 629, and a rejoinder by Robinson and Marris, *Economic Journal*, vol. 61, no. 241, March 1951, p. 176. See also Austin Robinson, 'The Cost of Agricultural Import-Saving', *Three Banks Review*, no. 40, December 1958, p. 3.

[3] See Chapter II, p. 21, and Part II, pp. 101 ff.

be shown that for small increases in the subsidy imports of food would eventually fall by £0·4 for every £1 increase in the subsidy.[1] For large changes in the subsidy the effect on imports per £ of subsidy would be smaller,[2] as it would also be if home-produced food is not a perfect substitute for imported food.[3]

7. TARIFFS ON IMPORTED MANUFACTURES

In this section we look at the effects of changes in tariffs on imports of manufactures only, since tariffs on imports of food and materials are usually small. In the negotiations over the European Free Trade Area the main reductions considered were in tariffs on manufactures. We must distinguish between (a) a unilateral reduction or increase in tariffs and (b) one which is accompanied by similar changes in other countries' tariffs on their imports of manufactures from the United Kingdom.

In the case of (a), it is estimated in Chapter VIII (pp. 168–9) that an increase of 1 in the percentage *ad valorem* tariff on imports of

---

[1] If the value of home-produced food at constant market prices is P (these being also the current prices) and if the index of prices paid to the farmer is $\overline{P}$, which is assumed equal to 1 before the change in subsidy, and if the price elasticity of supply is $\overline{p}_S$, and if R is the ratio of the value of home-produced food at factor cost to its value at market prices (currently about 1·15), then for small changes

$$\frac{\Delta P}{P} = \overline{p}_S \Delta \overline{P},$$

and the change in the subsidy bill $= PR\Delta\overline{P} + \Delta P(R-1)$. Whence it follows that

$$\Delta P = \frac{\overline{p}_S}{R + \overline{p}_S(R-1)} \times \text{the change in the subsidy bill. If home-produced food is a}$$

perfect substitute for imports, ΔP is also the reduction in imports.

[2] For example, taking the assumptions of footnote 1 above, and assuming the elasticity of supply $= 0·5$, an increase in the *ad valorem* rate of subsidy by 50 % would reduce imports by about 0·3 instead of 0·4 times the increase in the subsidy bill.

[3] See Chapter II, p. 23. It can be shown that for small changes in the subsidy, and taking the assumptions and notation described in Part II, the change in imports is given by

$$\Delta M = \frac{\overline{m}_P}{\overline{p}_P} \cdot \frac{\overline{p}_S}{R + \overline{p}_S(R-1)} \times \text{the change in the subsidy bill.}$$

This is the same as the formula in footnote 1 above, except that the change given there is multiplied by the additional factor $\dfrac{\overline{m}_P}{\overline{p}_P}$. Taking the best estimates of these given on p. 100, this additional factor is approximately 0·8, so that the change in imports may be only four-fifths as big as was estimated in the text for the case of perfect substitutability. This assumes that the subsidies are paid more or less evenly on all home food output. If they were concentrated on those foods which were close substitutes for imports, or whose elasticity of supply was above average, the reduction in imports would be greater.

manufactures would probably reduce the demand for imports by less than 7 %, but possibly by as much as 4 %. This estimate assumes that employment and the general level of factor prices in this country are not changed, and allows for a fall in the price of imports (exclusive of tariff) resulting from the imposition of the tariff.

In the case of (*b*), the effects would almost certainly be greater. An increase in tariffs on our imports of manufactures accompanied by a similar increase in other countries' tariffs on our exports to them would lead to a bigger reduction in our imports of manufactures. For as a result of the increase in foreign tariffs, there would be a diversion of British manufactures from export markets on to the home market, and this would tend to reduce imports of manufactures.[1] In the opposite case, the abolition of nearly all tariffs on imports of manufactures from other European countries in return for similar concessions to the United Kingdom would be likely to lead to a large increase in trade in manufactures, but no precise estimates can be given here.

8. CONCLUSION

The great importance of relative price changes as a factor influencing the demand for imports, especially imports of manufactures, is probably the most important implication of this study for economic policy. In this chapter a number of estimates of the effects of such price changes has been given. It cannot be pretended that these are firm estimates; the range of uncertainty is large. But it seemed better to give the estimates, together with this warning, rather than to seek refuge in a number of vague qualitative statements. The evidence for the view that the demand for some imports is sensitive to relative price changes was briefly summarized in Chapter II, but the persistent and sceptical reader will also wish to consult Part II and especially Chapter VIII. While he may not be completely convinced by what he finds there— for it is hard indeed to find convincing evidence in empirical economics —at least he may feel that the view taken by the writer is not implausible.

---

[1] This second case of reciprocal tariff changes has effects on imports similar to those of a change in the domestic price level relative to foreign price levels. It is estimated in Part II (p. 167) that a 1 % change in the price level would change the demand for imported manufactures by something like 7 %, assuming a constant level of employment in this country.

PART II

THE BEHAVIOUR OF IMPORTS OF FOOD MATERIALS AND MANUFACTURES

This part consists of a more detailed study of the behaviour of imports of food, materials and manufactures. It gives the evidence for some of the statements in Part I, as well as conclusions and speculations omitted there. The going is heavier, partly because of the greater detail, partly because of the numerous footnotes and partly because of the mathematics. These features are regrettable but inevitable in an empirical study of this kind. Although the algebra is elementary, some readers may find both it and the numerical calculations laborious. An attempt has been made to explain the general drift of the argument so that it can be understood without detailed references to the mathematics. Some readers may therefore wish to omit Chapter V, as well as certain parts of the succeeding chapters.

CHAPTER V

MATHEMATICAL INTRODUCTION

I. SYSTEM OF NOTATION

Variables are shown by capital letters, and if these are without super-scripts they mean a value at constant prices of the base year, or else an index of volume. For all index numbers, whether of volume or price, the base-year value $= 1$.

For any particular commodity:

$M =$ imports
$X =$ exports
$P =$ home production
$V =$ change in stocks
$H =$ sales on the home market for consumption or further processing

It follows, if the letters stand for values at constant market prices, that

$$M+P \equiv X+V+H.$$

These letters may refer to any group of imports, exports, etc. Thus M may mean imports of food, materials, fuels or manufactures, or a sub-group of any one of these groups. Where the context requires it, different commodity groups or different periods are distinguished by numerical suffixes; for example, M_1, M_2 might mean imports of group 1 or group 2, or imports in period 1 or period 2.

Other definitions are:

$C =$ Consumers' total current expenditure on goods and services at constant market prices
$N =$ Population
$G =$ Gross domestic product at constant factor cost
$I =$ Index of the volume of industrial production
$T =$ Time in years
$U =$ Percentage unemployed

A bar denotes the corresponding price or average value (that is, the price index obtained by dividing an index of current value by an index of volume). Thus:

$\overline{M} =$ Price of imports (exclusive of taxes or subsidies, base year $=$ 1)
$\overline{X} =$ Price of exports (base year $=$ 1)
and so on.

We use such expressions as $\overline{C-H}$ to mean the price of all C excluding H (for example, all non-food consumer goods, H being sales of food).

An asterisk denotes an index of one plus the *ad valorem* rate of net indirect tax or subsidy (the latter being negative) on the corresponding goods. If, for example, the average indirect tax on imports was currently 5 % *ad valorem* and nil in the base year, M^* would be 1·05. If, as well as this tax, there was a subsidy of 6 % *ad valorem* (also nil in the base year), M^* would be 0·99 approximately. If the net indirect tax had been 2 % *ad valorem* in the base year, the current value of M^* would be 0·97 instead of 0·99.

Hence $M\overline{M}M^* =$ the current value of imports at market prices.

The current value of imports at *market* prices in the base year is M (because $\overline{M}$ and M^* each equal unity).

Functional relations are shown as, for example:

$$M = d\ (\overline{M},\ \overline{P},\ .\ .\ .\ \text{etc.}),\ \text{or}$$
$$P\ = s\ (\overline{P},\ T,\ .\ .\ .\ \text{etc.})$$

In these examples, M and P are variables dependent on the variables within the brackets, and 'd' and 's' indicate demand and supply relations respectively.

A dash, for example $\overline{M}'$, shows that lagged values for the variable in question enter into the functional relation. Thus the demand for imports might depend on the price of imports in previous periods as well as on the price in the current period.

Parameters are shown by small letters corresponding to the independent variable in question, with suitable suffixes to distinguish them as necessary. To take an example, the demand for home consumption of food is assumed to depend on the price of food, the price of other consumer goods, the volume of consumers' total expenditure and the population. Hence

$$H = d(\overline{H},\ \overline{C-H},\ C,\ \mathcal{N}).$$

Suppose now that $\overline{H}$ changes by $\varDelta\overline{H}$, and that all the other variables on the right-hand side remain constant, and that the resulting change in H is $\varDelta H$. Then we define

$$h_H = \frac{\varDelta H}{\varDelta \overline{H}}.$$

This notation s abbreviated where the context permits to $\overline{h}$. On some other occasions a more elaborate system of suffixes is required, which is explained where necessary.

In most of the equations in this study we are dealing with the logarithms of the variables H, $\overline{H}$, etc. Hence usually

$$\overline{h} = \frac{\varDelta \log H}{\varDelta \log \overline{H}}.$$

In this case $\overline{h}$ is a price elasticity of demand, and as we usually assume the various elasticities are constant, it is immaterial whether $\varDelta$ indicates a large or a small change.

2. DEMAND

Most of the functional relations are assumed to be linear in logarithms. Thus the demand relation for home food[1] consumption described in the previous section would be

$$\log H = a_H + \overline{h} \log \overline{H} + \overline{c - h} \log \overline{C - H} + c \log C + n \log \mathcal{N} \ldots \ldots (1)$$

where a_H is a constant depending on the choice of units. The meaning of this type of relation is discussed briefly in Part I (p. 8), and is most easily grasped if we rewrite it in the form of *changes* from one period to another, thus:

$$\varDelta \log H = \overline{h} \varDelta \log \overline{H} + \overline{c - h} \varDelta \log \overline{C - H} + c \varDelta \log C + n \varDelta \log \mathcal{N} \ldots (2)$$

If we interpret $\varDelta \log H$ as the proportionate change in H, and likewise $\varDelta \log \overline{H}$, etc., then (for *small* proportionate changes) the equation tells us that the proportionate change in the volume of food consumption may be analysed into four parts. Each part is found by multiplying the proportionate change in a causal factor by a constant (a parameter). If, for example, $\overline{h} = -0.25$, and if $\overline{H}$ increases by 1 %, then the equation shows that the demand for food will fall by $\frac{1}{4}$ % on account of this rise of 1 % in its price. If $C = 0.3$ and if C increases by 2 %, then the demand for food will rise by 0.6 % on account of this rise of 2 % in consumers' total real expenditure. Taken together, the rise in the price of food and the rise in consumers' total real expenditure will increase the demand for food by $0.6 - 0.25 = 0.35$ %. This interpretation of the equation in terms of proportionate changes is only approximately true for small proportionate changes in the variables, but the process of multiplication of *logarithmic* changes by the parameters and then the addition of these to get the total logarithmic change in the dependent variable applies to large or small changes in the logarithms of the variables.

This form of relation seems rather more plausible than one which is linear in ordinary values or index numbers. It seems more plausible to

[1] In this section we draw most of our examples from the equations referring to food imports, consumption, etc. This kills two birds with one stone, since the examples have a more general application and we can also dispense with much further discussion of the food equations in later sections.

believe, for example, that a 1 % increase in the price of food relative to other goods will lead to the same *percentage* reduction in the quantity demanded whether total consumption is large or small than to believe that the percentage reduction is greater the smaller is total food consumption (because, for example, of a lower population or real total expenditure per head). It must be admitted, however, that there is not much to choose between the two hypotheses on grounds of plausibility, and if the changes in the variables are not large there is little difference between them.

Another reason for preferring the linear logarithmic relation is that the values of the parameters are then independent of the choice of units. This makes it easier to interpret the results, and to compare them with other similar estimates. The parameters are, in fact, elasticities. $\bar{h}$ and $\overline{c-h}$ are price elasticities, and c is an expenditure elasticity (similar to an income elasticity) of demand. A final argument of convenience is that many of the simplifying assumptions which are described below only lead to the simplest algebraical expressions when the equations are of the linear logarithmic form.

Our general strategy is to make as many plausible *a priori* simplifying assumptions about the form of the relations as possible. Two such assumptions which apply to equation (1) are

$$\bar{h}+\overline{c-h} = 0 \dotfill (3)$$
$$c+n = 1 \dotfill (4)$$

The first of these assumptions is that an equal proportionate change in the price of food and in all other consumer prices will leave the demand for food unaffected. Only *relative* price changes are assumed to matter.

The second assumption is equivalent to assuming that equal proportionate changes in consumers' total expenditure and in population (which must leave *per capita* total expenditure unchanged) cause the demand for food to change in the same proportion. Some might prefer to write equation (1) in terms of *per capita* total expenditure and if this is done the coefficient of log N becomes one: i.e. with *per capita* total expenditure unchanged, any change in population will lead to the same proportionate change in the demand for food. Algebraically the transformation is as follows

$$c \log C + n \log N = c \log C - c \log N + c \log N + n \log N$$
$$= c \log \frac{C}{N} + (c+n) \log N$$
$$= c \log \frac{C}{N} + \log N, \quad \text{if } c+n = 1.$$

If imported and home-produced food are assumed to be perfect substitutes (and this is one of the hypotheses we take), the demand for imports can be regarded as the difference between the demand for food for consumption and the home supply of food, after allowing for changes in stocks and exports of food. Thus, in the identity

$$M+P \equiv H+V+X \dots\dots\dots\dots\dots (5)$$

we explain P by means of a supply equation (discussed below), H by means of equation (1), and take V and X as they are without attempting to explain them.

Where the imported and home-produced food are not perfect substitutes (the usual case) we need a demand equation for each.

$$\log M_c = a_M + \overline{m}_M \log \overline{MM^*} + \overline{p}_M \log \overline{PP^*} + \overline{c-h}_M \log \overline{C-H}$$
$$+ c_M \log C + n_M \log N \dots\dots\dots\dots\dots (6)$$

$$\log P_c = a_P + \overline{m}_P \log \overline{MM^*} + \overline{p}_P \log \overline{PP^*} + \overline{c-h}_P \log \overline{C-H}$$
$$+ c_P \log C + n_P \log N \dots\dots\dots\dots\dots (7)$$

Each of these demand equations is very similar to equation (1), the main difference being the introduction of an additional variable on the right-hand side, which is the price of the closely competing substitute. If M and P were perfect substitutes, $\overline{m}_M$ and $\overline{p}_M$ would become infinite (with opposite signs), so that $\overline{MM^*}$ and $\overline{PP^*}$, which are the market prices of M and P, could never diverge so long as *some* of both M and P were demanded. For any divergence would lead to an infinite switch away from the more expensive to the less expensive substitute. In equations (6) and (7), however, we allow for the more usual case in which *some* switching would take place, but a finite and not an infinite amount. It is evident that $\overline{m}_M$ is negative, while $\overline{p}_M$ and $\overline{c-h}_M$ are positive. Similarly, $\overline{p}_P$ is negative and $\overline{m}_P$ and $\overline{c-h}_P$ are positive. Once again, if all prices were to change by the same proportion we assume demand would be unchanged, hence

$$\overline{m}_M + \overline{p}_M + \overline{c-h}_M = 0 \dots\dots\dots\dots\dots (8)$$
$$\overline{m}_P + \overline{p}_P + \overline{c-h}_P = 0 \dots\dots\dots\dots\dots (9)$$

M_c and P_c in equations (6) and (7) mean the demand for imports and home produce for consumption. They are defined so that

$$M_c + P_c \equiv H \dots\dots\dots\dots\dots (10)$$

In order to measure them, we need some method of allocating the effects of changes in stocks and exports between imports and home production. For want of any better hypothesis in the case of food we assume that these changes lead to equal proportionate changes in the demand for imports and home production. If we call this proportionate effect A, then we can put

$$\log M = \log M_c + \log A \dots \dots \dots \dots \quad (11)$$

$$\log P = \log P_c + \log A \dots \dots \dots \dots \quad (12)$$

and we can then re-write equations (6) and (7) with $\log M$ and $\log P$ on their respective left-hand sides and an additional $\log A$ on each of their right-hand sides. (For manufactures we proceed rather differently since for them exports of home produce are large and clearly influence the demand for home production in the first place rather than the demand for imports. Our procedure is to subtract exports from home production, and to use the resulting difference, $P-X$, in a demand equation similar to (7). We ignore stock changes as the data are inadequate.)

We also assume that other 'third' factors (such as the price of non-food consumer goods, consumers' total real expenditure and the population) influence the demand for M and P equi-proportionately. Thus we assume that

$$\overline{c-h}_M = \overline{c-h}_P \dots \dots \dots \dots \dots \dots \dots \dots \quad (13)$$

$$c_M = c_P \dots \dots \dots \dots \dots \dots \dots \dots \dots \quad (14)$$

$$n_M = n_P \dots \dots \dots \dots \dots \dots \dots \dots \quad (15)$$

In writing these parameters it is convenient to omit the subscripts, since the equalities make the distinctions unnecessary.

The main justification for making these assumptions about the influence of third factors is that M and P each consist of a wide range of similar goods, and so the demand for each of them is quite likely to be equally affected by changes in the prices of other goods, in consumers' real total expenditure and in the population (or in whatever the factors happen to be). It is a convenient assumption to make, for it means that the *relative* quantities of M and P demanded depend only on their relative prices. This implication of the assumption may be obvious intuitively, and it may also be seen if we re-write equations (6) and (7) in terms of changes in the logarithms (as in equation (2)), and substitute M and P for M_c and P_c by means of equations (11) and (12), and then subtract (7) from (6). This gives

$$\Delta \log M - \Delta \log P = \Delta \log \overline{M}M^* \; (\overline{m}_M - \overline{m}_P)$$
$$- \Delta \log \overline{P}P^* \; (\overline{p}_P - \overline{p}_M) \dots \quad (16)$$

Now, if we subtract equation (9) from (8), and make use of equation (13), we have

$$\overline{m}_M - \overline{m}_P = \overline{p}_P - \overline{p}_M = (\text{say}) \; \sigma \dots \dots \dots \dots \quad (17)$$

It follows from (16) and (17) that

$$\sigma = \frac{\varDelta \log M - \varDelta \log P}{\varDelta \log \overline{MM^*} - \varDelta \log \overline{PP^*}} \quad \dots\dots\dots\dots (18)$$

This is, in fact, a common definition or measure of σ, the elasticity of substitution between M and P. It is simply the relative change in the quantities of M and P demanded divided by the relative change in their prices. Defined in this way, σ is negative, and is infinite for perfect substitutes, since then

$$\varDelta \log \overline{MM^*} - \varDelta \log \overline{PP^*} = 0.$$

The arithmetically smallest value for σ (if we rule out the case where M and P are complements, and $\overline{m}_P$ and $\overline{p}_M$ are negative) occurs when the cross-elasticities $\overline{m}_P$ and $\overline{p}_M$ are zero. In that event, changes in the price of imports have no effect on the demand for the home product, and changes in the price of the home product have no effect on the demand for imports. σ does *not* then equal zero. From equation (17) it may be seen that $\sigma = \overline{m}_M$ or $\overline{p}_P$. Since, from equations (8) and (9), putting the cross-elasticities zero, we know that

$$\overline{m}_M = -\overline{c-h} = \overline{m}_P$$

while from equation (3)

$$\overline{h} = -\overline{c-h},$$

the arithmetically smallest value for σ is simply $\overline{h}$.

We make a fair amount of use of this concept of the elasticity of substitution. It is only useful provided the assumptions made above in regard to the equi-proportionate effects of third factors on the demand for M and P are granted. Otherwise, it must be admitted that 'it is a combination, with little intuitive appeal, of price elasticities, cross-elasticities, income elasticities, and supply elasticities'.[1]

A final simplifying assumption we make is known as the 'reciprocity theorem'. For *small* changes in the variables, and assuming perfect competition, it can be shown that

$$M\overline{M}M^* . \overline{p}_M = P\overline{P}P^* . \overline{m}_P. \dots\dots\dots\dots (19)$$

The simplest proof of this theorem known to the writer is that given by Professor Hicks.[2] It is clear that there is *some* relation between the

---

[1] See Irving Morrissett, 'Some Recent Uses of Elasticity of Substitution', *Econometrica*, vol. 21, no. 1, January 1953, p. 41. See also K. W. Meinken, A. S. Rojko and G. A. King, 'Measurement of Substitution in Demand from Time Series Data— a Synthesis of Three Approaches', *Journal of Farm Economics*, vol. 38, no. 3, August 1956, p. 711. Also R. J. Nicholson, ' "Product-Elasticities of Substitution" in International Trade', *Economic Journal*, vol. 65, no. 259, September 1955, p. 445, footnote 1.

[2] J. R. Hicks, *A Revision of Demand Theory* (Oxford, The Clarendon Press, 1956), p. 126.

two cross-elasticities $\bar{p}_M$ and $\bar{m}_P$. If, for example, M and P are very close substitutes, $\bar{p}_M$ will be large and also $\bar{m}_P$ will have to be large. If one is small the other must be too. One might also be prepared to accept, intuitively, that the relative amounts of expenditure on M and P (i.e. the relation of $M\bar{M}M^*$ to $P\bar{P}P^*$) must come into the relation. Given, in some sense, the closeness of substitutability between M and P, the magnitude of the proportionate change in the demand for M following a given proportionate change in $\bar{P}$ (which is what $\bar{p}_M$ measures) will be greater the smaller is expenditure on M relative to expenditure on P— loosely speaking, a given amount of switching between M and P will have a greater proportionate effect on M. If one accepts that there is some relation of the kind shown in equation (19), the simplest hypothesis to take is that equation, though it must be admitted that the assumptions on which it rests (perfect competition) are unlikely to be fulfilled.

Let us define

$$r = \frac{M\bar{M}M^*}{P\bar{P}P^*} \dots\dots\dots\dots\dots\dots (20)$$

i.e. the ratio of expenditure on imports to expenditure on home produce (strictly speaking we should use M_e and P_e, but the difference is usually negligible). Then we may re-write (19) as

$$r\,\bar{p}_M = \bar{m}_P.$$

Now, from (17)

$$\sigma = \bar{m}_M - \bar{m}_P$$
$$= \bar{m}_M - r\,\bar{p}_M$$
$$= \bar{m}_M - r(-\bar{m}_M - \overline{c-h}),\ \text{using (8)},$$
$$= \bar{m}_M(1+r) + r\,.\,\overline{c-h} \dots\dots\dots\dots\dots\dots\dots (21)$$

This is a relation which enables us to derive $\bar{m}_M$, provided we know σ, r and $\overline{c-h}$, and we use it in this way in the sequel. It can only hold strictly for small changes in the variables, for otherwise r will generally change, and then the equation is inconsistent with our assumption that the elasticities are all constant. In fact, however, we apply it as if it were true for large changes, and take r as the mean value of the ratio of expenditures on M and P in the initial and final periods. This means that we do not assume that the reciprocity theorem holds exactly in these periods (such an assumption would be inconsistent with our assumption that the elasticities are constant); instead, we assume it holds in some average sense for a position between both periods. Since the assumptions on which the reciprocity theorem rests are unlikely to be fulfilled, this modification of it seems justifiable on grounds of expediency.

3. SUPPLY

We turn now to consider the supply equations, again taking food for the sake of example. The home supply of food is assumed to be given by

$$\log P = a + \bar{p} \log \bar{P'} + \bar{g} \log \bar{G'} + t \cdot T \ldots \ldots \ldots (22)$$

The effects of changes in prices on supply are assumed to act with a lag, so that supply in the current period is influenced by prices in several previous periods. Thus, if suffix t denotes the current period we may expand $\bar{p} \log \bar{P'}$ to

$$\bar{p}(w_t \log \bar{P}_t + w_{t-1} \log \bar{P}_{t-1} + \ldots + w_{t-n} \log \bar{P}_{t-n}).$$

Here, the w_i's are weights showing the influence of prices in period t, $t-1, \ldots t-n$ on supply in the current period. The sum of these weights is unity. Consequently, if $\log \bar{P}$ were to change by $\varDelta \log \bar{P}$ and then to maintain this new level indefinitely, the resulting change in $\log P$ would be $\bar{p} \, w_t \, \varDelta \log \bar{P}$ in the first year, $\bar{p}(w_t + w_{t-1}) \, \varDelta \log \bar{P}$ after one year and so on until eventually production would stabilize at a new level which would be $\bar{p} \, \varDelta \log \bar{P}$ greater than the original one. Hence $\bar{p}$ is the *long-run* price elasticity of supply of P. It shows the amount by which we must multiply the proportionate change in the price of output to get the *eventual* change in output induced by this change in price.

A rise in the price received for output will stimulate output, so that $\bar{p}$ is positive. Likewise, a rise in the prices paid by producers for the factors of production which they hire will depress output. These factor prices are represented by $\bar{G}$, an index of the average value of total domestic output, in equation (22). Hence $\bar{g}$ is negative.

The last term in our supply equation is T, the time in years. This is a rag-bag which contains a great variety of influences on the level of production, such as applications of new techniques, shifts in the labour supply due to the expansion of the population and to any migration into or out of the industry which is unassociated with relative price movements, similar shifts in the supply of other factors of production, and (in the case of food) the weather. As a convenient starting-point we assume that, at least over a number of years, the proportionate rate of change in supply per annum due to these factors is a constant measured by t (which is, in fact, the annual change in the *logarithm* of output due to these factors). We do not, however, maintain this assumption throughout our analysis, so that t may vary from one period to another. It is still convenient to measure these influences as shifts in supply per annum and hence we retain this mode of expression. We shall refer to these factors as the *trend* factors influencing supply, although this title begs the question of whether they tend to be persistent and uniform through time, a question which is discussed in later sections.

It is evident that this supply equation, like the demand equations, is a very much simplified view of reality. Some other variables are introduced for particular groups of commodities and are discussed in their appropriate sections.

One simplification we may discuss here is the use of an index of the general level of factor costs, $\bar{G}$, in place of an index of the particular costs incurred by the producers whose supply we are considering. For farmers we might have been better advised to use an index of the prices paid by them for labour, land, capital and materials, which might show quite different movements from $\bar{G}$. The latter is used mainly because of the statistical difficulty of constructing the former index. Another justification is that this is a convenient consolidation or synthesis of more elementary relations. To explain this, let us suppose we have an appropriate index of costs of factors employed by farmers, $\bar{F}$. Then in place of $\bar{g} \log \bar{G}'$ in equation (22) we would have $\bar{f} \log \bar{F}'$. Now suppose we have a supply function for these factors of production

$$F = s\,(\bar{F},\, \bar{G},\, T),$$

i.e. suppose the supply of labour, land, etc. to farming depends on the prices paid for these factors ($\bar{F}$), on the average rewards available to factors of production throughout the economy (measured by $\bar{G}$, with a qualification to be discussed) and on a trend factor of the kind already discussed, T. The qualification to $\bar{G}$ as a measure of average factor rewards in the economy is that it is really a measure of factor costs per unit of *output* and not per unit of factor *input*. However, if we assume that output per unit of input in the whole economy changes uniformly through time, the replacement of $\bar{G}$ by a true measure of factor rewards would merely lead to a different coefficient for T.

Next suppose we have a demand function for these factors of production by farmers

$$F = d(\bar{F},\, \bar{P},\, T).$$

From these two equations we can eliminate F, and express $\bar{F}$ in terms of $\bar{G}$, $\bar{P}$ and T. Hence we can replace $\bar{f} \log \bar{F}'$ in equation (22) by $\bar{g} \log \bar{G}'$, at the same time modifying the coefficients of $\bar{P}'$ and T. The resulting equation in effect consolidates the three other equations (i.e. the original supply equation with $\bar{F}$ instead of $\bar{G}$, and the supply and demand equations for F) into one. In general, the effect of this consolidation is to make $\bar{p}$ and t smaller. $\bar{p}$ is made smaller because a given proportionate increase, say, in $\bar{P}$ is likely to lead to a smaller increase in P if $\bar{G}$ is held constant than if $\bar{F}$ is held constant. If $\bar{G}$ is held constant, the rise in $\bar{P}$ will increase farmers' demand for factors of production and will cause them to bid up $\bar{F}$, so there will be *some* rise in $\bar{F}$, and so a smaller stimulus to supply than if $\bar{F}$ had remained constant. t is made smaller because if both $\bar{P}$ and $\bar{G}$ are constant the rightward shift of the supply curve through time will be smaller than if $\bar{P}$ and $\bar{F}$ are constant. One would generally expect output per unit of input to rise through time, and hence if $\bar{G}$ is constant, factor prices on average must be rising, hence either $\bar{F}$ will be rising or else factors of production will be leaving farming. In either event the rightward shift of the food supply curve will be less than if $\bar{F}$ is constant.

If we can assume that equi-proportionate changes in the prices of $\bar{P}$, $\bar{F}$ and $\bar{G}$ (T being constant) in our three elementary equations lead to no net effect on the appropriate quantities demanded or supplied, then it follows that equi-proportionate changes in $\bar{P}$ and $\bar{G}$ in the consolidated supply equation (22) will have no net effect on the supply of P. Hence (as we shall usually assume)

$$\bar{p}+\bar{g} = 0 \dots\dots\dots\dots\dots\dots\dots\dots (23)$$

4. DEMAND AND SUPPLY TOGETHER

The diagram on p. 3 shows imports as the difference between home demand and home supply in the simple case in which imports and the home product are perfect substitutes for each other. Let us consider this case and construct a demand equation for imports which allows for repercussions on home supply—which is, in a sense, a 'net' demand curve for imports.

We have already indicated the way in which such an equation could be obtained (on p. 81). We use the identity (5) (p. 81), which may be rearranged to give

$$M \equiv H - P + V + X.$$

We then replace H by the right-hand side of (1) (p. 79), and P by the right-hand side of (22) (p. 85). This gives

$$M = \text{Anti-log } (a_H + \bar{h} \log \overline{M}M^* + \overline{c-h} \log \overline{C-H} + c \log C + n \log N)$$

$$-\text{anti-log } (a + \bar{p} \log \left(\frac{\overline{M}M^*}{P*}\right)' + \bar{g} \log G' + t \cdot T) + V + X \quad (24)$$

We have replaced $\bar{H}$, the price of food consumed at home, by $\overline{M}M^*$, the market price of imports (i.e. after allowing for tariffs and subsidies on imports), since under the assumption of perfect substitutability between M and P these two prices must be identical in a free market. Similarly, we have replaced $\overline{P}$, the price received by farmers, by $\dfrac{\overline{MM^*}}{P^*}$ which must equal it, since, with perfect substitutability, $\overline{PP^*} = \overline{MM^*}$. The equation is not simple to handle algebraically unless the changes in all the variables are small. If the changes *are* small, and writing $\mathrm{d}M$ for a small change in M, and putting $\mathrm{d} \log \overline{M} = \dfrac{\mathrm{d}\overline{M}}{\overline{M}} = \mathrm{d}\overline{M}$ (taking the initial value of $\overline{M}$ as one as also the initial values of M^*, $\overline{C\!-\!H}$, C, N, $\overline{G}$), and similarly for other logarithmic changes, we get (ignoring time-lags)

$$
\begin{aligned}
\mathrm{d}M &= \mathrm{d}H - \mathrm{d}P + \mathrm{d}V + \mathrm{d}X \\[4pt]
&= H\frac{\mathrm{d}H}{H} - P\frac{\mathrm{d}P}{P} + \mathrm{d}V + \mathrm{d}X \\[4pt]
&= H \,\mathrm{d}\log H - P \,\mathrm{d}\log P + \mathrm{d}V + \mathrm{d}X \\[4pt]
&= H(\bar{h}\,(\mathrm{d}\overline{M} + \mathrm{d}M^*) + \overline{c\!-\!h}\,.\,\mathrm{d}\,\overline{C\!-\!H} + c\,\mathrm{d}\,C + n\,\mathrm{d}\,N) \\
&\quad - P(\bar{p}(\mathrm{d}\overline{M} + \mathrm{d}M^* - \mathrm{d}P^*) + \bar{g}\,\mathrm{d}\,\overline{G} + t\,\mathrm{d}\,T) + \mathrm{d}V + \mathrm{d}X \\[4pt]
&= (H\bar{h} - P\bar{p})\,.\,(\mathrm{d}\overline{M} + \mathrm{d}M^*) \\
&\quad + H\,.\,\overline{c\!-\!h}\,.\,\mathrm{d}\,\overline{C\!-\!H} \\
&\quad + H\,.\,c\,.\,\mathrm{d}C \\
&\quad + H\,.\,n\,.\,\mathrm{d}N \\
&\quad + P\,.\,\bar{p}\,.\,\mathrm{d}P^* \\
&\quad - P\,.\,\bar{g}\,.\,\mathrm{d}\overline{G} \\
&\quad - P\,.\,t\,.\,\mathrm{d}T \\
&\quad + \mathrm{d}V + \mathrm{d}X \dots\dots\dots\dots\dots\dots\dots\dots\dots\dots\dots\dots\dots\dots (25)
\end{aligned}
$$

This equation shows how a small change in any one of the factors on the right-hand side affects the demand for imports of food. These factors are 'exogenous' so far as this study is concerned—we do not seek to explain them, although they do in fact interact. In the equation there are, therefore, ten exogenous factors whose separate influences on the demand for imports can be determined. The endogenous factors, determined by our three equations (one identity, one demand and one supply) are $\mathrm{d}M$, $\mathrm{d}P$ and $\mathrm{d}\overline{P}$, and we have eliminated the last two so as to obtain $\mathrm{d}M$.

The equation can be expressed so that the coefficients of the variables are elasticities by dividing both sides of it by M.[1] The price elasticity

---

[1] An alternative procedure is to put the change in imports for consumption, $\mathrm{d}M - \mathrm{d}X - \mathrm{d}V$, on the left-hand side and divide both sides by $M - X - V$, or M_C as we may call it (see p. 81).

of demand for imports, allowing for repercussions on home supply, is then

$$\frac{H\bar{h}-P\bar{p}}{M}$$

or, if we put $r = \dfrac{M}{P}$ as in equation (20) (the initial values of $\bar{M}$, $M*$, $\bar{P}$ and $P*$ all being unity), and if we assume $H \simeq M + P$,

$$\bar{h}\left(1+\frac{1}{r}\right)-\frac{1}{r}\,\bar{p}.$$

This expression for the price elasticity of demand for imports is similar to that derived by other writers.[1] It is useful in that it shows how the elasticity is made arithmetically greater if *either* $\bar{h}$ or $\bar{p}$ is made arithmetically greater (remembering that $\bar{h}$ is negative as defined here), or if the ratio of imports to home supply, r, is reduced. It shows how a change in the price of imports exerts a double effect on the demand, by reducing consumption and by stimulating home supply (compare the diagram on p. 3). It must be borne in mind, however, that the expression rests on the assumption that imports and home supply are perfect substitutes for each other. Although it takes supply repercussion into account, there are many other repercussions left out of account.[2]

A similar consolidation of demand and supply equations can be made when the elementary equations are like (6) and (7) on p. 81 and the supply equation is as before on p. 85, that is, when we no longer assume that imports and the home product are perfect substitutes. We eliminate P and $\bar{P}$ from our three equations and are left with a single demand equation for imports. The workings are not given here, but the formula for the price elasticity of demand for imports is given for comparison with the preceding formula. It is

$$\frac{\bar{h}\left(1+\dfrac{1}{r}\right)-\dfrac{1}{r}\,\bar{p}\left(1+\dfrac{r\bar{h}}{\sigma}\right)}{1-\dfrac{(\bar{p}-\bar{h}+r\bar{p})}{r\sigma}}.$$

It is clear that as σ approaches $-\infty$, the above formula approaches the preceding one. If σ is made arithmetically smaller, however, the elasticity is also made arithmetically smaller. The smallest value for σ is $\bar{h}$, as was shown on p. 83, and when σ is given this value the above formula also becomes equal to $\bar{h}$. This is what might be expected—if

[1] See, for example, Sir Donald MacDougall, *The World Dollar Problem* (1957), p. 560.

[2] See 'Interdependence and Foreign Trade', by M. FG. Scott, *Oxford Economic Papers* (New Series), vol. 9, no. 1, February 1957, p. 88.

M and P are not substitutes at all, then the price elasticity of demand for M is simply the same as the price elasticity of demand for consumption of M, and the demand for and supply of P are irrelevant.

5. MEASURING THE EFFECTS OF DIFFERENT FACTORS ON IMPORTS

The above system of equations provides us with a means of measuring the effects of a change in any one of the factors influencing imports. We need to know the change in the factor, the various parameters, and given these we want to be able to calculate the resulting change in imports. Succeeding sections deal with the problems of measuring the changes in the factors and of estimating the parameters. Here we must consider two problems which must be solved before we can apply this knowledge to obtain the results discussed in Part I. The problems are how to deal with large changes in the variables and how to deal with the effects of lagged factors.

The kind of problem which arises when we attempt to estimate the effects of large changes in the various factors on imports is illustrated by equations (24) and (25) (pp. 87 and 88). Equation (24) shows how imports are determined by ten exogenous factors, after allowing for repercussions on home supply. We want to calculate the effect of a change in any one of these factors on imports, using this equation. If the changes are small, this can be done quite simply by means of equation (25), but if the changes are large (as they usually must be if we are to attach any importance to them), then there is no simple and uniquely correct method of performing the calculation. This difficulty is discussed in Part I (p. 24), and what follows is an elaboration of the argument there given.

Mathematically, the difficulty may be expressed as follows. Suppose that in equation (24) we are told that over a certain period $\log \overline{M}$ has changed by $\varDelta \log \overline{M}$, while the other variables have also changed, all by large amounts. We are required to calculate the effect of the change in $\overline{M}$ on M. Now the size of this effect will depend on whether we measure it on the assumption that the other variables have *not* changed at all, or on whether we measure it on the assumption that the other variables have already taken up their new positions before $\overline{M}$ changes, or on whether we adopt some intermediate assumption. Hence there is no uniquely correct answer. Furthermore, some of the answers we might give will lead to the sum of our 'effects' being greater or less than the actual change in M. All this may be illustrated by an arithmetical example.

Suppose that, initially, consumption of food is 160 (value at constant prices), home food production is 60 and imports of food 100. Suppose the only changes which occur are a rise in the price of imports and a rise in population, and that the former would, by itself, halve food consumption and double home food production, while the rise in population would, by itself, treble food consumption. The outcome may then be summarized as follows:

Item	Initial value at constant prices	Effect of change in $\overline{M}$	N	Final value at constant prices	Change in value at constant prices
H	160	$\times \frac{1}{2}$	$\times 3$	240	+80
P	60	$\times 2$	—	120	+60
M	100	?	?	120	+20

What we require is some way of filling in the spaces occupied by the question marks. If our only task were to measure the effects on consumption H, say, of the changes in $\overline{M}$ and N, the simplest solution would be to say, as in the table, that one halved consumption and the other trebled it. But when we attempt to translate these changes into effects on imports, there is no obvious solution. If, for example, we say that the halving of consumption caused by the change in the price of imports would, by itself, have led to a fall of 80 in imports, while the rise in population would have led to an increase of 320, then the sum of these is an increase of 240 in imports, whereas we know that the whole increase in consumption caused a rise of only 80 in imports. This procedure would understate the importance of the rise in price which halved consumption, and would overstate the importance of the rise in population. The opposite fault occurs if we do a similar calculation for the effect of the rise in the price of imports, only we assume population to have changed to its final position instead of remaining at its initial position. If we assume, instead, that population remains at a position half-way between its initial and final position, then the effect of the change in import price works out at a fall of 120 in consumption and imports, while the corresponding calculation for the effect of the change in population gives an increase of 240.[1]

This solution still suffers from the defect that the sum of the effects does not equal the total change ($-120+240 = 120$ and not 80). It is nevertheless approximately the same as the solution adopted in this study, namely, to divide the absolute change in consumption amongst the causal factors in proportion to their *logarithmic* effects on consumption. The effect of the change in the price of imports on imports via

[1] The arithmetic is:
$$(\tfrac{1}{2}-1) \times 1\tfrac{1}{2} \times 160 = -120$$
$$\text{and } (3-1) \times \tfrac{3}{4} \times 160 = 240.$$

consumption then works out at about -137, and the effect of the change in population is about 217. In this way the *ratio* of the effects is properly stated, given our basic assumption that these factors influence consumption through an equation which is linear in logarithms. In addition, the sum of the effects equals the actual change in imports.[1]

This procedure is used throughout this study, and, on occasion, has been used in the reverse fashion as well, i.e. for translating arithmetic effects into logarithmic effects.

The problem of measuring the effects of lagged factors need only be discussed very briefly, since it is largely evaded in the following chapters. First we may make a relatively simple point which may be illustrated by reference to the supply equation (22) on p. 85, which shows the supply of food, P, as a lagged function of its price, $\bar{P}$. Usually in what follows, we shall mean by the effect on P of a change in $\bar{P}$ between two periods *not* the actual change in $\bar{P}$ multiplied by the price elasticity of supply (i.e. *not* $\bar{p}(\log \bar{P}_t - \log \bar{P}_{t-x})$) where t and $t-x$ are the later and earlier periods respectively) but the *lagged* change in $\bar{P}$ multiplied by the price elasticity of supply (i.e. $\bar{p}(w_t \log \bar{P}_t + w_{t-1} \log \bar{P}_{t-1} + \ldots + w_{t-n} \log \bar{P}_{t-n}) - \bar{p} (w_{t-x} \log \bar{P}_{t-x} + w_{t-x-1} \log \bar{P}_{t-x-1} + \ldots + w_{t-x-n} \log \bar{P}_{t-x-n}))$. This second measure gives us the change in P caused actually during the interval in question by the change in prices. The first measure shows us how much output would have changed from, first, the level it would have reached given time to adjust itself fully to the prices ruling in the earlier period to, second, the level it would have reached given time to adjust itself fully to the price situation in the later period. The more complex difficulties arise if we try to measure the direct *and indirect* effects of various factors, some of which have lagged effects. Thus, where imports and home production are not perfect substitutes, the level of $\bar{P}$ in any period is influenced by all our exogenous factors. Since changes in $\bar{P}$ have lagged effects on P (via the supply equation) and so on M, it follows that *every* factor has a lagged effect on M. These lagged effects are calculable only if the initial effects on $\bar{P}$ in the earlier periods are calculable. In the actual case in which we might want to make these calculations (i.e. the analysis of changes in food imports during the post-war period), these initial effects are not calculable, since there was no free market for food in the earlier years. In the absence of a free market we cannot be sure what the effects of changes in our exogenous factors on $\bar{P}$ were. Hence we do not in fact make these calculations, but instead adopt a different procedure which is described on pp. 114–15.

---

[1] Using this method, the entries in the table in place of the question marks would be, under $\bar{M}$ and N respectively, -197 and 217.

CHAPTER VI

FOOD, DRINK AND TOBACCO

I. INTRODUCTION

This chapter is mainly concerned with the behaviour of imports of food and non-alcoholic beverages. A brief mention is made at the end of it of imported alcoholic beverages and tobacco; these were excluded from the main study because of the great importance of duty payments which might have tended to obscure changes in food prices, and also because they are probably less easily substitutable for foodstuffs than are the different foodstuffs for each other. Also, the study of tobacco imports amounts to the study of tobacco consumption, since there is virtually no home production, and this has been studied by other writers.[1]

There is no need in this chapter, unlike the following ones, for a section describing the analytical framework. The energetic reader of Chapter V has already received a complete exposé, so that no further equations are required. The outline given in Chapters I and II suffices for the rest, further details being described as they arise in the subsequent discussion.

Table 14. *United Kingdom retained imports of food, drink and tobacco in 1957*

	£ million, c.i.f.
Live animals chiefly for food	45
Meat and meat preparations	306
Dairy products, eggs and honey	137
Fish and fish preparations	33
Cereals and cereal preparations	211
Fruits and vegetables	227
Sugar and sugar preparations	148
Coffee, cocoa and preparations, tea and spices	179
Feeding stuffs for animals and food wastes	45
Miscellaneous food preparations	17
Oil seeds, oil nuts and oil kernels	62
Animal and vegetable oils, fats, etc.	61
Total food	1,472
Alcoholic beverages	28
Tobacco and tobacco manufactures	85

Source: Trade and Navigation Accounts, December 1957.

[1] In particular, Richard Stone, *The Measurement of Consumers' Expenditure and Behaviour in the United Kingdom, 1920–1938, Vol. I,* Studies in the National Income and Expenditure of the United Kingdom, 1 (Cambridge University Press, 1954).

Table 14, which shows the composition of imports of food in a recent year, illustrates the great variety of products which are grouped together in this chapter as 'food'. Imports include animal feeding stuffs, non-alcoholic beverages and manufactured foodstuffs as well as the more 'ordinary' things like meat and wheat.

The opening sections of this chapter deal first with the demand for all food consumed on the home market and then with the supply of food produced in this country. There follow two sections, one of which is an addendum to Chapter II and explains how some of the estimates relating to food consumption and imports were made, the other a concluding section on consumption and imports of alcoholic drink and tobacco.

Section 2 on the demand for food summarizes the results obtained by some other workers in this field. Their estimates of the price and expenditure elasticities of demand for food, whether measured at retail or at the farm gate, are accepted without further inquiry. The estimates used in this study, which are based on them, are summarized on p. 97. Some rather arbitrary limits to these estimates are also given which are thought to be sufficiently wide to make larger or smaller values of the elasticities not worth considering.

Section 3 analyses the demand for food into the demand for imported and home-produced food. This is necessary if these two groups of food are not close substitutes for each other, and some evidence bearing on this is examined. This shows that there was, apparently, a substantial increase in the average market price of imported food relative to that of home-produced food from 1935–8 to 1954–5 which accompanied the decrease in the consumption of the former relative to that of the latter. This supports the view that the two groups are not very close substitutes. For various reasons, however, this evidence is unreliable, and there is evidence from other periods to the contrary. In view of this uncertainty, in subsequent calculations two sets of values for the relevant demand elasticities are taken: one assuming imperfect and one assuming perfect substitutability. The former set is given in Table 16, p. 100, together with upper and lower limits. For the latter, the estimates in Section 2, Table 15, suffice.

Section 4 is a study of the determinants of home agricultural production, which is approximately equivalent to the supply of home-produced food. The main determining factors are assumed to be the price of output received by farmers (i.e. inclusive of price subsidies), an index of the general price level, the percentage unemployed in all industries and trend factors (changes in techniques, etc.). As a first step, the separate influence of each of these factors on agricultural production is estimated by the usual least-squares regression procedure from data extending over the past eighty years. An attempt is then made to assess the reliability of these estimates, and to put upper and lower limits to the values of the various parameters. Since there is reason to believe that the trend factors caused a faster increase in production after 1939 than before, so that less of the subsequent rise in production can properly be attributed to price factors, the price elasticity of supply which is finally selected (i.e. 0·5) is lower than that estimated by the least-squares procedure (i.e. 0·9). The final best estimates and limits are on p. 102.

From these estimates of the price elasticities of demand for and supply of food one can calculate a price elasticity of demand for *imports* of food, using the formulae given in Chapter V, Section 4 (pp. 87–90). Likewise, one can estimate the appropriate parameters relating consumers' expenditure on all goods and services to imports of food (similar to an income elasticity of demand for imports of food), and population to imports of food. The values of all these parameters depend upon the ratio of imports to home food production. No estimates for them are given in this chapter, but estimates which are appropriate to the ratio in 1957 are given in Chapter III, Table 12, p. 49.

2. CONSUMERS' DEMAND FOR FOOD

The main determinants of the demand for food are assumed to be the market price of food, the prices of other consumer goods, the population and its real total current expenditure (or expenditure per head, if that is preferred). Since the demand for food has been the subject of study by many econometricians, many of whose estimates are in agreement with each other, it was decided to accept these estimates without further inquiry. What follows is mainly a summary of the relevant results.[1]

For the most part, investigators of the relationship between prices and incomes and food consumption, where they have used time series, have used annual figures and not lagged variables. Where lagged variables have been used, the estimates of the lagged effects are small compared with the unlagged ones. Accordingly, we assume that food consumption in the current year is determined by income and prices in that year, and we ignore lagged effects.

Both the price and the income elasticity of demand for food measured at the farm gate appear to be significantly smaller than for food measured at retail. After reviewing a large number of estimates made by

---

[1] The works consulted were: L. Juréen, 'Long-term Trends in Food Consumption: a Multi-country Study', *Econometrica*, vol. 24, no. 1, January 1956, p. 1; T. W. Schultz, *The Economic Organization of Agriculture* (New York, McGraw-Hill, 1953); Richard Stone, *The Measurement of Consumers' Expenditure and Behaviour in the United Kingdom, 1920–1938, Vol. I* (1954). The first two works summarize some of the results achieved by many research workers in this field.

different people, Professor Schultz gives the following estimates for food demand in the United States.[1]

| | For food measured at | |
	Farm gate	Retail
Income elasticity	0·25	0·50
Price elasticity	−0·25	−0·50

Food measured at the farm gate excludes a large part of the costs of processing and distribution which enter into food measured at retail. The demand for these processing and distribution services appears to be considerably more elastic in response to changes in incomes than is the demand for crude food.

Mr Juréen shows that the income elasticity of food varies with real income. The richer the community, the lower the income elasticity appears to be. He also shows (as do the other writers cited) that the income and price elasticities vary quite considerably for different food-stuffs. The income elasticities are lowest for cereals for human consumption (for which they appear to be negative) and higher for livestock products and fruit and vegetables. Taking unprocessed food measured at constant prices he gives estimates of income elasticities at different levels of income varying from 0·11 to 0·59. For the lowest of these elasticities, 'income' per head is shown as $U.S. 600, and for the highest $U.S. 25. The United Kingdom's 'income' is given as $U.S. 226, and at this 'income' level the income elasticity lies between 0·21 and 0·30.[2] The estimate he takes of the price elasticity of demand for total food is −0·20.

Professor Stone's work is concerned with final consumers' expenditure and hence the elasticities tend to be higher than those for unprocessed food given above. He gives an estimate of the expenditure elasticity of demand for all food of 0·59, and income elasticity 0·53, each with a standard error of 0·04. His estimate of the price elasticity is −0·35, with a standard error of 0·28.[3]

---

[1] Schultz, *The Economic Organization of Agriculture*, pp. 61 and 188. The elasticities at retail are those corresponding to food expenditure as measured by the United States Department of Commerce.

[2] Juréen, 'Long-term Trends in Food Consumption', *Econometrica*, January 1956, table V. Mr Juréen's measure of food appears to be the result of adding the calorie value of three categories of foodstuffs (cereals, livestock products, and all other) using their average prices per calorie as weights. It therefore does not correspond exactly to the ordinary concept of consumption of food at constant prices. The figures of 'income' per head cited above refer to the pre-war value of commodities available per head, the source being the *Economic Survey of Europe in 1949* (Geneva, Economic Commission for Europe, 1950), table IV, pp. 276–7.

[3] Stone, *Measurement of Consumers' Expenditure . . . 1920–1938, Vol. I*, tables 105, 106.

There seems to be no need to allow for variations in these elasticities through time as a result of changes in the level of real income per head, at least if we confine our attention to the present century. So far as can be judged,[1] from 1900 to 1955 real consumers' total expenditure per head increased by only about a quarter—an astonishingly small amount in terms of the rate of increase experienced over the last few years. An increase of this amount, according to Mr Juréen,[2] would only change the income elasticity by about 0·03. Hence, although most of the studies on which the elasticities are based relate to the pre-war period, their results may be applied to the post-war one.

0·3 and 0·6 are taken as best estimates for the expenditure elasticity of demand for food measured at the farm gate and at retail respectively, and −0·25 and −0·5 for the corresponding price elasticities of demand. We also give (arithmetically) upper and lower limits for these elasticities. These are meant to be wide, so that most informed observers would probably agree that the elasticities did not have higher or lower values than these. They are therefore taken as follows.[3]

Table 15. *Elasticities of demand for consumption of food*

Elasticity		Food measured at	
		Farm gate	Retail
Expenditure, c	high	0·6	1·2
	best guess	0·3	0·6
	low	0	0
Price, h	high	−0·5	−1·0
	best guess	−0·25	−0·5
	low	0	0

The remaining elasticities we have to determine are those measuring the influence of changes in non-food consumer prices and in population. Both follow at once from the elasticities we have just determined, given two assumptions mentioned in Chapter I (pp. 8–10). If we assume that an equal proportionate increase in food and non-food prices leaves the

[1] The following estimates of changes in real consumers' expenditure per head are derived from figures kindly supplied by Mr D. A. Rowe for the period 1900 to 1938, and the estimates of the Central Statistical Office thereafter.

[2] 'Long-term Trends in Food Consumption', Table V.

[3] It is customary to take twice the standard error of estimate as a confidence limit for estimates obtained by the method of least squares. There are various reasons for distrusting this procedure, and it is not followed here. In any case, the estimates given here are not derived from any single simple statistical procedure, so that it would be difficult to measure the standard error of estimate. For other estimates made in this study, various crude procedures are used for deriving limits. In this case, where the best guess estimates are based on others' work, we have simply taken zero as a lower limit in each case, and then chosen the upper limit so that the best guess is always in the middle of the range.

demand for food unchanged, then the price elasticity of demand for food with respect to non-food prices must simply be the negative of the elasticity with respect to food prices (i.e. $+0 \cdot 25$ and $+0 \cdot 5$, best guesses). Secondly, we assume that changes in population, *per capita* real total current expenditure of consumers being constant, lead to equal proportionate changes in the demand for food (i.e. an elasticity of 1).

3. THE SEPARATE DEMANDS FOR IMPORTED AND HOME-PRODUCED FOOD FOR CONSUMPTION

The bulk of imports consist of relatively unprocessed commodities which are more or less comparable to food produced on British farms. We must now consider how closely substitutable the two groups, imports and home production, are for each other. For unless they approximate to perfect substitutes we need separate demand functions for each.

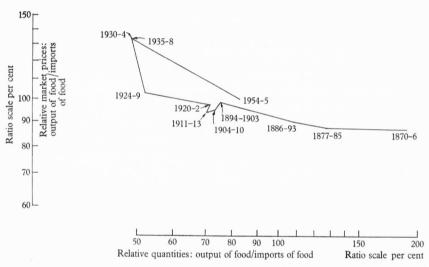

Chart 8. Relative quantities and prices of United Kingdom food imports and food output

We review past changes in the relative quantities and relative prices of the two groups. Both groups are bought by consumers,[1] and if they were very close substitutes for each other we might expect that large changes in the relative quantities purchased would have been accom-

---

[1] Though—in both cases—only after a considerable amount of processing and distribution costs have been incurred, but this should not substantially affect the following argument.

panied by only small changes in their relative market prices. On the other hand, if they were not very close substitutes, it would have required a fairly large change in relative prices to induce consumers to make the necessary switch in their purchases from one to the other.

Chart 8 provides a convenient summary of the evidence. If we omit the 1930's, the points in the chart lie on a line which is nearly horizontal, showing that large changes in relative quantities were accompanied by small changes in relative market prices, i.e. that substitutability between the groups was probably high. The change from the 1920's to the 1930's and from the 1930's to post-war contradicts this. Thus, if we take the changes from 1935–8 to 1954–5 we find a large reduction in the quantity of imports relative to the quantity of home output accompanied by a substantial cheapening in the price of home output relative to that of imports.

It is possible that some unusual or uneven distribution of shifts in demand or supply may have produced this result, and that it is misleading as a general guide to the behaviour of relative prices and quantities. This is a possibility which must always be borne in mind when considering the behaviour of groups, as is shown in the Appendix (p. 204). The writer was unable to find an explanation along these lines, however.[1]

There are also statistical deficiencies in the series which may account for some of the apparent relative price changes, but it seems unlikely

[1] Weighting differences do not appear to account for much of the divergence. An index of food prices, weighted in accordance with the relative values of foods in the value of the output of British farms, but using as price relatives (a) prices paid to British farmers and (b) prices paid for imports, shows the following changes from 1935–8 to 1954–5 (see K. R. Clark, 'Some Indicators of General Price and Cost Movements affecting Agriculture in the United Kingdom', *Farm Economist*, vol. 8, no. 10, 1957, p. 58).

Index, 1911–13 = 100

	1935–8	1954–5	Percentage change
(a) Farm	116	392	239
(b) Import	103	410	299

Import prices weighted in this way rose by about 18 % relative to United Kingdom farm prices, and the rise was due to relative increases in the prices of fairly narrowly defined commodity groups rather than to any difference in weighting as between the groups. The index numbers used in Chart 8 show a larger relative increase in import prices, about 33 % from 1935–8 to 1954–5. About 9 % of this, however, is due to adjustments for indirect taxes and subsidies, since the index numbers in Chart 8 show market prices. The remaining relative increase in import prices c.i.f. over prices paid to British farmers was thus 24 %, and, to judge by the 18 % divergence in the *Farm Economist* index numbers quoted above, not much of this was attributable to weighting differences.

that they account for them all.[1] It was therefore decided to make two
sets of calculations, one on the assumption that the substitutability of
imports of food for home food production was perfect (infinite), and
one on the assumption that it was as suggested by the behaviour of
relative prices and quantities between 1935–8 and 1954–5.

For the second assumption we need separate demand functions for
imported and home-produced food. The determinants of demand are
the same as in the previous section with the addition of the price of the
close substitute, so that in each function there are now three price
elasticities instead of only two. Thus the demand for imports is determined by the market price of imports, the market price of home-
produced food (which need not be identical) and the prices of all other
non-food consumer goods, as well as by the population and its real total
current expenditure.

We assume that imported and home-produced food are influenced in
equal proportions by changes in third factors—prices of non-food goods,
population and real expenditure, the elasticities being the same as those
just determined. It follows that the relative quantities of imports and
home produce demanded depend only on their relative prices, and the
relation between the two is shown in Chart 8, p. 98. Taking the change
from 1935–8 to 1954–5, the elasticity of substitution (obtained by dividing the relative change in quantities by the accompanying relative
change in prices, all measured in logarithms) works out at −1·9.

Table 16. *Elasticities of demand for imported and home-produced food
assuming imperfect substitutability*

		Price elasticity of demand for	
		Imported food (Suffix M)	Home-produced food (Suffix P)
With respect to changes in price of			
Non-food consumer goods, $\overline{c-h}$	high	0·5	0·5
	best	0·25	0·25
	low	0	0
Imported food, $\overline{m}_M$ and $\overline{m}_P$	high	−0·99	0·88
	best	−0·83	1·04
	low	−0·67	1·20
Home-produced food, $\overline{p}_M$ and $\overline{p}_P$	high	0·49	−1·38
	best	0·58	−1·29
	low	0·67	−1·20

[1] The estimates of the changes in the price and quantity of agricultural output
and of imports of food appear to be inconsistent with those of food consumption at
retail for the period 1935–8 to 1946–9, and again for the period 1946–9 to 1954–5.
But there is no marked inconsistency as regards the change from 1935–8 to 1954–5
(see Appendix II, pp. 223–4).

From this, and using the results of the previous section, we can compute the price elasticities of demand by means of equation (21) (p. 84). The results are summarized above, all estimates referring to food at the farm gate.

A word of explanation may be necessary about the meaning of the high and low estimates. Only one value for the elasticity of substitution was used throughout the calculations, since this was already an extreme value, the other extreme being perfect substitutability. The high estimates in the table are those consistent with the high estimate for the price elasticity of demand with respect to non-food consumer goods (i.e. 0·5), while the low ones are those consistent with the low estimates for that elasticity (i.e. 0).

4. HOME FOOD SUPPLY

Home food supply comes mostly from farms, and most farm output consists of food. In what follows we treat home food supply, farm output and agricultural production as equivalent, although this is not strictly accurate. The statistical problems are discussed in Appendix II (pp. 225–6).

The determinants of agricultural production were assumed to be the prices received by farmers, an index of the general level of factor costs per unit of output in the whole economy, the percentage of unemployment in the economy,[1] and a group of other so-called 'trend' factors (from which the effects of changes in the weather were partially eliminated by confining attention to averages for periods of five years or more). These factors are discussed in Chapter II (p. 21) and in Chapter V, Section 3 and some further discussion is given below.

As a first step in the process of estimating the effects of these factors an equation (similar to equation (22) on p. 85, but with the addition of the percentage unemployed as an explanatory variable) was fitted, using the usual method of least squares. Prices were lagged according to the six-year lagging system set out on p. 107. The choice of this system was largely arbitrary, but, as is shown below, it seems unlikely that the choice of any other plausible lagging system would make much difference. The results are shown in Chart 2, and the fitted equation was the following:

$$\log P = -0\cdot121 + 0\cdot86 \log \overline{P}' - 0\cdot86 \log \overline{G}'$$
$$+ 0\cdot0023\,T + 0\cdot0013\,U.$$

The estimated price elasticity of supply was therefore 0·86, the estimated trend was equivalent to an increase of the anti-log of 0·0023,

[1] See pp. 103–4 for an explanation of this factor.

or to 0·5 % per annum, and the estimated effect of an increase of 1 in the percentage unemployed was to raise production by the anti-log of 0·0013, or by 0·3 %.

The chief implausibility in the above estimating procedure is the assumption that the trend factors, which represent all factors influencing supply other than relative prices and unemployment, were constant over time. In what follows we first give some reasons for thinking it unlikely that the true price elasticity of supply was negative, so that we can take zero as a lower limit for it. This then enables us to set either lower or upper limits for the value of the trend factor over each of various periods in the past. On the further assumption that the highest and lowest observed values of these was not exceeded in any other period we can place an upper limit on the price elasticity of supply. Finally (pp. 108–9), we give some reasons for thinking that the least squares estimate of the price elasticity of supply is too large, and that 0·5 is a better estimate.

As the non-specialist reader may prefer to omit the following pages (102–9), the limits estimated for the various parameters are summarized below:

> Trend factor　　　−1 to 3 % per annum,
> Elasticity of supply 0 to 2.

The lower limit chosen for the long-run elasticity of supply was zero. One can justify this limit on general grounds, as well as by an appeal to the figures. The usual reasons for expecting a backward-sloping supply curve in agriculture are the lack of effective alternative employment for farm workers, the tendency to prefer additional leisure to additional income as real income increases, and the tendency to consume more of one's own produce as real income increases, thus leaving less available for sale to the rest of the community. The last reason may be dismissed at once, since the figures of agricultural production used here include production consumed on the farms. Even if they did not (and the estimates may be unreliable) the point could hardly be important since by far the greater part of output is sold off the farms, and since farmers in this country are sufficiently rich to have a low income elasticity of demand for food. The first reason is not applicable to this country either. Only about one-twentieth of all workers are engaged in agriculture and over the last century there has been a very large shift of workers from the countryside to the town. There remains the effect of increased income on the 'consumption' of leisure. Even if one grants that the more one pays farm workers the less hard do they work, it does not follow that less will be produced. In the first place, it does not even follow that there will be fewer *man-hours* worked on farms, since more people will be attracted into agriculture. In the second place, direct labour, including the farmers' as well as labourers' incomes, forms only about a half of total inputs into agriculture.[1] Even if direct labour inputs are reduced when agricultural prices rise, other inputs are likely to be increased, so that on balance total production may rise. Farming in this country is in many ways similar to any other business. The position is very different from that of peasant cultivators in a predominantly agricultural country. One expects the different sectors of manufacturing industry to have positively inclined supply curves and there seems little reason to suppose that farming in this country is essentially different in this respect.[2]

Besides these general reasons one can quote various authorities in support of the view that agricultural supply in this country or in the United States has some positive elasticity, at least in the long run and in periods of fairly full employment.[3] It is true that in the United States from 1929 to 1932 the index of 'parity'[4] fell by close on 40 %, while production fell scarcely at all until the drought years 1934–6. This phenomenon has supported some writers in their conclusion that the supply of agricultural output is very inelastic in response to changes in price, so that zero might seem a best guess rather than a lower limit for the elasticity of supply. However, the explanation for the maintenance of output despite the fall in prices may have been the increase in industrial unemployment after 1929. Since the alternative to work in agriculture was not work at a relatively higher wage-rate in industry, but more probably no work at all, farm workers did not leave agriculture for industry. Indeed, statistics of the farm population in the United States show that the downward drift in population was halted and reversed after 1929. It was resumed again after 1933, the peak year of

[1] See table 209 of the *Annual Abstract of Statistics* for 1956. The ratio of farming net income plus expenditure on labour to total revenue was 48 % in 1937–8, 60 % in 1946–7 and only 41 % in 1954–5.

[2] The arguments in the above paragraph apply with more force to the current situation than to past years. Especially before 1914, when Southern Ireland was included in the statistics, the elasticity of supply may very well have been lower than it is now. However, the conclusions drawn below about the probable size of the long-run elasticity of supply refer to recent years, and are not based to any great extent on the pre-1914 statistics.

[3] See J. R. Bellerby, *Agriculture and Industry: Relative Income* (London, Macmillan, 1956); D. Gale Johnson, 'The Nature of the Supply Function for Agricultural Products', *American Economic Review*, vol. 40, no. 4, September 1950, p. 539; T. W. Schultz, *The Economic Organization of Agriculture* (1953), chs. 11 and 13.

[4] This index measures the ratio of an index of prices received by farmers for their produce to an index of prices they pay, both for ordinary living expenses and for purchases of materials needed on the farm.

104 UNITED KINGDOM IMPORTS

industrial unemployment.[1] It seems plausible, therefore, to believe that changes in industrial unemployment affect agricultural output,[2] and so we have allowed for this by introducing unemployment as an explanatory variable in our supply equation.[3]

Table 17. *Rates of change in United Kingdom* agricultural production caused by factors other than prices under certain assumptions*

| | Percentage per annum Assuming long-run elasticity of supply is | | | | | | | | | |
| | 0 (i.e. actual rate of change of output) | 0·5 | | | 1·0 | | | 2·0 | | |
		3 yr.	6 yr.	10 yr.	3 yr.	6 yr.	10 yr.	3 yr.	6 yr.	10 yr.
1877–85 to 1886–93	0·4	0·8	0·6	0·4	1·2	0·8	0·5	2·1	1·3	0·6
1886–93 to 1894–1903	−0·3	0	0	0·1	0·2	0·3	0·4	0·7	0·9	1·1
1894–1903 to 1904–10	0·5	0·8	0·8	0·8	1·0	1·0	1·0	1·5	1·6	1·5
1904–10 to 1924–9	−0·4	0·2	0	−0·2	0·7	0·4	−0·1	1·9	1·3	0·3
1924–9 to 1930–4	0	0·5	1·0	1·8	1·0	1·9	3·6	1·9	3·8	7·2
1930–4 to 1935–9	0·4	0·1	0·5	0·6	−0·2	0·6	0·9	−0·7	0·8	1·4
1935–9 to 1946–50	2·7	1·0	0·9	1·2	−0·8	−0·8	−0·3	−4·2	−4·3	−3·2
1946–50 to 1951–5	2·5	2·7	2·3	1·7	3·0	2·1	0·9	3·5	1·7	−0·6

Note: The assumptions on which this table is constructed are described in the text. The reader who wants to derive values for other elasticities can easily do so since there is an approximately linear relation between the figures in the table for any particular period and lagging assumption.

* An adjustment has been made to remove the discontinuity in the series caused by the secession of Southern Ireland from the United Kingdom in 1923, but it is subject to a wide margin of error.

Sources: See pp. 225 ff. and S36 and 37.

[1] See United States Bureau of the Census, *Historical Statistics of the United States, 1789–1945* (Washington, U.S. Government Printing Office, 1949), series B 231. The statistics include all persons living on farms without regard to occupation.

[2] D. Gale Johnson in 'The Nature of the Supply Function for Agricultural Products', *American Economic Review*, September 1950, argues that a rise in industrial unemployment reduces the *price elasticity of supply* of agricultural output, and not just that it directly increases supply itself. This seems an unnecessarily complicated explanation of the failure of United States agricultural output to fall after 1929. Moreover, this view would imply that a rise in agricultural prices during a prolonged depression would not lead to greater agricultural output, even though it would in a period of relatively full employment. With labour easier to get, it is difficult to see why this should be so. Alternatively, if one granted that a rise in prices, but not a fall, would affect output in a depression, then one must suppose that a series of rises followed by equal falls in a prolonged depression would lead to a gradual expansion of agricultural output, which also seems implausible.

[3] The effects of changes in industrial unemployment on agricultural output in the United Kingdom are probably smaller than in the United States, however. The existence of minimum wage legislation would prevent an influx of cheap labour during a depression such as occurred in the United States and Canada during the 1930's. See Bellerby, *Agriculture and Industry: Relative Income*, pp. 56, 75, 113–16, 122.

If it is accepted that the elasticity of supply is unlikely to be as low as zero, it is possible to establish lower and upper limits for the 'trend' factor in agricultural supply, and also an upper limit for the price elasticity of supply. The basic data are given in Table 17, which shows the rates of change in United Kingdom agricultural production between various periods for which the data are available, and what rate of change must have been due to factors other than relative price changes on various assumptions about the elasticity of supply and the time lags involved. Table 18 gives average percentage total unemployment in the years in question.

Table 18. *Percentage unemployed in the United Kingdom*

1877–85	5·6	1904–10	6·0	1935–9	12·8
1886–93	5·3	1924–9	10·6	1946–50	2·1
1894–1903	4·0	1930–4	19·2	1951–5	1·6

Sources: Up to 1926 the Trades Union unemployment rate was used as given by Lord Beveridge in *Full Employment in a Free Society* (London, Allen and Unwin, 1944), pp. 312, 313. Thereafter the unemployment percentages given in the March 1956 issue of the *London and Cambridge Economic Bulletin* were used. The percentages are not strictly comparable over all these periods, but it is thought that they do not give a misleading impression.

From the rates of change in United Kingdom agricultural output given in the first column of Table 17 we can derive with some confidence the maximum rate of *fall* in output which is likely to be due to factors other than changes in prices and unemployment. Up to 1939 the relative price of agricultural output was falling (Chart 2). If, for the reasons given above, we take as an extreme assumption that this fall had no effect at all on output, we can attribute the whole of any actual fall to non-price factors. In the sixty years to 1939 the maximum rate of fall seems to have been about one-half of 1 % per annum. In none of these periods was unemployment falling at any great rate (see Table 18), and during the inter-war years it increased. But for this increase in unemployment the fall in output from 1904–10 to 1924–9 might have been greater, and there might have been a fall from 1924–9 to 1930–4. However, the experience of the other periods suggests that a greater fall in output is unlikely; we are taking an extreme assumption about the effects of relative price changes; and the actual fall from 1904–10 to 1924–9 is dubious on statistical grounds (because of the secession of Southern Ireland). Hence it seems unlikely that factors other than changes in unemployment and prices would cause production to fall by more than, say, 1 % per annum.

This conclusion is supported by American experience. After 1910, if we exclude the middle 1930's when output was severely affected both by droughts and by government restrictions, there is no pair of five-year periods between which agricultural production[1] fell.

It is less easy to derive a likely *maximum* for the effects of factors other than prices and unemployment. For the United Kingdom in the period under review, price movements were clearly favourable to the farmer only during the two World Wars. No estimates of production during the First World War seem available. From 1935–9 to 1946–50 production rose by 2·7 % per annum. Changes in prices were very favourable during these years, and hence it would be an extreme assumption to suppose that the whole of the increase was due to other factors were it not for the large fall in unemployment which occurred at the same time. Since the latter tended to reduce agricultural production, it is still possible that other factors tended to raise it by more than 2·7 % per annum. From 1946–50 to 1951–5, however, unemployment did not change appreciably, and relative prices were fairly stable. Even if we allow for lagged effects there cannot have been much change in output due to either of these. Production rose by only 2·5 % per annum. Hence a proponent of the view that other factors tended to raise production by more than 2·7 % per annum from 1935–9 to 1946–50 would have to explain why production did not increase faster from 1946–50 to 1951–5, when changes in unemployment were no longer adverse. If we are content to generalize on the basis of this experience, then, we might regard an increase in output of as much as 3 % per annum, due to factors other than changes in prices or unemployment, as unlikely.

Again, we turn to the United States for confirmation. As in this country, the maximum rates of growth since 1910 occurred during the last war, when price movements were exceptionally favourable, but changes in unemployment were adverse. Excluding the drought years, the maximum rate of growth of output was 4 % per annum. In view of the price changes accompanying this increase, and since one might expect output to rise faster in the United States than in this country (because, *inter alia*, of the more rapid increase in population), it does not seem necessary to modify the above conclusion.

Given that the net effect on production of factors other than changes in relative prices and unemployment has lain between the limits −1 and +3 % per annum, we can set an upper limit to the long-run price elasticity of supply. Table 17 shows the rates of change in production which must have been due to factors other than changes in relative prices under various assumptions about the size of the elasticity and its

---

[1] As measured by the United States Department of Agriculture's index of farm output available for eventual human use, and given in *Agricultural Statistics: 1955*.

distribution over time. The three lagging systems used were as follows (see also Chapter V, p. 85):

W_t when $t =$	t	$t-1$	$t-2$	$t-3$	$t-4$	$t-5$	$t-6$	$t-7$	$t-8$	$t-9$	$t-10$
3-year lag	0	0·4	0·4	0·2							
6-year lag	0	0·1	0·2	0·2	0·2	0·2	0·1				
10-year lag	0	0·1	0·1	0·1	0·15	0·15	0·1	0·1	0·1	0·05	0·05

W_t is the weight used to distribute the long-run elasticity of supply over previous years.[1] The effects of the non-price factors in Table 17 were calculated as the difference between the actual increase in output in each period and the increase due to the lagged effect of changes in prices paid to farmers relative to the average value of the gross domestic product, this lagged effect being calculated as described in Chapter V, p. 92. It can be seen from what follows that the conclusions reached are similar whichever lagging system is used.

If we take the assumption that the elasticity of supply lies somewhere between 0 and 1, with a lag extending possibly up to ten years, we find only one period in which our limits for the trend factor are exceeded. From 1924–9 to 1930–4 non-price factors would have to account for an increase of 3·6 % per annum in output if the effects of changes in prices are lagged over ten years. Since unemployment increased in these years, thus tending to raise agricultural output, even this period does not conflict with our findings. If we suppose the elasticity to be as high as 2, not only do we get high rates of increase for the period 1924–9 to 1930–4, but we also get very large reductions for the period 1935–9 to 1946–50. It is still *possible* that these could be explained by changes in unemployment, but let us see what this implies, taking only the six-year lag for simplicity's sake. In every period except 1935–9 to 1946–50 the rate of increase in production due to non-price factors was at least 0·8 % per annum. Hence it is implausible to suppose that, if unemployment and prices had not changed, it would have been much less than 0·8 % per annum from 1935–9 to 1946–50. It is true that during the war farmers must have faced many difficulties, but on the other hand they received help from the government in a wide variety

[1] In recent years, when the government has guaranteed minimum prices, or sometimes fixed prices for a year or more ahead, the above simple model would seem less appropriate. It is unlikely that this alters the conclusions drawn about the size of the long-run elasticity of supply, although the point would be more important if one were considering the behaviour of agricultural production over the next few years. In general, farmers' production plans are related to their expectations of future prices. These expectations will not be related as simply as is assumed above to past prices, and they will be influenced by other factors, such as the government's guarantees.

of ways other than by a direct increase in prices. In addition to technical assistance, some grants were made which are not included in the value of agricultural output, and hence do not effect our price index, but which undoubtedly stimulated output. It seems unlikely, then, that output would have done worse than stagnate if there had been no change in unemployment or prices. This means that we must suppose that the fall in unemployment would, by itself, have caused a fall in output of at least 35 % (and probably more) between 1935–9 and 1946–50, which seems implausible.

The conclusion that the long-run elasticity is unlikely to be as high as 2 is somewhat reinforced if we consider the period 1930–4 to 1935–9; but here the figures are less reliable. Taking them at their face value, and assuming that the lag for price effects is six to ten years, the effect of non-price factors is shown to be to increase output by 0·8 to 1·4 % per annum. Since unemployment fell sharply over this period, and since we have to assume that this had a large effect on output (if we are to accept the figures for 1935–9 to 1946–50), these rates of increase seem on the high side—to judge by the figures for other years.

We may conclude that the long-run elasticity of supply is probably less than 2 and more than zero. Furthermore, if one thinks it is as high as 2, it seems one must, to be consistent, accept the view that changes in unemployment have a large effect on agricultural production. *Per contra*, if one thinks it is as low as zero, one must believe that changes in unemployment have virtually no effect on agricultural production.

To narrow these limits one needs to know how much weight to attach to the effect of changes in unemployment on production, and also how far production was depressed during the war and early post-war years by difficulties later removed. If one knew the answer to these questions one might be able to say whether the difference in the effects of non-price factors shown in the last two lines of Table 17 should be large or small. Otherwise, it is hard to say whether 0·5 is a better guess for the elasticity than 1.

The writer is inclined to take the lower estimate. It seems probable that the effects of changes in unemployment are small in this country.[1] If so, there is no reason why the rate of increase in output due to non-price factors should have been *substantially* less between 1935–9 and 1946–50 than between 1946–50 and 1951–5. Hence it is more plausible that the elasticity is 0·5 than 1 (compare the last two lines of Table 17).[2]

[1] See footnote 3 on p. 104. The regression coefficient for unemployment given on p. 101 also suggests the effects are small (and see also Chart 2).

[2] On the other hand it is possible, for the reasons given in Appendix II, p. 224, that the index of agricultural production used here understates the true increase in output from 1935–9 to 1946–50, and overstates the increase from 1946–50 to 1951–5. If this

An estimate of 0·5 seems preferable to the 0·86 yielded by the regression analysis (p. 101). Instead of maintaining the assumption that the trend factor was constant throughout the period, as is done in the regression analysis, it is more plausible to assume that there was a more rapid upward trend after 1935–9, in view of the wide range of 'non-price' measures taken to stimulate output during and after the war. If this is granted, it follows that *less* of the rise in output after 1935–9 was due to relative price changes than is assumed in the regression analysis, i.e. that the elasticity is probably less than 0·86. This also implies that, given a continuation of the governmental measures, the upward trend in output in the future may be more than 0·5 % per annum. From 1948–52 to 1953–7, on the assumption of a price elasticity of supply of 0·5 and a six-year lagging system, the residual upward trend in output was about 1·9 % per annum. The rate of growth of output may, how-ever, have been less than the official index of output suggests over this period (see p. 224).

5. EXPLANATION OF SOME ESTIMATES GIVEN IN CHAPTER II

This section gives some details of the calculations on which the statements and tables relating to food in Chapter II are based. Only the results of using the best guesses for the elasticities are given there, but here we also give the results when upper or lower limits are used. We start with the estimates relating to food consumption (pp. 18–19), and then consider the estimates in Table 4, p. 22.

The data on which the calculations are based are summarized below.

Table 19. *Data for estimating changes in the demand for food*

Item	Percentage change from 1935–8 to 1946–9	1954–5
Consumers' total real expenditure, C	1	15
Population, N	4	8
Food measured at farm gate		
Consumption of food, H	−5	14
Price of food, $\overline{H}$	125	218
Price of non-food consumer goods, $\overline{C-H}$	87	148
Food measured at retail		
Consumption of food, H	3	20
Price of food, $\overline{H}$	70	169
Price of non-food consumer goods, $\overline{C-H}$	101	151

Sources: See p. 238.

were so, there would be less difference between the last two lines of Table 17 calculated on the assumption that the long-run elasticity of supply was 1, and that assumption would seem more plausible.

In making estimates relating to food consumption, we confine our-selves to the single demand equation for total food. It can be shown that, given the assumptions described in Chapter V (and in particular, the reciprocity theorem, equation (19), p. 83) it makes no significant difference to the demand for total food whether we assume that imported and home-produced food are perfect or imperfect substitutes for each other.

The logarithmic changes corresponding to the above percentage changes were inserted into equation (2) (p. 79). For the change over the whole period 1935–8 to 1954–5 it was found that the sum of the effects of the causal factors on the right-hand side of the equation fell short of the actual change in consumption. If this discrepancy is attributed to the operation of factors excluded from the analysis, such as the levelling of incomes, the welfare food schemes, cheap canteen meals and propaganda for better nutrition (as is suggested on p. 19) the influence of these factors on consumption amounted to the following percentage changes. The different combinations of assumptions of the values of the parameters are chosen so as to obtain upper and lower limits for the discrepancy, as well as the best guess.

Table 20. *Discrepancy between the actual and calculated change in demand for food from 1935–8 to 1954–5*

Nature of estimate	Parameters $\bar{h}$	c	Discrepancy, percentage change in consumption of food
(a) Food measured at farm gate			
High	−0·5	0	20
Best	−0·25	0·3	10
Low	0	0·6	2
(b) Food measured at retail			
High	−1	0	19
Best	−0·5	0·6	11
Low	0	1·2	3

It makes little difference to the calculation whether we take food measured at farm gate or at retail.

In the next set of calculations we compare the demand for food in 1946–9 with that in 1935–8, taking different sets of assumptions about the values of the parameters. In each case, for the reasons discussed on p. 19, we assume that there were factors tending to increase demand over this period, in addition to the factors mentioned in equation (2), p. 79, and that their effects were equal to the discrepancies just given. In this way it makes no difference whether we estimate the demand for food in 1946–9 by comparison with 1935–8 or by comparison with

1954–5. The resulting estimates of free demand in 1946–9 are compared with actual food consumption, and the following table shows the percentage deficiency of the latter compared with the former. Again, we chose the parameters so as to give the highest and lowest as well as the best estimates of this deficiency.

Table 21. *Estimated deficiency in the actual consumption of food in 1946–9 compared with the free demand for it*

	Parameters		Percentage deficiency of actual food consumption compared with free demand
Nature of estimate	$\bar{h}$	c	
(a) Food measured at farm gate			
High	−0·5	0	16
Best	−0·25	0·3	12
Low	0	0·6	8
(b) Food measured at retail			
High	−1	0	29
Best	−0·5	0·6	16
Low	0	1·2	0

In this case the range of uncertainty for the estimate with food measured at retail is greater than with food measured at the farm gate, mainly because of the larger range for the price elasticity coupled with the big change in relative prices which occurred.

As is explained in the note to the statistics on pp. 223–4, the estimates of food consumption at the farm gate are not consistent with those of food consumption at retail for the change from 1935–8 to 1946–9, or from 1946–9 to 1954–5, although there is little evidence of inconsistency for the change from 1935–8 to 1954–5. Because of this inconsistency, it is possible that the true quantity of food consumption at the farm gate was higher in 1946–9, and its price lower, than the estimates used here suggest. Hence the percentage deficiency of actual consumption compared with free demand in 1946–9 may not have been as great as in Table 21. On the other hand, the reverse may have been true of food consumption at retail, for which the percentage deficiency may have been larger than in Table 21.

The rest of this section gives details of the calculations on which Table 4 in Chapter II is based, with some upper and lower limits of the estimates and a discussion of the effects of the different factors after allowing for further interactions of supply and demand. This also serves as an example of the procedure followed in making similar calculations for the other groups of imports, for which similar details are not given.

The equations used and the method followed in these calculations are described in Chapter V (see especially Sections 4 and 5). The data are summarized below in the form of percentage changes from 1935–8 to 1954–5. In the equations, logarithmic changes were used. Percentage changes in non-food consumer prices, $\overline{C-H}$, in consumers' total real current expenditure, C, and in the population, N, are the same as in Table 19, p. 109, and so are not repeated.

Table 22. *Data used for Table 4*

Item	Percentage change from 1935–8 to 1954–5
1 Volume of imports of food, M	−9
2 Price of imports of food, $\overline{M}$	291
3 Index of one plus net indirect tax on imports, M^*	−8
4 Price paid to farmer, $\overline{P}$	216
5 Index of one plus net indirect tax on home food, P^*	−14
6 Price of gross domestic product at factor cost, $\overline{G}$	144
7 *Lagged* change in $\overline{P} \div \overline{G}$ (six-year lag)	49
8 Volume of home food output, P	54

Sources: Lines 1 and 2, see pp. 209 ff., S 4 and 5.
Line 3, derived from S 5 and S 40.
Line 4, see pp. 225 ff., S 37.
Line 5, derived from S 37 and 38.
Line 6, see pp. 216 ff., S 19.
Line 7, see lines 4 and 6, and p. 107.
Line 8, see pp. 225 ff., S 36.

The effects of the various exogenous factors listed in Table 4 on imports of food via their effects on food consumption (part A of Table 4) were obtained as follows. For the first column, assuming perfect substitutability between imported and home-produced food, the effect of each factor on food consumption was determined from equation (2) (p. 79), the logarithmic effects being translated into absolute effects (i.e. £ million at 1948 prices) by the procedure described in Chapter V, Section 5. Item 3 in Table 4, the 'residual food price', is simply the effect of the discrepancy between the actual change in the market price of food at the farm gate, $\overline{H}$, and the actual change in the market price of imports, $\overline{MM^*}$. On the assumption of perfect substitutability the two should be equal, but in fact there is a discrepancy. Item 7 in Table 4 is the residual change in consumption which could not be explained by changes in the other factors in equation (2). This is given in Table 20, p. 110. For the second column, equations (6) and (7) (p. 81) were used, home food output for consumption, P_c, being taken as fixed (being determined by $\dfrac{\overline{P}'}{\overline{G}'}$ and T whose effects on imports are given in part B of Table 4), and the market price of home food, $\overline{PP}*$, being eliminated. Again, the logarithmic effects on imports were translated into absolute effects.

Part B of Table 4 shows the effect on imports of the factors determining home food supply. The effects on home food supply were computed from equation (22) (p. 85) for both columns, the 'other' factors' effects in line 9 being simply the difference between the actual change in output and the change attributable to the lagged changes in relative prices, $\dfrac{\overline{P'}}{G'}$. For the first column, the absolute effect on home food supply is equal and opposite to the absolute effect on imports. For the second column, however, the effect is smaller, and can be computed from equations (6) and (7) (p. 81).

Part C of Table 4 shows the effect on imports of changes in food stocks and exports of food. For the first column, the effect of the change in stocks is simply the change in the rate of investment in stocks valued at constant 1948 market prices for imports. The effect of exports is not simply the change in the 1948 market value of exports, since a large part of them consist of processed foodstuffs and beverages such as

Table 23. *Upper and lower limits for the estimates of the effects of different factors on imports of food, 1935–8 to 1954–5†*

Factor		£ million (1948 market prices)
A. Effects via changing consumption of food		
1 Price of imports of food, $\overline{M}$	0	—1030
2 Net indirect taxes on imports of food, $M*$	0	60
3 Residual food price	0	100
4 Price of consumer goods, non-food, $\overline{C-H}$	0	690
5 Population, N	110	110
6 Real expenditure per head, C/N	70	0
7 Other	20	270
	200	200
B. Effects via changing home output of food		
8 Price paid to farmers relative to general price level, $\overline{P'}/\overline{G'}$	0	—490
9 Other, T	—270	220
	—270	—270
Total of 'price factors', lines 1, 2, 4, 8	0	—770

† As given in Table 4, p. 22.

whisky, biscuits and chocolates. Instead, half the market value was taken as a rough guess at the value of the 'crude food content' of exports. For the second column, the absolute changes in stocks and exports were divided between imports and home food output in proportion to the values of the last two. These changes were then expressed as logarithmic effects on the demand for imports and home food output and introduced into equations (6) and (7) in this form. Their effects on imports were then determined in the same way as for any other factor in these equations.

To illustrate the margin of uncertainty attached to the estimates in Table 4, we give on p. 113 upper and lower limits for the figures in the first column of that table (the limits for the second column are similar, but rather narrower in absolute terms). These limits are obtained by choosing *consistent* combinations of the limiting values of the various parameters as given in preceding sections of this chapter. The combinations are consistent in that, for example, a lower price elasticity of supply for home output is taken to imply a bigger increase in home output due to non-price factors. As may be seen, the limits are very wide.

Table 24. *Effects of different factors on imports of food, 1935–8 to 1954–5, allowing for interactions between demand and supply*

		£ million (1948 market prices) Assuming substitutability between home and imported food	
	Factor	Perfect	Imperfect
1	Price of imports of food, $\overline{M}$	−920	−630
2	Net indirect taxes on imports of food, $M*$	60	40
3	Residual food consumption price†	50	—
4	Net indirect taxes on home-produced food, $P*$	−40	−20
5	Residual food supply price‡	80	—
6	Price of consumer goods, non-food, $\overline{C-H}$	340	280
7	Population, N	110	90
8	Real expenditure per head, C/N	30	20
9	'Other' influences on food consumption	150	100
10	General price level, $\overline{G}$	260	140
11	Non-price factors in food supply, T	−140	−70
12	Stocks and exports of food	−20	−20
	Total above = change in imports	−40	−70
	(the actual change was −90)		
	Total of 'price factors' (lines 1, 2, 4, 6, 10)	−300	−200

† I.e. effect of discrepancy between $\overline{M}M*$ and $\overline{H}$.

‡ I.e. effect of discrepancy between $\dfrac{\overline{M}M*}{P*}$ and $\overline{P}$.

As was pointed out in Chapter II (p. 24), the above series of estimates are unsatisfactory in that they assume that home food supply is determined by factors which are independent of those which determine the demand for food for consumption. Yet, as explained in Chapter V, Section 5, we cannot make any very plausible allowances for the interactions of supply and demand because of the existence of rationing and price controls before 1954. What we can do, however, is to calculate the effects which the various factors would have had on imports if they had been allowed to work themselves out fully. That is, we take the actual changes in the various exogenous factors between 1935–8 and 1954–5 and, using the methods described in Sections 4 and 5 of Chapter V, we calculate their eventual effects on imports. The results, using only the best guesses for the various parameters, are given on p. 114. The sum of the effects no longer equals the actual change in imports, but it is not so very different.

6. ALCOHOLIC DRINK AND TOBACCO IMPORTS

Imports of alcoholic drink and tobacco are considered separately from imports of food for the reasons given on p. 93. Their importance in the total import bill is small, but they are extremely important sources of tax revenue. Customs duties on these imports amounted to roughly £700 million in 1955, mostly on tobacco.

Table 25. *Retained imports of drink and tobacco at 1948 c.i.f. prices*

Annual rates (£ million)

	1935–8	1946–9	1954–5
Tobacco	43	50	50
Wine	15	9	11
Spirits	2	8	2
Beer	5	4	5
Total	65	71	68

Sources: Tobacco obtained in same way as other imports, see pp. 209 ff. Wine, spirits and beer obtained by multiplying quantities in the *Annual Statement of Trade* by average values in 1948.

Table 25 shows imports of these products at constant prices. Unlike imports of food, these imports were higher just after the war than before it, and subsequently showed a slight fall. To explain these movements, we take each product in turn.

Most of the change in tobacco imports from pre-war to post-war can be accounted for by the increase in domestic consumption of tobacco (measured by net clearances from bond, line 2 of Table 26). Changes in stocks were large in individual years, but on average were similar in the three periods considered, and changes in exports and other uses were also fairly small and cancelled each other out.

Table 26. *Tobacco*

		Annual rates		
		1935–8	1946–9	1954–5
		Million pounds weight		
1	Retained imports*	275	326	324
2	Net clearance from bond (= consumption)	178	225	235
3	Change in stocks in bond	34	35	28
4	Exports†	40	50	43
5	Other use of tobacco (wastage, etc., residual)	23	16	18
		£ million (1948 market prices)		
6	Consumers' expenditure on tobacco	630	802	821
		1948 = 100		
7	Average value of consumers' expenditure on tobacco	26	89	106
8	Average value of all consumers' expenditure	50	96	128

* Almost all unmanufactured.
† Almost all manufactured.

Sources: Lines 1, 2 and 4, *Annual Abstract of Statistics*.
Line 3, *Annual Statement of Trade*, vol. IV.
Lines 6, 7 and 8, as for consumers' expenditure on food at retail and all consumers' expenditure in Table 19, see p. 238.

Professor Stone, using inter-war data, has estimated the price elasticity of demand for tobacco at retail to be about −0·5 and the income elasticity to be about 0·25. In addition, he states that there was an upward trend of about 3 % a year in tobacco consumption not accounted for by changes in incomes or prices (but which may have been due partly to an increase in the population as well as to a change in tastes, since the effects of changes in population were not explicitly allowed for).[1] These elasticities, in conjunction with the data in Table 19, explain the changes in tobacco consumption from 1935–8 to 1954–5 fairly well. Because of the great increase in tobacco duty, tobacco rose far more in price than did consumer goods in general; but the continuing rise in population, and in real income, and the apparently continuing shift in tastes more than offset the effects of this price rise. If, however, a similar attempt is made to explain the rise in demand from 1935–8 to 1946–9, the actual increase in consumption of tobacco

[1] Richard Stone, *Measurement of Consumers' Expenditure . . . 1920–1938, Vol. I*, ch. XXI. The price elasticity in his preferred equation is given as −0·27 for current year prices and −0·26 for the previous year's prices. Changes in population, too, were not explicitly allowed for in the estimated demand functions for alcoholic drinks.

appreciably exceeds the amount which the calculations suggest. Tobacco was officially unrationed (though some brands of cigarettes and other products were often difficult to buy) and it seems probable that the shortage of other consumer goods stimulated the demand for smoking. The demand for some alcoholic drink was similarly affected (see below).

Table 27. *Wine*

| | | Annual rates | | |
		1935–8	1946–9	1954–5
			Million gallons	
1	Retained imports	16·4	9·6	12·2
2	Duty paid withdrawals from bond	15·5	8·0	11·9
3	Change in stocks in bond	0·7	1·4	−0·1
4	Other use (residual)	0·2	0·2	0·4
			1948 = 100	
5	Average value of wine imports plus duty	22	92	89
6	Average value of all consumers' expenditure	50	96	128

Sources: Lines 1–5 from data in the *Annual Statement of Trade.*
Line 6, see notes to Table 19, p. 238.

The changes in imports of wine are again largely accounted for by changes in domestic consumption (line 2), although there was also an appreciable increase in the rate of investment in stocks just after the war. Home production of wine is not shown.

Professor Stone estimates the price elasticity of demand for imported wine to be about −0·6 and the income elasticity to be 1·4, with no significant residual trend. Again, these elasticities in conjunction with the data in Table 19 provide a fairly good explanation of the change in consumption from 1935–8 to 1954–5. The very great increase in the price of wine (here only *very* roughly measured by an index of the average value of imports plus duties) offset the effects of rising real incomes, so that wine consumption fell. The estimates for 1946–9, however, do not suggest that consumption was abnormally high (as was tobacco consumption, for instance). Professor Stone's equation does not introduce the prices of other alcoholic drinks as causal factors explaining changes in the demand for wine. The price of wine rose by more than the price of spirits or beer from 1935–8 to 1946–9, and by rather less from 1946–9 to 1954–5. It is possible that this might explain the seemingly low level of demand for wine in 1946–9. There may also have been shortages of supplies just after the war.

The very large increase in imports of spirits in 1946–9 compared with pre-war is only partly explained by an increase in the amount drunk at home (line 2). There was also an increase in the rate of investment in stocks, and an increase in the residual, which was mainly rum used in

Table 28. *Spirits*

		Annual rates		
		1935–8	1946–9	1954–5
		Million proof gallons		
1	Retained imports	2·2	9·6	2·4
2	Duty paid withdrawals from bond for drinking	1·2	3·8	2·5
3	Change in stocks in bond	0·4	2·5	—1·3
4	Other use of imports (residual)	0·6	3·3	1·1
5	Consumption of home-produced and imported spirits	10	9	12
			1948 = 100	
6	Average value of imported spirits plus duty	38	90	111
7	Average value of all consumers' expenditure	50	96	128

Sources: Lines 1–4 and 6 from data in the *Annual Statement of Trade*.
Line 5, *Annual Abstract of Statistics*.
Line 7, see note to Table 19, p. 238.

industry or redistilled into, for example, gin. The increase in the consumption of imported spirits for drinking consisted mainly of rum, and was probably stimulated by the shortage of whisky. Consumption of all spirits in 1946–9 (line 5) was below the pre-war level. In later years consumption of rum declined, but in 1954–5 it was still between two and three times as much as in 1935–8, and consumption of other imported spirits had also increased, as had consumption of home-produced spirits.

Professor Stone, in the study referred to above, estimates the price elasticity of demand for all spirits to be about $-0·57$ and the income elasticity of demand to be $0·6$; in addition he states that there was a residual trend downwards in demand (presumably reflecting a change

Table 29. *Beer*

		Annual rates		
		1935–8	1946–9	1954–5
		Bulk barrels		
1	Retained imports	1·2	0·9	1·1
2	Duty-paid withdrawals from bond	1·2	0·9	1·1
3	Consumption, home and imported	24	29·5	25
		£ million (1948 market prices)		
4	Consumers' expenditure on beer	580	592	544
			1948 = 100	
5	Average value of expenditure on beer	32	92	97
6	Average value of all consumers' expenditure	50	96	128

Sources: Lines 1 and 2, from data in the *Annual Statement of Trade*.
Line 3, *Annual Abstract of Statistics*.
Lines 4, 5 and 6, as for food expenditure at retail and all consumers' expenditure in Table 19, see p. 238.

in tastes) of some 3 % per annum. These estimates do not, however, provide a satisfactory explanation for the apparent rise in consumption of spirits from 1935–8 to 1954–5, and it is probable that there was a shift in taste *towards* consumption of spirits rather than a continuation of the shift away from them.

Imports of beer dropped slightly from 1935–8 to 1954–5, as did total beer consumption measured in terms of expenditure at constant prices (consumption measured in bulk barrels rose slightly). In 1946–9, however, imports of beer were appreciably lower still, whereas total beer consumption was higher. There may have been difficulties in obtaining imports shortly after the war.

Professor Stone estimates the price elasticity of demand for all beer (home-produced and imported) to be about −0·87, the income elasticity of demand to be about zero, with no significant residual trend. This leaves the whole of any change in beer consumption to be explained by shifts in relative prices. The rise in the price of beer relative to all consumer goods does, in fact, account for rather more than the fall in beer consumption from 1935–8 to 1954–5 (as given in line 4) on this basis. Since beer was even dearer relatively to other goods in 1946–9, the high level of consumption then is presumably attributable to shortages of other consumer goods.

We may conclude this section with some comments on the price elasticity of demand for *imports* of alcoholic drink and tobacco. There is no reason to suppose that the income elasticities of demand for imports of these goods are very different from Professor Stone's estimates, even though the latter refer to sales at retail and include home-produced spirits and beer. The price elasticities of demand, however, are likely to be appreciably smaller than his estimates, because imports represent such a small proportion of the total costs to the consumer. About 80 % of the retail price of imported alcoholic beverages, and over 90 % of the retail price of tobacco, consists of tax or distribution and manufacturing costs incurred in this country. It would therefore require a large change in the price of imports to produce a significant change in the retail price.[1] On the other hand, imports of beer and spirits compete with home-produced substitutes; this would tend to increase the price elasticity of demand for them as compared with Professor Stone's estimates, which refer to the total consumption of beer and spirits.

[1] The customs duties on tobacco and alcoholic beverages are specific (i.e. so much per physical unit), and so would not be affected by a change in import prices. Retail and wholesale margins might be slightly reduced, but only slightly (even if they are fixed in percentage terms) because of the large element of duty in the price.

CHAPTER VII

MATERIALS

I. INTRODUCTION

The materials studied in this chapter are those for which we draw the bulk of our supplies from abroad. The main items are given in Table 30. Some important industrial materials are not included: steel, and many semi-manufactures such as textile yarns and piece-goods, leather, paper and many chemicals. Although they are 'materials', they differ from the ones studied in this chapter in that home production and exports of them are large in relation to imports. On grounds of statistical convenience, however, the choice of materials for inclusion is not wholly determined by our given criterion. All materials in Class B, 'Basic Materials', of the trade returns are included, other than animal and vegetable oils and fats, nuts and oilseeds (these being treated as imports of food or feeding stuffs). Non-ferrous base metals, which are in Class D of the official trade returns, are included here since the bulk of our supplies is imported.

Imports of materials are equal to home consumption less home production plus investment in stocks and exports of materials. Had the

Table 30. *United Kingdom retained imports of materials in 1957*

(£ million, c.i.f.)

Hides, skins and fur skins undressed	29
Wool and other animal hair and tops	188
Cotton	107
Other textile fibres and waste, jute yarn and manufactures, and pulp for rayon	60
Total textile materials	386
Metalliferous ores and metal scrap	201
Non-ferrous base metals	188
Total metal materials	389
Rubber, including synthetic and reclaimed	66
Wood and cork	173
Pulp and waste paper	90
Crude fertilizers and crude minerals excluding fuels	40
Miscellaneous animal and vegetable crude materials, molasses and titanium ores	41
Total 'other' materials	411
Total materials	1,185

Source: Trade and Navigation Accounts, December 1957.

data been available, this chapter might have followed the same sequence as the previous one: a study, first, of the determinants of home consumption and then of home production. Unfortunately, estimates of home production could only be made for the years since 1935, and of stock changes only since 1946, and even so the coverage of the estimates is far from complete. Hence the behaviour of consumption and production in the United Kingdom over a long period of years could not be studied.

Instead, imports[1] had to be directly related to the determinants of consumption and production. Consumption of materials is assumed to depend on the level of industrial production, the price of materials in relation to the general price level, and trend factors. Production of materials is assumed to depend on the same relative prices, and on trend factors. Hence the determinants of imports are assumed to be industrial production, relative prices, and trend factors. The mathematical relationships involved are set out in Section 2.

Before proceeding to this study of imports, and as a background to it, we examine in Section 3 trends in raw materials consumption in the United States and the rest of the world, for which statistical information is available for the years from 1900 to 1952. The evidence from this section suggests that relative price changes are not an important determinant of total raw materials consumption, that the combined effect of changes in manufacturing production and of trend factors is to cause materials consumption to rise by less than manufacturing production, with some weak evidence that the production elasticity of demand is less than one[2] and that trend factors are negative.[3]

---

[1] Adjusted for changes in stocks and exports of materials as far as possible, that is, for the years 1946–55 (and for 1935–8 for exports only) imports *minus* the increase (or plus the decrease) in stocks of materials and *minus* exports of materials were related to the determinants mentioned. This adjustment assumes that imported and home-produced materials are perfect substitutes (see p. 123). A further adjustment was made, for 1935–8 and 1946–55, on account of some imports and exports of semi-manufactures with a high material content. Thus the raw wool content of exported wool tops was subtracted (just as exports of raw wool were) from imports of textile materials, and the raw cotton content of imported cotton yarns was added. A consequential adjustment was made to production of textiles, to which imports of textile materials were related, by subtracting the processing element in the exported semi-manufactures, with a corresponding addition for imported semi-manufactures. Similar adjustments were not made to metals and engineering production or to total industrial production, since they would have been negligible.

[2] That is, that when manufacturing production rises by x per cent, and abstracting from changes due to trend factors, the demand for materials for consumption rises by less than x per cent.

[3] That is, that materials consumption tends to fall through time, abstracting from changes in manufacturing production.

Since imports account for the bulk of United Kingdom consumption of raw materials,[1] one would expect them to behave in broadly the same way, although the price elasticity of demand and the production elasticity of demand might both be larger for reasons given in Section 2. At first sight, however, there is a contrast in behaviour, for the drop in the ratio of imports to industrial production in the United Kingdom nearly all took place during the two world wars, and the downward trend in the ratio in peace-time, so noticeable for the United States and the rest of the world, is much less marked for the United Kingdom (Chart 4). Section 4 is mainly an examination of the reasons for this contrast in behaviour. Despite it, the conclusion is reached that a downward trend in the ratio is to be expected in peace-time in this country.

In Section 5 we estimate the effects of the three determinants of imports by means of least-squares regression analysis, concluding that the production elasticity of demand is about 1, the price elasticity of demand about $-0 \cdot 2$, and that trend factors (with a qualification discussed below) cause a fall in imports of about 1 % per annum. Before making the analysis, the crude data for imports, relative prices and industrial production are adjusted in various ways so as to eliminate as far as possible the effects of other determinants of imports not allowed for in the analysis. The effects of changes in the pattern of industrial production as between the metals and metal-using industries and the textile, clothing and leather industries are separately estimated and eliminated, since they led to irregular falls in imports rather than the smooth fall assumed by the trend factor. Allowing for these, the downward trend in imports would normally be more than the 1 % per annum mentioned above. Other adjustments are made for bias in the index numbers, for stock changes and for exports of materials, and some years are excluded from the analysis because, for example, of import controls whose effects could not be allowed for. Section 5 concludes with an attempt to estimate limits for the probable values of the various elasticities.

The last section in the chapter, 6, is an addendum to Chapter II, giving further details about the behaviour of imports of three groups of materials (metals, textiles and other) from 1935–8 to 1954–5.

[1] Home production of substitutes for imports amounted to about 20 % of imports in 1935–8 and about 30 % in 1954–5, taking a rather narrow definition of 'substitute' (excluding, for example, cement and steel, although these are substitutes for timber) and excluding many minor materials for which statistics are not readily available. See Table 5, p. 26, and, for the three subdivisions of materials, Tables 36, 37 and 39, pp. 147, 148 and 149. These percentages are calculated from values at 1948 prices.

2. MATHEMATICAL FORM OF THE ASSUMPTIONS

The demand for imported materials is assumed to be given by the following equation:

$$\log M_c = a_M + \overline{m}_M \log \overline{M}' + \overline{g}_M \log \overline{G}' + i_M \log I + t_M T \ldots \ldots \ldots (26)$$

The symbols have the meanings given in Chapter V. $\overline{M}$ is an index of the price of imports, $\overline{G}$ an index of the general level of prices, I an index of industrial production and T the time in years. a_M, $\overline{m}_M$, etc. are parameters. M_c is the volume of imports for consumption and is the same as 'adjusted imports' in the preceding section.[1] Hence (ignoring exports and imports of semi-manufactures, which are in principle treated in the same way as X and V):

$$M_c \equiv M - X - V.$$

If we differentiate equation (26) we obtain an equation very similar to (25) (p. 88), which shows the effect of small changes in various causal factors on the demand for imports of food after allowing for repercussions on the home supply of food and on the assumption that home-produced and imported food are perfect substitutes. It is only if home-produced and imported materials are perfect substitutes that we can calculate M_c in the way shown above. If they are not perfect substitutes we must adopt some such procedure as in equations (11) and (12) on p. 82. In what follows we provisionally assume that they *are* perfect substitutes, though this can be only approximately true.

It is useful to consider the probable relations between the parameters in equation (26) and those in a corresponding equation relating the demand for the consumption of materials (imported *and* home produced together) to the same causal factors. In Section 3 we consider the behaviour of *consumption* of materials, and if we are to apply our results to the behaviour of *imports* of materials, we need to know something about the relations between these parameters.

Let us assume a demand function for consumption of materials by industry of the form

$$H = d(\overline{H}, \overline{G}, I, T) \ldots \ldots \ldots \ldots \ldots (27)$$

where H is the consumption of materials, and a supply function for home produced materials

$$P = s(\overline{P}, \overline{G}, T) \ldots \ldots \ldots \ldots \ldots (28)$$

where P is home production of materials. Since M, H and P are all assumed to be perfect substitutes for each other, their prices must all change in the same proportions, so we can substitute $\overline{M}$ for $\overline{H}$ and $\overline{P}$ in the above functions.

[1] See p. 121 and footnote 1.

Putting $r = \dfrac{Mc}{P}$, the ratio of imports for consumption to home output of materials (which was about 3 in 1954–5) we can show by similar reasoning to that given in Chapter V, Section 4, that (for small changes):

$$\bar{m}_M = \bar{h}_H\left(1+\frac{1}{r}\right) - \frac{1}{r}\,\bar{p}_P = -\,\bar{g}_M \dots\dots\dots\dots (29)$$

$$i_M = i_H\left(1+\frac{1}{r}\right) \dots\dots\dots\dots\dots\dots\dots\dots (30)$$

$$t_M = t_H\left(1+\frac{1}{r}\right) - \frac{1}{r}\,t_P \dots\dots\dots\dots\dots\dots (31)$$

Here, suffix H shows that the parameter comes from (27), and suffix P that it comes from (28). $\bar{h}_H$ is therefore the price elasticity of demand for consumption of materials by industry, i_H is the production elasticity of demand for materials, and t_H is the trend parameter—all these referring to the *total* consumption of materials (adjusted imports plus home production). $\bar{p}_P$ is the (long-term) price elasticity of supply of home-produced materials and t_P is the trend parameter in the home supply equation.

Equation (29) shows that the price elasticity of demand for imports, $\bar{m}_M$, is arithmetically greater than the price elasticity of demand for materials for consumption, $\bar{h}_H$, and would be finite even if $\bar{h}_H$ were zero, so long as there was *some* responsiveness of home production of materials to price changes. Equation (30) shows that the production elasticity of demand for imports, i_M, is greater than the production elasticity of demand for consumption of materials. In equation (31), it is probable that t_H is negative, i.e. that there is a downward trend in materials consumption per unit of output, while t_P might be positive or negative, so that one cannot be certain how t_M compares with t_H.

Equations (29), (30) and (31) are modified if we allow for the link between home production of materials and imports of them due to the importance of scrap and waste products in home production. If we assume that a given (small) proportionate expansion in imports for consumption causes a proportionate expansion in the supply of home-produced materials m_P times as big, then it can easily be shown that equations (29), (30) and (31) all hold if we divide their right-hand sides by $1+\frac{1}{r}\,m_P$. Scrap and waste products probably account for a half or less of home-produced materials, and so it is likely that m_P is less than 1. The general effect of this modification is therefore to bring $\bar{m}_M$, i_M and

t_M all nearer to $\bar{h}_H$, i_H and t_H, respectively, though $\overline{m}_M$ will still remain arithmetically greater than $\bar{h}_H$, and i_M will remain arithmetically greater than i_H.

Another fact which also tends to make the elasticities in the import demand function more like those in the consumption demand function is that imported and home-produced materials are unlikely to be perfect substitutes.[1] Even if the individual products were physically identical, grouping them leads to the groups behaving as imperfect substitutes (see Appendix I). Furthermore, they may be sold in imperfect markets.

3. THE CONSUMPTION OF MATERIALS

In this section we consider the relation between the consumption of materials and industrial or manufacturing production. For the reasons just stated the behaviour of consumption of materials is a good guide to the behaviour of imports of materials.

Chart 3 shows the ratio of materials consumption[2] to manufacturing production in the United States and the rest of the world since 1900. The materials included are similar to those included in our series for United Kingdom imports. The ratio has a strong downward trend averaging $-1\cdot9$ % per annum for the United States and $-1\cdot1$ % per annum for the rest of the world.[3]

This downward trend might have been due to changes in any one (or all) of our three determinants of the consumption of materials. It might have been caused by a rise in the price of materials relative to prices in general, or by a production elasticity of demand for materials which was less than one, or by what we have called 'trend factors', that is, factors

---

[1] See Chapter V, p. 89, for the reasons why imperfect substitutability makes the price elasticity of demand for imports approximate to that for home consumption. Similar reasons apply to the production elasticity of demand and trend factor.

[2] It might be better to say 'apparent consumption', since the series are derived from statistics of materials production, imports and exports, and no account is taken of changes in stocks. This is important for short-run, but not long-run, comparisons.

[3] This tendency to economize in the use of raw materials has been noticed and commented on by several writers. See *World Economic Survey, 1955*, United Nations Department of Economic and Social Affairs (New York, 1956), pp. 36–9; *Raw Materials in the United States Economy, 1900–1952*, United States Department of Commerce, Bureau of the Census, Working Paper no. 1 Preliminary (Washington, U.S. Government Printing Office, 1954); C. T. Saunders, 'Consumption of Raw Materials in the United Kingdom: 1851–1950', *Journal of the Royal Statistical Society*, Series A (General), vol. 115, part 3, 1952, pp. 332–5; Sir Donald MacDougall, *The World Dollar Problem* (1957). H. Neisser and F. Modigliani, however, state that 'The downward shift in the United States propensity to import raw materials . . . is an indication of a trend towards economizing in the input of raw materials, which is rather exceptional in the development of capitalism', *National Incomes and International Trade* (University of Illinois Press, 1953), p. 40, footnote 5.

which operated independently of changes in relative prices or manufacturing production.

It seems unlikely that relative price changes had much effect on the ratio. No price series corresponding exactly to the quantity series in Chart 3 are available, but the ratio of United Kingdom import prices of materials to the general price level in the United Kingdom, which is shown in Chart 4, provides a reasonably good guide. There was no sustained rise in the relative price of materials corresponding to the sustained fall in the ratio of consumption of materials to manufacturing production. Although raw materials became relatively much cheaper in the inter-war period, the downward trend in the ratio of materials consumption to manufacturing production was not on average much less steep than in the first decade of the century, nor during the great relative rise in material prices after 1939.

The fall in the ratio must therefore have been due to one or both of the other two factors mentioned, but it is exceedingly difficult to allocate the responsibility between them. The main reason for the difficulty is that manufacturing production has generally risen through time. Consequently, one cannot be sure whether the fall in the ratio would have gone on even if production had not risen, or whether it was dependent on that rise. For many purposes, indeed, there is no need to distinguish the two factors. The conclusion that consumption of materials increases more slowly than manufacturing production when the latter is rising is the one that matters, and it is a reasonably firm one.

There were various changes in techniques and tastes, leading to changes in the nature and pattern of production, which must have reduced the ratio of materials consumption to manufacturing production independently of changes in the level of production. Substitution of plastics, cement and steel[1] for the materials included in the index numbers was probably one example. Increased reliance on scrap was another.[2] The growth of the electrical engineering and aircraft industries are examples of the increasing complexity of production leading to materials being more highly processed. It is difficult to think of factors tending in the opposite direction, so that the general presumption might be that trend factors, independently of changes in production, were tending to reduce materials consumption.

---

[1] Iron ore, but not steel as such, is included in the index numbers of consumption of materials in Chart 3, as well as in United Kingdom imports of materials in Chart 4 and elsewhere.

[2] Scrap is not included in the index numbers of consumption of materials used for Chart 3. For data on the increased use of scrap in the United Kingdom, see C. T. Saunders, 'Consumption of Raw Materials in the United Kingdom: 1851–1950', *Journal of the Royal Statistical Society*, vol. 113, part 3, 1952.

There are some reasons for thinking that the production elasticity of demand for materials was less than one, so that some of the fall in the ratio of materials consumption to manufacturing production was also caused by the rise in production itself. In the first place, a rise in production usually implies a rise in consumers' real incomes, and consumers' income elasticity of demand for at least some engineering goods (cars, washing machines, refrigerators, wireless and television sets) is probably greater than for clothing. Since the materials content of engineering goods is much smaller than that of clothing, as consumers get richer the composition of their purchases of manufactures may shift in such a way as to reduce its average materials content.[1] Secondly, a period in which

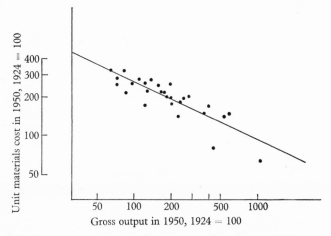

Chart 9. Relation between changes in output and unit materials costs, 1924–50, for 28 trades in the United Kingdom

production is increasing more rapidly than usual is also likely to be one in which investment in plant and equipment is higher than usual. This may reduce the ratio of materials consumption to manufacturing production for two reasons. First, the new plant and equipment may simply use materials more economically[2]; and, second, the expansion

[1] On the other hand, the engineering goods mentioned were all recent innovations during the period covered by our statistics, so that one cannot attribute all, or perhaps even the greater part, of this particular shift to rising incomes. Even if there had been no rise in incomes there would probably have been a shift as consumers altered the pattern of their expenditure to take advantage of the new possibilities open to them. In other words, much of the shift may have been what we have called a 'trend factor'.

[2] This reason was suggested by Dr W. E. G. Salter's 'A Consideration of Technological Change with particular Reference to Labour Productivity', a dissertation submitted to the University of Cambridge for the degree of Doctor of Philosophy,

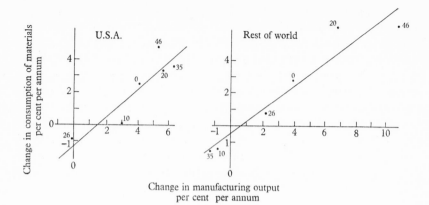

Change in manufacturing output
per cent per annum

KEY TO PERIODS

0 = 1900–03 to 1910–13	26 = 1926–9 to 1935–8
10 = 1910–13 to 1920–3	35 = 1935–8 to 1946–7
20 = 1920–3 to 1926–9	46 = 1946–7 to 1951–2

Chart 10. Relation between rates of change in output and in consumption of materials:
United States and rest of world

of investment may shift the pattern of output towards the engineering industries, with their lower than average materials content.

The data for the United States and the rest of the world provide some confirmation of the view that trend factors were tending to lower the ratio of materials consumption to manufacturing production and that the production elasticity of demand was less than one, so that to some extent the observed fall in the ratio was due to the rise in production itself. In Chart 10 one can see how the rate of change of consumption of materials over six periods subdividing the years 1900 to 1952 varied

1955. (See also his *Productivity and Technical Change*, Cambridge University Press, 1960.) Dr Salter examined, *inter alia*, the changes in output, output per head, and unit materials cost (at current prices) in about thirty different trades in this country from 1924 to 1950. He found that the trades showing the greatest increases in output also showed the greatest increases in output per head, and those showing the latter had the smallest rises in unit materials cost. His explanation for this may be inadequately summarized as follows: technological progress tends to economize in all factor inputs per unit of output and it is fastest in those industries for which output is expanding fastest, partly because they have a higher rate of investment and attract better men. There is also a causal process working through the demand side: where costs and prices are reduced fastest, the quantity demanded expands fastest. While it is true that some part of the connexion which Dr Salter found between greater expansion of output and less expansion of unit materials cost (see Chart 9) was probably due to the lower prices of materials in some industries enabling them to cheapen their outputs relatively to those of other industries, and so to sell relatively more, part may also have been due to the higher rate of investment.

with the rate of change of manufacturing production. As one would expect, the faster the rate of growth of production in any period, the faster was the rate of growth of consumption, so that the points lie approximately on a line which slopes upwards to the right. The lines shown in the chart were fitted by the usual least squares procedure,[1] and, if one assumes that they represent the 'true' relationship, the above conclusions follow. Thus, for a zero rate of growth of manufacturing production it can be seen that both in the United States and in the rest of the world there was a drop in materials consumption (of about 1·2 % per annum for the United States and about 0·4 % per annum for the rest of the world). Also the slope of the line in each case is less than 1 (0·86 for the United States and 0·73 for the rest of the world) showing that an extra growth of 1 % per annum in manufacturing production was associated with an extra growth of less than 1 % per annum in materials consumption. It must be recognized, however, that this evidence is unreliable. The points do not lie very closely on the lines in either diagram.

4. THE BEHAVIOUR OF UNITED KINGDOM IMPORTS OF MATERIALS SINCE 1900

In this section we review the behaviour of United Kingdom imports of materials since 1900 and explain the apparent differences between that behaviour and the behaviour of materials consumption which we have just examined. This explanation is qualitative. In the next section we attempt a quantitative explanation of the changes in the demand for imports of materials.

If we turn to Chart 4 we see that the ratio of total imports of materials[2] to total industrial output has fallen considerably over the last fifty years, but that nearly all of the fall occurred over the two wars. There is little sign of a strong downward trend in peace-time. On a simple view, therefore, we might be inclined to say that the experience of the United

---

[1] The equation fitted in each case was of the form

$$\frac{\Delta \log H}{\Delta T} = a + b \frac{\Delta \log I}{\Delta T},$$

where H is materials consumption and $\Delta \log H$ the change in its logarithm over any particular period, I is manufacturing production, T the time in years (so that ΔT is the number of years in a period and $\dfrac{\Delta \log H}{\Delta T}$ is the annual logarithmic change in consumption within a period). Then a gives the trend factor, in terms of the annual logarithmic change in consumption, and b gives the production elasticity of demand.

[2] Neither imports of materials nor industrial production in Chart 4 are adjusted in any of the ways described on pp. 121–2 or 134–6. They are simply the series S6 and the index described on p. 218.

Kingdom is not at all like that of the United States and the rest of the world. For in their case there was no reason to suppose that the wars had greatly affected the downward trend in the ratio[1] and there was certainly a strong downward trend in peace-time. This marked contrast in behaviour can be accounted for by the following factors.

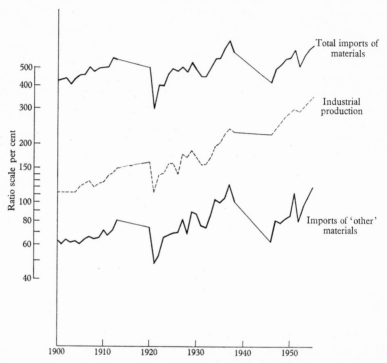

Chart 11. Total industrial production and volume of imports of total and 'other' materials

In the first place, part of the explanation of the great fall in the ratio of imports to output in the United Kingdom over the whole period after 1913 lies in the changes in the composition of output as between the metals and textiles industries (see also Chapter II, p. 29). Since then, the output of the metals industries, which have a low imported material content, has expanded more rapidly than industrial production as a whole, whereas the output of the textile industries, which have a high

[1] In Chart 10 the points showing the relation of changes in materials consumption to manufacturing production in the periods which included the wars (these are marked 10 and 35 in each diagram) do not appear to diverge markedly from the line of best fit.

imported material content, has expanded less rapidly (and indeed has fallen). But from 1900 to 1913 the output of the textile industries grew faster than industrial production as a whole, and possibly faster even than metals production. This partly accounts for the failure of the ratio of imports of materials to industrial production to fall in the period 1900 to 1913.

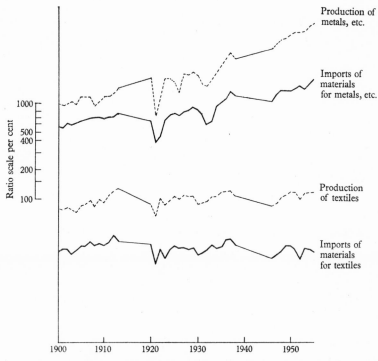

Chart 12. Textile, metal and engineering production and volume of imports of textile and metal materials

It is interesting to estimate the effect on imports of materials of the changes in the pattern of output as between the metals and textiles industries, and an attempt has been made to do this in Table 31. It can be seen that, on the assumption made in the calculation, imports of materials would have fallen by about 8 % more than they did from 1900–3 to 1910–13 had it not been for the shift in the pattern of production towards textiles. Over the whole period from 1900–3 to 1952–5, however, the shift in the pattern was tending to reduce imports. They would have risen about 27 % more than they did but for the shift, and in fact the shift accounted for roughly a third of the whole of the fall in the ratio of imports of materials to industrial production over this period.

Table 31. *Adjustments to imports of materials for changes in the relative importance of metals and textiles production**

Period	Percentage change from previous period	Cumulative index 1900–3 = 100
1900–3	×	100
1905–8	−1	99
1910–13	−6	92
1922–5	10	102
1926–9	3	105
1931–4	5	111
1935–8	3	114
1946–9	8	123
1952–5	3	127

* The index numbers show the amount by which imports must be multiplied so as to make them change as they would have done if both metals and textiles production had changed in the same proportion as all industrial production, assuming the production elasticity of demand for imports to be one.

A second reason for the failure of the ratio of imports to production to fall much in peace-time, and an explanation of its rapid fall over the periods including the two wars, is that in the years immediately following the wars there were special and temporary factors which tended to reduce imports. There were, for example, large supplies of metal scrap left over from war production, and while these were being used up imports of metals were reduced. Large stocks of rubber, left over after the First World War, were also run down, and there may have been other unrecorded changes in stocks. More information is available on stock changes of imported materials after the Second World War. In the years 1946–9 the run-down in recorded stocks was equivalent to about $2\frac{1}{2}$ % of pre-war imports. In addition, the fall in exports of crude materials, or of semi-manufactures with a high material content, together with the rise in imported semi-manufactures with a high material content, may have reduced imports of materials by about 8 % compared with the pre-war period (see Table 5, p. 26). Restrictions on the consumption and imports of certain materials after the Second World War must also have temporarily lowered the ratio of imports to industrial production.

A third reason, though perhaps not a very powerful one, is to be found in the behaviour of raw material prices. Chart 4 shows an index number of the price of imported materials divided by an index number of the general level of prices in the United Kingdom. The great cheapening of materials in the period between the wars must have stimulated imports of them to some extent and may partly explain why the ratio of imports to production fell so little in this period. Likewise, their rise in price during the Second World War may have induced some economy in their use, and so helps to explain the large fall in the ratio which took place then. Allowing for lagged effects, the rise in material prices during the First World War may also have caused some of the fall in the ratio of imports to production from 1913 to 1920. Before 1913 the relative price movements were not very large.[1]

If adjustments for the effects of all these factors could be made to the index of the ratio of imports of materials to industrial production shown in Chart 4 it would look very different. Some downward slope would appear in the line from 1900 to 1913. After each of the wars the line would be raised, thus reducing the drop over each war period, and the downward trend from 1920 to 1938 would be increased. So the behaviour of United Kingdom imports of materials may be reconciled with the conclusions reached in the previous section about the behaviour of materials consumption. It seems possible, that is to say, that the demand for imports of materials does not increase as rapidly as industrial production, and that this tendency operates in peace-time as well as during a war.

5. QUANTITATIVE ANALYSIS OF THE DEMAND FOR IMPORTS OF MATERIALS

Equation (26), p. 123, shows how the demand for imports of materials is assumed to be determined by their price, the general price level in this country, industrial production and time (which represents the effects of various trend factors). We first discuss (pp. 134–6) some adjustments which were made to the data to eliminate, so far as possible, the effects of factors not included amongst the determining variables. Estimates of the parameters in the equation are then given (Table 33, p. 137), derived by the usual method of least squares. Finally, an attempt is made to assess the reliability of these parameters and to gauge upper and lower limits for them by a procedure similar to that used in connection with the supply of home-produced food (Chapter VI, Section 4). These limits are given in Table 35 (p. 145).[2]

The demand equation was fitted both to the data for total imports

[1] Although—since prices rose—one might have expected imports to fall, so that this rather contradicts the line of argument given above. Before 1900, however, material prices were falling, so that if one allows for lagged effects and for the smallness of the movements there is no substantial contradiction involved.

[2] The non-specialist reader may prefer to omit pp. 143–5 which explain how they were derived.

of materials and to the data for imports of each of the three groups of materials—metals, textiles and other. The price index of the appropriate group of imports was used in each case, and for metals and textiles the index numbers of production used were those of the main consuming industries (i.e. metals, engineering, shipbuilding and vehicles for metal materials; and textiles, clothing, leather and leather goods for textile materials, including hides and skins). For total imports of materials and 'other' materials the index of total industrial production was used.

Total imports of materials were adjusted for the effects of changes in the composition of output as between metals and textiles in the manner described in the previous section, i.e. they were multiplied by the factors given in Table 31 *before* being fitted to the other data. This was done so as to make the elasticities found in this equation directly comparable to the average of those found in the three equations for the sub-divisions of imports. It also seemed best to remove the effects of the changes in composition since they were largely due to different factors from those given in equation (26). They were probably scarcely influenced by relative price changes of materials, and they did not occur uniformly over time. It is true that they may have been partly influenced by changes in real incomes (see p. 127) and so linked to the level of total industrial production. But for the most part they were probably determined by other influences, such as our competitive position in the markets for our exports.

To eliminate the effects of stock changes, for which data were not available for most years, only four-year averages of imports were used. In addition, imports were adjusted (as explained on p. 121) for exports and changes in stocks of materials and trade in semi-processed goods with a high import-content, wherever the data permitted. The consequential adjustments to industrial production were only significant for textiles, and had the effect of lowering output in 1935–8 by about 5 % in relation to post-war years (see footnote 1 on p. 121, and Appendix II, p. 227).

Some periods were omitted in the fitting procedure because it was thought that imports were subject in them to the influence of other important factors not mentioned in equation (26). The periods omitted for this reason were 1920–1 and 1946–9, as well as the war years. The years 1900–3 were also omitted because of the unreliability of the index of production. The behaviour of imports in these years (other than the wars) is compared with the behaviour implied by our estimating equation to see whether the discrepancies seem plausible.

Consideration was given to the likelihood of there being any bias in the results due to the different weighting systems used for production and imports. The systems used are bound to be arbitrary to some extent. The general aim was to choose similar formulae and base periods for production and imports (for reasons discussed in Appendix I, p. 206). The series were not readily available in this form, however, and the actual systems used are set out in Table 32.

Table 32. *Weighting systems used for index numbers of industrial production and imports of materials*

Industrial production		Imports of materials	
Period	System	Period	System
1900–7	No particular system, but similar to Hoffman's index with 1907 prices	1900–22	Mainly 1913 prices
		1922–3	1922 prices
1907–24	Geometric average of 1907 and 1924 prices	1923–4	1923 prices
		1924–30	1924 prices
1924–35	1924 prices		
		1930–5	1930 prices
1935–48	Geometric average of 1935 prices and 1946 prices	1935–55	1948 prices for main groups, but *within* groups prices
1948–55	1948 prices		of 1935, 1938, 1947, 1950, 1954 at various periods

Note: Both sets of index numbers use weighted arithmetic averages, the weights being the prices of the years shown. For the index numbers of production the 'prices' are in principle net values added.

Sources: See p. 218 for the index of production, and pp. 209 ff. for imports of materials, S 6.

It is generally true that an index of the volume of production or imports which is weighted by prices in an earlier year shows an upward bias compared with an index weighted by prices in a later year. An index which is a geometric average of early- and late-year weighted index numbers might be expected to change in much the same proportions as an index weighted by prices of an intermediate year.

While it is not possible to estimate the extent of the bias in the import index relative to the production index, there is reason to believe that it cannot be very large, taking the period as a whole. What follows is only a qualitative appraisal, but since the biases mentioned would each be fairly small and since they tended to cancel out, it provides some support for the above conclusion. For the period 1900–7, the import index may be biased downwards in relation to the production index (except for imports of metals, for which the bias is the other way, since for these 1900 prices were used). For the period 1907–24 it is hard to say what the bias is, since the year from which the import prices are drawn (mainly 1913) is between the years used for the production index

(1907 and 1924). At a guess one might say the import index was biased upwards. For 1924–30 both series use 1924 weights. For 1930–5 there is probably little bias either way, since a production index with 1930 weights (i.e. the same as the import index) shows similar changes to one with 1924 weights.[1] For 1935–48 it is again uncertain what the bias is, both index numbers being an amalgam of index numbers using prices of both pre-war and post-war years, but imports are probably biased upwards slightly. After 1950 the import index is probably biased somewhat downwards in relation to the production index, since the subgroups of imports are weighted by prices of 1950 or 1954, while production is weighted by 1948 prices.

The only adjustment made for bias in the weighting was for the years 1935–8 compared with post-war. For metals and textiles, the index numbers of production used were virtually entirely weighted by 1948 prices (Table 32 only refers to the *total* index of production and the weights used for metals and textiles production were not exactly the same, see Appendix II, p. 218). Since imports were partially weighted by pre-war prices, the change from pre-war to post-war was biased upwards. Consequently, imports in 1935–8 were raised in relation to post-war imports (see Tables 37 and 39 and Appendix II, p. 234). A similar adjustment was made to total imports of materials and to imports of 'other' materials, and, in Tables 5 and 6 in Chapter II, and Table 36 in this chapter, the index of industrial production in 1935–8 was also adjusted to bring it on to a fully 1948 price weighted basis (see Appendix II, p. 219 for details).[2] It should be noted that these adjustments for bias in the weighting system were only made in fitting equation (26) to the data and in the computations for Tables 5 and 6 in Chapter II and for Tables 36, 37 and 39 in this chapter. The series given in Appendix II and in Charts 11 and 12 and Chart 4 are *not* adjusted in this respect.

In estimating the effects of prices only a 6-year lagging system was used, the weights for the current year t, $t-1$, $t-2$, etc. being respectively 0·2, 0·3, 0·2, 0·15, 0·1 and 0·05. Most of the weight was therefore given to the current year and the two immediately preceding years. Some experiments with 3-year and 10-year weighting systems suggested that using these would not have greatly affected the results.[3]

---

[1] See C. F. Carter, W. B. Reddaway and R. Stone, *The Measurement of Production Movements*, University of Cambridge Department of Applied Economics Monographs, 1 (Cambridge University Press, 1948), p. 126.

[2] In the least-squares fitting, however, this last adjustment to the index of total industrial production was erroneously omitted, hence the rise in production from 1935–8 to post-war is exaggerated. It is not thought that this was a serious error, since the adjustment consisted in multiplying the 1935–8 average by only 1·027.

[3] Since the lagging system was in any case very rough, the estimates of lagged prices for the three separate groups of materials were made by a simpler and more

The estimates for the parameters are given in Table 33. In what follows we attempt to appraise their reliability.

Table 33. *Results obtained by least-squares fitting of equation* (26)

Parameter in equation	Value obtained for parameter (approximate average weight of each group in total imports is in brackets)				Weighted average of last 3 columns
	Total (1·0)	Metals (0·2)	Textiles (0·5)	Other (0·3)	
Price elasticity, m_M	−0·20	−0·12	−0·06	−0·40	−0·17
Production elasticity, i_M	1·23	1·05	0·82	1·13	0·96
Trend, t_M	−0·0064	−0·0088	−0·0025	−0·0061	−0·0048
Trend as percentage per annum	−1·5	−2·0	−0·6	−1·4	−1·1

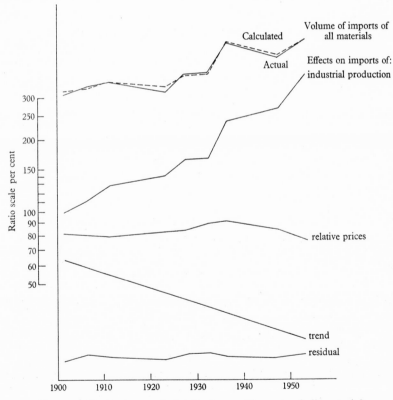

Chart 13. Regression analysis of volume of imports of all materials

approximate procedure than that followed for the estimates for total imports of materials.

As has already been remarked, because of the correlation between production and time the estimates of their separate effects on imports are unreliable. What is reasonably certain is that their combined effect in most cases is to cause imports to rise more slowly than production.[1]

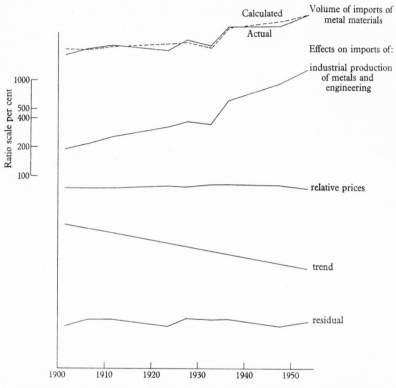

Chart 14. Regression analysis of volume of imports of metal materials

Our aim is to get plausible estimates for the parameters for *total* imports of materials, rather than for each of the three groups. It is clear from Charts 13 to 16 that the fit is worse for the latter, as was to be expected in view of the smaller opportunity for cancelling of erratic factors which we have failed to take into account, and also the greater

[1] Taking the results in the first column of Table 33, industrial production would have to rise by more than $6\frac{1}{2}$% per annum for imports to rise faster. Taking the last column of the table, imports would rise more slowly than production regardless of the rate of growth of the latter. The conclusion is strengthened if we allow for the general tendency for metals production to expand faster than, and textiles production slower than, the average for all industries (the effects of this tendency being excluded from the estimates in Table 33).

errors of measurement involved.[1] For these reasons we cannot be sure that the differences between the groups are significant. Nevertheless, the three separate groups provide a useful test of the plausibility of the values found for the parameters for total imports of materials and this, on the whole, is satisfied.

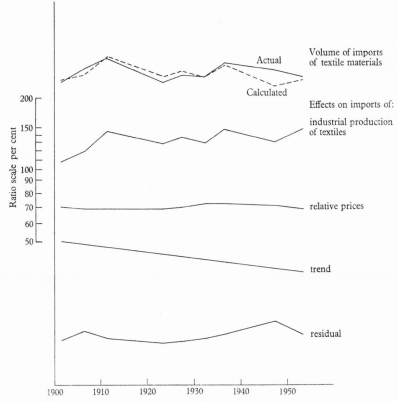

Chart 15. Regression analysis of volume of imports of textile materials

A further test is to see whether we can reasonably explain the divergences between actual imports and those given by the equations, both for the years used in the fitting procedure,[2] and for the years

[1] The index of total industrial production is probably more reliable than the index numbers of metals or textiles production: see 'Indices of Industrial Output', by R. and W. M. Stone, *Economic Journal*, vol. 49, no. 195, September 1939, p. 476. The same is probably true of the index number of total materials imports compared with the index numbers for groups. Also, some metal material imports are used outside the metals industries and some textile materials are used outside the textile industries.

[2] 1905–8, 1910–13, 1922–5, 1926–9, 1931–4, 1935–8 and 1952–5.

excluded, of which 1900–3 and 1946–9 are shown on the charts. Small changes in t, the trend factor, are only to be expected. Technical progress does not proceed at a uniform constant rate. We must also expect margins of error for measurement of a few per cent. Together, these could easily account for the divergences in the total, the maximum for any period being only 4·5 % (in 1900–3) and the maximum rate

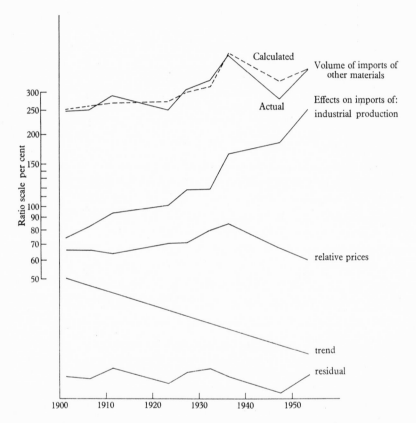

Chart 16. Regression analysis of volume of imports of 'other' materials

of change over any two successive periods only 1·3 % per annum from 1922–5 to 1926–9.

The greatest divergences in Chart 13 occur in 1900–3, 1922–5 and 1946–9. The first of these could not be explained (and the years were excluded from the fitting procedure). The lowness of imports in 1922–5 is discussed below, and their lowness in 1946–9 may be attributed to import controls. The divergences between actual and calculated imports before 1913 were also large for the sub-groups, and could not be explained, though there is reason to suspect the accuracy of the index numbers of industrial production in this period.[1]

In 1922–5 metals are about 15 % below their calculated level (Chart 14). The only explanation the writer can suggest is that the consumption of scrap left over from the First World War was still substantial in this period. There was also a run-down in stocks of scrap and metal accumulated during the war, and if recorded changes are taken into account the discrepancy is reduced to about 12 %. Unrecorded stock changes may account for some of the remainder.[2] If these explanations were right, it would be true to say that the war tended to depress (temporarily) the demand for imports by giving a boost to home production of substitutes (i.e. scrap). The Second World War had the same effect (see p. 148). In the same period textiles and other imports were 6 % and 9 % respectively below their calcu-lated levels. If account is taken of a large fall in stocks of rubber,[3] the discrepancy for 'other' becomes only 5 %, and both are then small enough to be dismissed. Nevertheless, their coincidence for all three groups makes it probable that some systematic factor has been omitted.

This is a useful point at which to consider the results for the years 1920–1, which were omitted from the calculations on the grounds that stock changes were known to be particularly large then. Thus, if we take into account the *recorded* changes in stocks of non-ferrous metals and scrap,[4] our import estimates for metals are raised by no less than 18 % in these two years, and even by as much as 13 % if we take the

---

[1] For a description of the index numbers used here see Appendix II, p. 218. More recently, K. S. Lomax has published some index numbers of industrial production for the years 1900 to 1938 which are the result of a thorough re-working of the field (see the *London and Cambridge Economic Bulletin*, no. 25, June 1958, p. v). These index numbers show slower rates of growth over the period 1900 to 1913 than the ones used here, which would tend to make the discrepancies mentioned above generally bigger. The slower growth may partly be due to a difference in weighting. Lomax places less confidence in the index numbers for the years before 1920, and emphasizes the unreliability of the index numbers of engineering output, especially before 1914.

[2] Attempts to explain the low level of imports by reference to changes in exports or home production of metals failed. It is worth noting that an index of consumption of the main non-ferrous metals based on the estimates made by Mr Saunders ('Consumption of Raw Materials in the United Kingdom: 1851–1950', *Journal of the Royal Statistical Society*, vol. 115, part 3, 1952) (but using price weights to combine the quantities of the different metals) shows a rise of 5 % from 1910–13 to 1922–5 as compared with a fall of 9 % in the index of imports used here. The writer has not been able to account for this difference. The recorded stock changes referred to above are those given in *Stocks of Staple Commodities*, London and Cambridge Economic Service Special Memoranda, 1 and 16 (1923 and 1926).

[3] Derived from figures given in the Special Memoranda referred to in the preceding footnote.

[4] Derived from figures given in the Special Memoranda referred to above.

four-year average 1920–3. Recorded changes in stocks of rubber were also large, but in the opposite direction. No information is available on changes in stocks of textile fibres. As was to be expected, actual imports of metals in 1920–3 were even further below their calculated levels than in 1922–5, while imports of other materials were much nearer to the calculated levels than in 1922–5. Imports of textiles were also rather nearer. The remaining substantial discrepancies occur in 1946–9 and are more fully considered in the following section.

Our examination shows that the actual movement of imports of materials, whether in total or by groups, can be fairly satisfactorily explained in terms of equation (26), with parameters whose values are something like those in Table 33. In most periods the discrepancies are small enough to be explained away in terms of stock changes not fully eliminated, errors in measurement, or slight changes in the trend factor. For some of the larger discrepancies we have also found some fairly plausible explanations. There remain some puzzles, but it is not thought that these are sufficiently important to make us discard the estimates.

There is no need, however, to accept the exact figures in the first column of Table 33 as our best guesses. While we have no other evidence which would lead to a rejection of the estimate of −0·2 for the price elasticity, the figure of 1·2 for the production elasticity seems on the high side when compared with our earlier conclusions on p. 129. The data for the United States and the rest of the world suggested that the production elasticity of demand for materials for *consumption* was probably less than 1, and we obtained admittedly shaky estimates of 0·86 and 0·73. In Section 2 above, however, we saw that the production elasticity of demand for *imports* of materials was probably slightly greater than for *consumption* of materials. Hence it seems reasonable to take 1·0 as our best guess for the former, instead of 1·2. This is also nearer to the weighted average of the separate estimates for the three groups (last column of Table 33). A lower production elasticity implies an arithmetically smaller trend factor, since they work in opposite directions most of the time. Again, we may take a figure nearer to the weighted average, say −1·0 % per annum. It will not have escaped notice that these figures are chosen partly for their statistical convenience: where the choice is rather arbitrary, this seems the best criterion to use. The fit which results from adopting these best guesses for the production elasticity and the trend factor rather than those yielded by the least squares estimates is only slightly less close.[1]

The estimates given above are the best the writer can make, but others might prefer slightly different ones, and it would be difficult to

[1] The mean deviation of the calculated from the actual values for imports is raised from 2·0 % to only 2·4 %.

show that they were wrong. Hence it is desirable to set limits for each of the parameters. These are meant to be values which all would agree are sufficiently improbable to make still higher or lower values not worth considering. If anything, we shall err on the wide side in setting these limits, the choice being rather arbitrary. Some basic assumptions are that the price and production elasticities are approximately constant, but that the trend factor may vary from period to period. We also assume that the price elasticity cannot be positive. Throughout, we shall speak of a maximum and minimum price elasticity in the *arithmetical* sense, but for the trend factor (which may be positive or negative) we shall use the algebraic sense.[1]

Certain general considerations set the limits for the production elasticity, i_M. For the reasons given on pp. 127–8, and to judge by the data for the United States and the rest of the world (pp. 128–9), it is unlikely that the production elasticity for consumption, i_H, is greater than 1. We have seen many reasons why the consumption of materials per unit of output should fall as output rises, but none as to why it should rise. If the maximum probable i_H is 1, we may put the maximum probable i_M at 1·3, since it is doubtful whether home production of materials is more than 30 % of imports for consumption and, even if it were as much, the multiplier to arrive at i_M from i_H should be less than 1·3 for the reasons given in Section 2 above. As regards the lower limit for i_M, the estimates of i_H derived from the data for the United States and the rest of the world were respectively 0·86 and 0·73, which suggests that i_M should not be much lower than, say, 0·7. To be on the safe side (since these are uncertain estimates) we take 0·6 as a lower limit for i_M.[2]

We may now calculate the trend factor, t_M, for total imports in each of 11 periods, putting i_M at each of its extreme limits and assuming for

[1] The non-specialist reader may wish to omit the following pages and turn at once to the results given on p. 145.

[2] Using Dr Salter's figures to derive an estimate of the relationship between changes in output and in unit materials cost in different industries in the United Kingdom between 1924 and 1950 (see p. 127, n. 2 and Chart 9) we find that for every 1 % per annum that an industry expanded its output over the period 1924 to 1950 more than the average, it increased its unit materials cost by 0·45 % per annum *less* than the average. If we assume that the whole of this reduction is due to factors which also operate to reduce the volume of materials consumption per unit of output in all industries taken together as between periods in which output is expanding at different rates, then we could put i_H at as low a figure as 0·55 (i.e. 1 minus 0·45), which is consistent with $i_M > 0·6$. In fact it is unlikely that the whole of the reduction of 0·45 % in unit materials cost could be attributed to such factors. For example, some of the reduction would have been due to the lower prices of materials in some industries enabling them to cheapen their outputs relative to those of other industries, and so to sell relatively more. Hence i_M is probably more than 0·6 to judge by this evidence.

the moment that $\overline{m}_M = 0$. We thus get a pair of values for i_M for each period, and one of these is an extreme value. Which it is, and whether it is an upper or lower limit, can easily be found. Consider, for example, the first line of the first five columns of Table 34. This shows that lagged prices rose (column (1)) from 1900–3 to 1905–8. Hence, if there was *any* price elasticity of demand at all, price effects were tending to reduce imports over this period. As we are assuming that price effects were zero $(\overline{m}_M = 0)$, we are crediting all the other factors with the minimum possible effect in the direction of increasing imports. We are therefore going to get a lower limit for t_M. We will get this lower limit if we credit production with having the maximum possible effect in increasing imports, thus leaving as little as possible to be caused by trend factors. Since production rose over the period (column (2)) this means putting i_M at its maximum of 1·3 (column (3)). In this way we arrive at the lower limit of $-0·7 \%$ per annum for t_M in this period (column 5)). We cannot find the corresponding upper limit for t_M since we do not know how big $\overline{m}_M$ might be. The other upper or lower limits for t_M in columns (4) and (5) were found by similar reasoning.

We now make the further assumption that amongst the limits for t_M given in columns (4) and (5) we have two, 2·7 % per annum for 1931–4 to 1935–8 and $-2·8 \%$ per annum for 1946–9 to 1952–5, which are at least as wide as the true ones. This seems to be a safe assumption, for the true value of i_M must lie between 0·6 and 1·3 and this would tend to reduce the limits we have found, as also would any value for $\overline{m}_M$ greater than zero. Hence, if we assume that t_M cannot vary more than from 2·7 to $-2·8 \%$ per annum, we are almost certainly on the safe side.

Finally, we need a maximum value for $\overline{m}_M$, the minimum being zero. For each of the periods in the table, we may select those values of i_M and t_M which yield a maximum $\overline{m}_M$, and the results are shown in column (8). Since $\overline{m}_M$ is assumed to be constant, it cannot exceed the least of these values, which is $-0·4$ for 1926–9 to 1931–4. If, for example, we supposed $\overline{m}_M$ to be as high as $-5·3$ (the largest value in column (8)) we could not reconcile this value with the data for other periods. To do so would mean assuming either i_M or t_M, or both, to be outside the limits already found for them.

The above analysis depends on the values found for *changes* in imports, prices and production over various periods. There is something to be said for confining our attention to changes over fairly long periods, in view of the possible errors of measurement, the arbitrariness of the weighting systems used, and the erratic influences of stock changes, etc. which, as we have seen, are not completely eliminated by our use of

Table 34. *Limits for the trend factor and the long-term price elasticity of demand for imports of materials on certain assumptions*

| | Sign of change in | | Extreme values for t_M | | | Maximum arithmetical values for $\overline{m}_M$ | | |
| | Lagged prices | Produc-tion | Value for i_M | Upper t_M | Lower t_M | Values for | | |
Period	(1)	(2)	(3)	(4)	(5)	i_M (6)	t_M (7)	$\overline{m}_M$ (8)
1900–3 to 1905–8	+	+	1·3	×	−0·7	1·3	2·7	−2·3
1905–8 to 1910–13	+	+	1·3	×	−2·2	1·3	2·7	−5·3
1910–13 to 1922–5	−	+	0·6	−1·0	×	0·6	−2·8	−1·1
1922–5 to 1926–9	−	+	0·6	2·1	×	0·6	−2·8	−3·4
1926–9 to 1931–4	−	+	0·6	0·2	×	0·6	−2·8	−0·4
1931–4 to 1935–8	−	+	0·6	2·7	×	0·6	−2·8	−2·8
1935–8 to 1946–9	+	+	1·3	×	−2·4	1·3	2·7	−1·4
1946–9 to 1952–5	+	+	1·3	×	−2·8	1·3	2·7	−0·7
1900–3 to 1910–13	+	+	1·3	×	−1·5	1·3	1·3	−2·3
1910–13 to 1926–9	−	+	0·6	−0·3	×	0·6	−2·5	−1·4
1926–9 to 1935–8	−	+	0·6	1·3	×	0·6	−2·5	−0·8
1935–8 to 1952–5	+	+	1·3	×	−2·5	1·3	1·3	−0·8

Note: The values given for t_M are measured as so many per cent per annum.

four-year averages. Over a short period these various sources of error could lead to large fluctuations in the values found for t_M, whereas over longer periods their influence would be reduced. Hence, in the lower part of Table 34 the results of similar calculations are given for rather longer periods. The lower limit for t_M is much the same at −2·5 % per annum, but the upper is now only 1·3 % per annum. Since the writer finds it difficult to believe in any sustained value of t_M much in excess of zero, in view of the numerous factors tending to reduce materials imports and input per unit of output, this seems to him a safe enough upper limit. The lowest $\overline{m}_M$ in column (8) is now −0·8, but, in fact, the limit can be set even lower, at −0·6, given our assumptions that $\overline{m}_M$ and i_M are constant.[1] These limits were finally chosen,

Table 35. *Parameters for determination of imports of materials*

Parameter	Lower limit	Best guess	Upper limit
Long-term price elasticity of demand $\overline{m}_M$	0·0	−0·2	−0·6
Production elasticity of demand, i_M	0·6	1·0	1·3
Trend factor, t_M	−0·0112	−0·0044	0·0057
Trend factor, t_M per cent per annum	−2·5	−1·0	1·3

[1] For $\overline{m}_M$ to be as large as −0·8, i_M must be 0·6 in 1926–9 to 1935–8 and 1·3 in 1935–8 to 1952–5 (column (6)). We can find what *constant* value for i_M yields the maximum $\overline{m}_M$ in these periods by putting t_M at the values shown in column (7) and then solving for $\overline{m}_M$ and i_M. The results are −0·59 for $\overline{m}_M$ and 0·90 for i_M.

and together with the best guesses for the parameters, are set out in Table 35, which summarizes the results of this section.

6. BEHAVIOUR OF IMPORTS 1935–8 TO 1954–5
(ADDENDUM TO CHAPTER II)

In Chapter II the behaviour of total imports of materials from 1935–8 to 1954–5 is described summarily. This section fills in the details of the behaviour of the three subdivisions of imports: metals, textiles and 'other' materials. Details of the calculations for Table 6 on p. 31 are not given. The method is described in Chapter V, Section 5, the basic equation is in Section 2 above, and the procedure was similar to that followed for food in Chapter VI, Section 5. About three-quarters of the saving in inputs of all materials per unit of industrial output in 1946–9 as compared with pre-war was in 'other' materials, and we discuss them first.

(a) 'Other' materials

The tremendous fall in inputs of 'other' materials is especially striking, but to some extent misleading since, as compared to metals and textiles, we may have failed to bring into our reckoning of inputs a larger part of home-produced substitutes. In the building industry, for example, much of the fall in timber consumption was probably offset by substitution of cement or steel,[1] neither of which is included in our index of home-produced substitutes. In Chapter II it was stated that import controls may have reduced the demand for imports of 'other' materials by about £40 million per annum in 1946–9. This estimate is simply the residual difference between actual imports of 'other' materials in 1946–9 and the demand for imports calculated from the known changes in relative prices, industrial production and time using the estimates for the various parameters given in Table 33 in the

---

[1] The following index numbers derived from the 1948 Census of Production give the quantities of materials purchased and used by larger private firms in the building and contracting trades in 1948 with 1935 = 100 (*Final Report on the Census of Production for 1948*, vol. 12, Trade A, *Building and Contracting*, p. 12/A/23).

Cement	188
Steel reinforcement	186
Other structural iron and steel	92
Timber, not fabricated, approximately	60 (obtained by dividing change in value by estimated change in average value).

Whereas the price of cement probably less than doubled and that of steel less than trebled from 1935 to 1948, the price of timber increased to nearly five times its 1935 level.

previous section. This estimate is a very uncertain one.[1] Nearly all the sharp drop and subsequent rise in imports could be explained by fluctuations in the trend factor which are within the limits given in the

Table 36. *Imports and consumption of 'other' materials, pre-war and post-war*

		Annual rates, £ million, 1948 c.i.f. prices		
		1935–8	1946–9	1954–5
1	Consumption	329	241	335
2	Production	26	44	42
3	Exports	5*	1	3
4	Change in stocks	..	4	9
5	Imports (1−2+3+4)	308*	202	305
	of which			
6	timber	165†	94	126
7	paper-making materials	64†	41	75
8	remainder	58†	68	104
		Index numbers		
		1935–8	1946–9	1954–5
9	Total industrial production‡	100	108	149
10	Building and contracting output	100	84	101
11	Paper and printing output	100	115	186
12	Chemicals output	100	158	280
13	Consumption of 'other' materials	100	73	102
14	Imports of 'other' materials	100	66	99

* Adjusted for bias in the weighting system by multiplying original estimates by 1·07, see p. 235.

† Unadjusted for bias, hence these do not add to 308.

‡ Adjusted for bias in the weighting system by multiplying original estimates for 1935–8 by 1·03, see p. 219.

Sources: Lines 1–5, see pp. 227 ff., S 58–62.
Lines 6–8, derived in the same way as line 5.
Line 9, see p. 218.
Lines 10–12, derived in the same way as S 24–9 for 1935–8 and 1948 and from the *Annual Abstract of Statistics* for other years.

last section. We may have omitted important adjustments for exports or changes in unrecorded stocks of materials. Still, attempts were made to restrict consumption of timber and wood pulp, and to use substitute materials, and our figures suggest that these attempts had some con-

[1] It is also incomplete. The effect of controls on exports of materials is ignored, and also any effects on the prices of imports, on the general level of industrial production, or on changes in stocks of materials, since we take all these factors as given. On the other hand, in so far as controls influenced the *composition* of output (e.g. by discouraging paper and building output), this is taken into account.

siderable success. From Table 36 it can be seen that timber and pulp were responsible for the fall in imports of other materials from before the war to 1946–9, and for much of the rapid increase thereafter. Part of the saving in pulp imports in 1946–9 in relation to paper output was due to the increased use of home-produced straw and waste paper by our mills. While their consumption of wood pulp nearly halved from

Table 37. *Imports and consumption of metal materials, pre-war and post-war*

		Annual rates, £ million, 1948 c.i.f. prices		
		1935–8	1946–9	1954–5
1	Consumption	146	183	243
2	Production	38	75	83
3	Exports	34*	32	26
4	Change in stocks	..	−3	—
5	Imports (1−2+3+4)	142*	137	186
		Index numbers		
		1935–8	1946–9	1954–5
6	Metals, engineering and vehicles output	100	147	221
7	Consumption of metal materials	100	125	166
8	Imports of metal materials	100	96	131

* Adjusted for bias in the weighting system by multiplying original estimates by 1·11, see p. 235.

Sources: Lines 1–5, see pp. 227 ff., S 47–51.
Line 6, see pp. 218 ff., S 20.

1935 to 1948, that of waste paper increased by about three-quarters, and that of straw and straw pulp seems to have multiplied about seven times.[1] The five-fold rise in pulp prices from 1935–48 no doubt encouraged this switch. The extra supplies of straw and waste paper came partly from increased home production, but also from a great reduction in exports of waste paper.

(b) Metal materials

A most striking point in Table 37 is the doubling of home production of metals from pre-war to post-war. A large part of this was due to the scrap available from war production, and it will be recalled that our estimates for 1922–5 suggested that the same thing may have happened after the First World War (p. 141). The boost given to home production was temporary, for it only increased by about 10 % from 1946–9 to

[1] *Report on the Census of Production for 1948*, vol. 10, Trade F, *Paper and Board*, pp. 10/F/21 and 22.

Table 38. *Changes in prices and consumption of non-ferrous metals*

	Average value* of imports in 1948 1935=100	Quantity consumed in 1946–9 1935=100
Lead	614	95
Zinc	516	122
Copper	375	138
Tin	239	137
Aluminium	82	496

* Allowing for import duty.

Sources: First column from the *Annual Statement of Trade*. Second column from C. T. Saunders, 'Consumption of Raw Materials in the United Kingdom: 1851–1950', *Journal of the Royal Statistical Society*, vol. 115, part 3, 1952.

Table 39. *Imports and consumption of textile materials, pre-war and post-war*

		Annual rates, £ million, 1948 c.i.f. prices		
		1935–8	1946–9	1954–5
1	Consumption	330	297	319
2	Production	70	57	85
3	Exports (including crude content of semi-manufactures)	76*	34	49
4	Imports (crude content of semi-manufactures)	1*	7	11
5	Changes in stocks	..	−21	−11
6	Imports (1−2+3−4+5)	336*	245	260
	of which			
7	cotton	157†	103	95
8	wool	75†	66	82
9	other textile materials	56†	44	59
10	hides and skins	31†	33	24
		Index numbers		
		1935–8	1946–9	1954–5
11	Textiles, clothing and leather and leather goods output‡	100	87	105
12	Consumption of textiles materials	100	90	97
13	Imports of textile materials	100	73	77

* Adjusted for bias in the weighting system by multiplying original estimates by 1·05, see p. 235.

† Unadjusted for bias, hence these items do not add to 336.

‡ Adjusted for processing element in exports and imports of semi-manufactures included in lines 3 and 4.

Sources: Lines 1–6, see pp. 227 ff., S 52–7.

Lines 7–10, derived in the same way as line 6.

Line 11, see pp. 218 ff., S 21

1954–5 despite the accompanying 50 % increase in the output of the metal industries which should have provided further sources of scrap. Within the group there was a shift away from those metals which rose most in price to those which become relatively cheaper, as is shown in Table 38.

(c) Textile materials[1]

Imports of textiles did not fall quite as much as imports of other materials from 1935–8 to 1946–9, but they failed to recover strongly thereafter. Raw cotton and hides and skins were about the only large groups of imports actually to *fall* from 1946–9 to 1954–5. Wool and other textile fibres made a better showing, reflecting, amongst other things, the greater strength of our exports of woollen goods.

Imports of textile materials for consumption in 1946–9 were considerably higher than our explanatory equation suggested they should be (see Chart 15). The reason seems to have been mainly the unusual behaviour of home production of substitutes which *fell* by about 20 % from pre-war to 1946–9, despite the great rise in the price of textile materials which should have stimulated home supplies. From 1946–9 to 1954–5, as if making up for lost time, home production increased by nearly 50 %. The fall was due partly to the fact that some home production (cotton and wool waste) is linked to imports which fell, partly to the war and the severe winter of 1947 which reduced flocks and so wool and sheepskin production. Cattle-hide production also seems to have fallen, not because herds were smaller but because of fewer slaughterings (perhaps because farmers were trying to build up herds more rapidly). Man-made fibre production (included in home production of textile materials) was up by two-thirds, but the pace of expansion became even more rapid after 1946–9. In general, it seems that the war and other factors mentioned prevented home production responding quickly to the rise in prices. There was therefore a delayed response which showed itself in the very rapid increase during the post-war period. The position was thus the reverse of that for metals, where the war boosted home supplies temporarily, and this largely accounts for the difference in the behaviour of imports as illustrated in Charts 14 and 15.

It does not altogether account for the difference, however. As may be seen from Tables 37 and 39, whereas consumption per unit of output fell for metals from 1935–8 to 1946–9, it is estimated to have risen slightly for textiles. This, again, on the assumption that the production elasticities of demand were less than one, may have been partly due to the fact that the output of the metals industries rose whereas that of the

---

[1] The term 'textile materials' is used here to include hides and skins.

textiles industries fell, but it is doubtful whether this is the complete explanation.

Various other explanations may be considered. The estimates of consumption may be faulty, but they agree with other estimates.[1] Further adjustments for the materials content of exports or imports of semi-manufactures only seem to make matters worse.[2] There may have been large unrecorded stock changes but this seems unlikely, given the wide coverage of the official figures.[3] The most likely explanation seems to be that the index of production of textiles and clothing is based mainly on the *yardage* of cloth produced, and that from 1935–8 to 1946–9 there was an increase in the weight of fibre used per yard.[4]

[1] Weighting Mr Saunders's estimates of consumption of the principal textile fibres ('Consumption of Raw Materials in the United Kingdom: 1851–1950', *Journal of the Royal Statistical Society*, 1952) by their 1948 average import values gives an index for 1946–9 of 78, with 1935–8 = 100. This may be compared with the estimates of consumption given in Table 39, but excluding hides and skins and excluding the adjustments for imports and exports of semi-manufactured textiles (which are not taken into account in Mr Saunders's estimates), for which the corresponding index is 79.

[2] The only woven cotton fibres included in the exports and imports were grey unbleached woven piece-goods. A large part of the imports of these goods (responsible for virtually all of line 4 of Table 39) was finished and then re-exported, and this alone would have increased the import : output ratio, unless the extra exports were also taken into account. However, it seems that by including more piece-goods (e.g. white, bleached and printed) the fall in exports (line 3 of Table 39) was made larger, and the fall in adjusted imports correspondingly smaller for the period 1935–8 to 1946–9.

[3] See the *Monthly Digest of Statistics Supplement, Definitions and Explanatory Notes*, January 1950, pp. 14 and 15.

[4] From 1935 to 1948 the weight of cotton piece-goods per square yard rose by about 24 % on average, and that of rayon, nylon, etc. and silk piece-goods by about 32 %. The weight of woven woollen tissues per square yard, however, fell a few per cent (see the 1948 *Census of Production*, vol. 6, Trade B, *Cotton Weaving*, p. 6/B/7; Trade C, *Woollen and Worsted*, p. 6/C/16; Trade D, *Rayon, Nylon, etc. and Silk*, p. 6/D/16).

CHAPTER VIII

MANUFACTURES

I. INTRODUCTION

As may be seen from Table 40, imported manufactures consist of a
wide variety of goods, destined for many different end uses. The most
appropriate single index to which one might relate them is probably an
index of the quantity of sales of manufactures on the home market.
Chart 17 shows this relationship for five groups of manufactures,
covering 60 to 80% of imports (depending on the period), for the

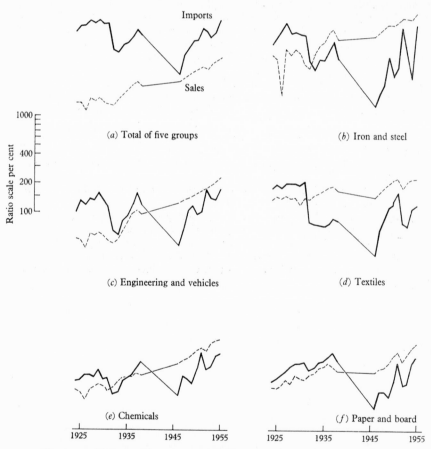

Chart 17. Volume of imports and total sales on the home market of various
manufactures, 1924–55

years 1924–38 and 1946–55. The behaviour of the quantity of all
imported manufactures[1] in relation to an index of industrial production
over a longer period is shown in Chart 7. Although there is less logic
in this comparison, since industrial production includes output of non-
manufactures and of exported manufactures, there is sufficient similarity
between the two charts to ensure that the second is not misleading; and
since it includes all imports and a greater number of years we will for
the present confine our attention to it.

The relative movements of the two series on the chart show some
striking features. In some periods the lines move quite closely together.
This is true of the periods 1900–13, 1925–30 (allowing for the general
strike in 1926), and 1932–8. What leap to the eye, however, are the
very dissimilar movements which have occurred. There are three
periods in which imports of manufactures fell sharply, although the
index of production was relatively unchanged. From 1913 to 1920
imports fell by about a quarter, although production rose by a tenth.
From 1930 to 1932 imports nearly halved, while production only fell a
tenth. Finally, from 1938 to 1948 imports fell by a third while production rose about a tenth. Two of these occasions followed the two wars,
and each time the fall in imports was succeeded by a very rapid
recovery. The recovery after the First World War restored the pre-war
relation of imports to output, but, at least up to 1955, the recovery after
the Second World War had not gone so far. The other big fall in
imports was due to the imposition of the tariff and the devaluation of
the pound in 1932. In this case, although imports rose rapidly after
1933, they only kept pace with output. The effects of the tariff and
devaluation seem to have been more permanent than those of the wars.

In what may be called 'normal peace-time' there is therefore some
tendency for imports to change in roughly the same proportions as
industrial production and also (Chart 17) as the volume of sales of
similar products on the home market. The connexion between the two,
however, is obviously nothing like as strong as that between imports of
materials and industrial production. It has been snapped on three
important occasions. Hence in this case it is more than usually inadequate to seek to explain the behaviour of imports purely in terms of
some income-type variable. Such an explanation would obviously be
very misleading for certain kinds of policy decisions, even if it might
appear to have some success in forecasting imports in certain periods.

It is the main purpose of this chapter to show that changes in the
price of imports of manufactures can greatly affect their quantity, that is,
that the price elasticity of demand for them is high. There are two
prima facie reasons for believing this to be so.

[1] As defined for this study, see Appendix II, p. 212.

The first is the behaviour of imports in 1932, when, as has been remarked, they fell very sharply, and when the most obvious explanation of this fall was their relative rise in price on account of the devaluation and tariff. In Section 2 the evidence from this period is examined, and an attempt is made to estimate various price elasticities of demand for imports using this data alone. Consideration has to be given to some conceptual problems raised by the need to take account of the importance of exports of manufactures and of the size of manufacturing in the whole economy. The simpler partial equilibrium approach used for imports of food and materials proves less useful here, so that different possible demand elasticities, allowing to different extents for repercussions on the rest of the economy, must be examined.

The second prima facie reason for believing in a high price elasticity of demand is that imports of manufactures provide only a small proportion of total sales of manufactures on the home market, the great bulk coming from home production. As was shown in Chapter V, the smaller the ratio of imports to home-produced sales, *ceteris paribus*, the larger is the price elasticity of demand for imports.[1]

Here, however, we meet a puzzle. For there appear to be different ways in which the ratio of imports to home-produced sales on the home market might be measured, and while for some the ratio is small, for others it is not. Thus from Tables 40 and 41 one can derive three measures of the ratio of imports to home-produced manufactures for sale on the home market in 1935. The smallest of these is only 8 % and is the ratio of total imports (plus duty) to total home-produced manufactures for sale on the home market in Table 40. Inspection of the last column of figures in that table shows, however, that for many of the largest groups of imports the corresponding percentage is well above 8. One might therefore weight the percentages in the last column by the corresponding values of imports and regard this as a better measure of the ratio for the typical import. The result is 14 % instead of 8 %. Table 41 shows what happens if an even finer commodity analysis is used, distinguishing some 450 different items instead of the 20 in Table 40. The ratio for the typical import now becomes about 120 %. In other words, using a fine commodity analysis, the typical import supplies more than half of the home market for that particular good. In principle one could proceed to such a fine analysis that each

---

[1] See pp. 88–9. These show that the elasticity of demand for imports is higher the smaller the ratio, given the elasticity of demand for consumption of imports plus home production ($\bar{h}$), the elasticity of supply of home production ($\bar{p}$) and the elasticity of substitution between imports and the home product (σ). A similar conclusion, but applicable only to the elasticity of demand for imports without allowing for repercussions on home supply, follows from equation (21), p. 84.

import was treated as unique, the ratio would become infinite, and the typical import would supply the whole of the home market for that particular good. What do we mean, then, when we say that the ratio of imports to home-produced sales of manufactures on the home market is small?

Table 40. *Total imports of manufactures in 1935 in relation to home-produced sales of similar products on the home market*

	£ million		
Item	Value of total imports including duty	Value of home-produced sales on the home market	(1) as percentage of (2)
	(1)	(2)	(3)
Building materials	3	60	4
China, glass, etc.	6	27	21
Chemicals, etc.	18	72	25
Soap, polishes	5	36	14
Iron and steel	9	170	5
Mechanical engineering	15	147	10
Electrical engineering	4	91	5
Motor and cycle	6	153	4
Aircraft	—	12	1
Railway rolling stock	—	42	—
Cotton and silk	12	150	8
Woollen and worsted	3	108	3
Hosiery and lace	3	46	6
Other textiles	5	43	11
Leather and fur	11	40	29
Clothing	8	214	4
Paper	16	72	22
Printing and publishing	1	137	1
Rubber	2	23	8
Miscellaneous manufacturing	3	21	15
Total	128	1,665	8

Note: The figures are taken from Dr T. Barna's 'The Interdependence of the British Economy', *Journal of the Royal Statistical Society*, Series A (General), vol. 115, part 1, 1952, pp. 49, 50. Imports include re-exports and have a slightly different coverage from those given elsewhere in this study. Home-produced sales on the home market are gross domestic output less exports and re-exports. 'Metal goods n.e.s.' have been omitted, since the bulk of imports in that category consist of precious metals not included in the definition of manufactures in this study. Non-ferrous metals are also excluded, since they are regarded as 'materials' in this study. Ship-building is excluded because imports consisted mainly of second-hand ships not recorded in the trade returns and therefore excluded from this study.

Table 41. *Distribution of imports of manufactures in relation to home-produced sales in 1935 using a fine commodity analysis*

£ million

Percentage ratio of imports to sales on the home market from home production	Value of retained imports including duty	Value of sales on the home market from home production
(1)	(2)	(3)
0 to 5	18	1,268
5 to 10	17	226
10 to 20	15	106
20 to 40	24	76
40 to 80	41	74
80 to 160	17	18
160 to 320	7	3
Above 320	8	1
	146	1,772

Note: The figures are taken from Dr T. Barna's detailed work sheets for 'The Interdependence of the British Economy' (referred to in Table 40). The totals differ on account of the different coverage. Also, in this table imports are *retained*, and home-produced sales equal gross domestic output less exports of United Kingdom produce.

To solve this puzzle one must remember that a smaller ratio implies a higher elasticity of demand only if other things are equal, and that one of these other things is the substitutability of the imported for the home-produced goods. For example, the elasticity of demand for imported steel might be higher than for imported wool because, although each has a very close substitute produced at home, the ratio of imports to home production is smaller for steel than for wool. But this ratio might be still smaller for books, and yet the elasticity of demand for imported books might be lower than for either steel or wool, if imported books were not at all close substitutes for home-produced books. The different values for the ratio of imports to home products mentioned in the preceding paragraph were found by considering different pairs of imported and home-produced goods. The pair for which the ratio was lowest was for all imports and all home products, each taken as a single group. Since these large groups consist of very different goods mixed in different proportions, substitutability between them is less close than it is between the pairs of imports and home products for the twenty subdivisions shown in Table 40. Imported building materials and home-produced building materials, for example, are likely to be closer substitutes than all imported manufactures and all home-produced manufactures taken together. Hence, although the

average ratio is bigger when we consider twenty subdivisions of manufactures, the average substitutability is also greater, and the elasticity
of demand may therefore be the same.[1]

To establish that the elasticity of demand for imported manufactures
is high, it is therefore not enough to show that imports *taken as a group*
are small in relation to home products, taken as a group. In addition
one must show that they are close substitutes *taken as a group*.

In Section 2 we try to show this using the data for 1930–5. Between
these years the quantity of imports fell sharply in relation to the
quantity of home-produced manufactures sold on the home market,
but the price of imports did not rise much in relation to the price of
home products; this suggests a high degree of substitutability between
the two groups.

Although the evidence from this period is persuasive, and constitutes
what is probably the strongest part of the case for believing in a high
elasticity, it is desirable to find supporting evidence as well. A review
of the behaviour of imports in other periods is given in Section 3. For
various reasons, no quantitative estimates of the elasticity of demand can
be made from the data for these other periods, but the behaviour of
imports is at least consistent with the elasticity being high. Since others
have used some of the same data to derive appreciably lower estimates
of the elasticity, some reasons are given for rejecting their estimates in
Section 4.

The behaviour of imports of some fifteen individual commodities[2] is
examined in Section 5. The supporting evidence here is of two kinds.
In the first place, one can check to some extent that the very small
increase in the price index of all imports relative to the price index of
home-produced manufactures, which took place between 1930 and
1935, was not some freak of index numbers. The same failure of the
price of imports to rise much relatively to the price of home products
over this period can be observed for most of the fifteen commodities.
Secondly, bearing in mind the preceding discussion of the relation
between the size of the groups and their substitutability one can check
that substitution between pairs of these individual commodities is
considerably higher than between all imports and all home products
taken as groups. An attempt is also made to reconcile this finding with
the commonly held view that the market for individual manufactures
is very imperfect.

---

[1] The reasoning in this paragraph is inevitably somewhat compressed. For a more
precise and lengthier discussion, see Appendix I.

[2] That is, of the smallest commodity groups distinguished in the statistical sources
available.

2. ESTIMATES OF PRICE ELASTICITIES FROM THE DATA FOR 1930-5

In the first part of this section we estimate the price elasticity of demand for imports of manufactures ignoring repercussions on the home supply, that is, assuming that the prices of home-produced manufactures remain constant. In the second part we consider various ways in which the estimates might be modified to allow for changes in these prices. The basic data are set out in Table 42, which shows percentage and logarithmic changes in various items from 1930 to 1935, and the symbols corresponding to these items in the equations of this section.

Table 42. *Data for 1930-5*

Item	£ million 1930	£ million 1935	Changes from 1930 to 1935 Percentage	Changes from 1930 to 1935 Logs	Corresponding symbols
United Kingdom retained imports of manufactures					
1 At current prices, c.i.f.	220	120	−46		
2 1930 prices	220	150	−33	−0·1720	M
3 Average value			−20	−0·0964	$\overline{M}$
4 Average value, corrected for change in tariffs			−9	−0·0414	$\overline{M}\overline{M}*$
Sales of manufactures from United Kingdom production on the United Kingdom market					
5 At current prices	1480	1680	14		
6 1930 prices	1480	2040	38	0·1311	P_C
7 Average value			−18	−0·0851	$\overline{P}_C$
8 United Kingdom wage rates and also average value national product excluding manufacturing			−3	−0·0132	$\overline{G-H}$
9 United Kingdom industrial production			21		Υ
10 United Kingdom imports of materials, average value			−24		
11 United Kingdom factor prices			−7	−0·0320	$\overline{W}_P$
United Kingdom exports of manufactures					
12 At current prices	420	310	−26		
13 1930 prices	420	380	−9	−0·0400	X
14 Average value			−19		$\overline{X}$
15 Wage rates abroad (in sterling)			19		
16 Factor prices abroad (in sterling)			10	0·0434	$\overline{W}_M$

Sources: See p. 238.

The data in lines 10, 11, 15 and 16 are not used in this chapter, but are used in Appendix I (see p. 201) and are included here for convenience.

(a) Demand without supply repercussions

The two equations show the demand functions for imports and home-produced manufactures respectively, and are similar to equations (6) and (7) on p. 81:

$$M = d(\overline{M'}, M^{*'}, \overline{P'_C}, \overline{G\text{–}H'}, Y) \dots\dots\dots\dots\dots\dots\dots\dots\dots \quad (32)$$

$$P_C = d(\overline{M'}, M^{*'}, \overline{P'_C}, \overline{G\text{–}H'}, Y) \dots\dots\dots\dots\dots\dots\dots\dots\dots \quad (33)$$

In these equations M, $\overline{M}$ and M^* mean the volume, price and duty[1] on imported manufactures respectively (see also Chapter V). Y is an income-type variable, discussed further below. P_C is the volume of home-produced manufactures for sale on the home market and is simply home production minus exports, $P\text{–}X$, since no stock changes are taken into account owing to the lack of data. $\overline{P_C}$ is a price index of P_C. $\overline{G\text{–}H}$ is a price index of non-manufactures. The primes show that the variables have lagged effects on M and P_C.

In deriving P_C from $P\text{–}X$, output minus exports, output is measured gross of duplication. It is simply the sum of the output for sale of each establishment. This differs from the usual method of adding up outputs, which is to subtract the consumption of purchased materials and fuels from output for sale, and to sum the resulting 'net' outputs. In this way a total is obtained which does not count the value of, say, yarn output several times over (as yarn, cloth, and clothing, for example). It seemed appropriate here, however, to use gross rather than net output. This is what we would obtain if we wrote down an equation similar to (33) for each commodity and then summed these equations (see Appendix I).

It must be admitted, however, that this is not a very secure theoretical justification for using gross output. As is shown in Appendix I, the assumptions required if a simple summation of equations is to be a valid procedure cannot be justified in practice. Some alternative estimates of the elasticity of demand for imports of manufactures were made, therefore, using different methods of measuring output. As it turned out, the increase in the volume of manufacturing output and of sales of home-produced manufactures on the home market from 1930 to 1935 was the same, whether one used index numbers of changes in gross or net output for the separate industries, provided that these index numbers were

---

[1] Measured in the way described on p. 78.

weighted by the same values of gross output in 1930.[1] The index
numbers of net output were also weighted by the estimated values of
output of each manufacturing industry net of purchases from other manufacturing industries in 1930.[2] This gave an estimate of the change in the
volume and price of output of manufactures from 1930 to 1935 free of
duplication within manufacturing industry taken as a whole, but
including sales to other non-manufacturing industries. After subtracting
exports, estimates of sales of manufactures on the home market free of
duplication were obtained. The use of these estimates in calculating
the price elasticity of demand for imports of manufactures, in place of
the estimates in Table 42, made little difference to the result.[3]

The symbols $\overline{G-H}$ and Y in equations (32) and (33) are only re-
minders of causal factors which should be taken into account. We make
no serious attempt to estimate the corresponding parameters. For an
individual semi-manufacture, for example, the appropriate income-type
variable corresponding to Y would be the output of the trades which
were the main users of the good in question. If all imports were semi-
manufactures (and most are), the index of industrial production might
be a fairly adequate variable to take. But for imports of finished
consumer goods we should use an index of consumers' total real current
expenditure, or real income, and for imports of finished capital goods
there is probably no single simple variable which is suitable.

There are other factors which might be considered to influence the
demand for M and P_C. We might introduce a trend, and in the short
period stock changes could be important. In fact, however, we cannot
measure the income-type variable at all accurately, so that the trend
can be combined (conceptually) with it. As for stock changes, there are
virtually no data which would enable us to distinguish effects on imports
from effects on home production, and here again we may assume that
the main movements affect both equi-proportionately and are included
in our income-type variable, Y.

[1] The index numbers of gross output and the gross output weights were those
given in A. L. Bowley (ed.), *Studies in the National Income, 1924–1938*, National Institute
of Economic and Social Research, Economic and Social Studies, 1 (Cambridge
University Press, 1944), p. 149, table III. The index numbers of net output were
those given in C. F. Carter, W. B. Reddaway and R. Stone, *The Measurement of
Production Movements* (Cambridge University Press, 1948), p. 125, table 2. These
index numbers were preferred to the net output index numbers given by Bowley for
various reasons.
[2] These estimates were approximate, and were based on the input-output matrix
for 1935 given in Dr Barna's 'The Interdependence of the British Economy', *Journal
of the Royal Statistical Society*, vol. 115, part 1, 1952.
[3] The elasticity, $\overline{m}_{m.d}$, worked out at $-6\cdot7$ as compared with the estimate of
$-6\cdot2$ given on p. 162.

We make similar assumptions to those set out in equations (8), (9), (13), (14), (15) and (19) of Chapter V, that is, we assume that equi-proportionate changes in all prices leave demand unaffected, that changes in third factors (in this case, $\overline{G-H}$ and Υ) affect the demand for imports and home products to the same proportionate extent, and that the reciprocity theorem holds.

As a partial test of the second of these assumptions for the period 1930–5, the change in the volume of total sales of manufactures was compared with the change in an index of the volume of sales, constructed by weighting the index numbers for eight separate groups of sales[1] by imports in 1930. These two index numbers therefore differed only in respect of their weights (total sales in 1930 for each group in one case and imports in 1930 in the other), and the object was to see whether this difference led to any difference in the change from 1930 to 1935. In fact, the index numbers were almost the same (131 and 129 respectively), so that there was no evidence here of imports being particularly favoured or disfavoured by changes in third factors in this period.

Given these assumptions, the relative quantities of imports and home products demanded depend only on their relative prices, and the relation between the two is expressed by the elasticity of substitution.[2] From the data in Table 42 we can therefore estimate this elasticity, which is equal to the relative change in quantities divided by the relative change in prices between 1930 and 1935, all measured in terms of their logarithms:

$$\sigma = \frac{-0\cdot1720 - 0\cdot1311}{-0\cdot0414 + 0\cdot0851} = -6\cdot9.$$

If we allow for possible errors of $\pm 5\%$ in estimating the relative changes in prices and quantities, we get limits for σ of -4 and -14. These limits are wide because the large change in relative quantities was accompanied by such a small change in relative prices.

From this estimate of the elasticity of substitution we can estimate the price elasticity of demand for imported manufactures, $\overline{m}_{m.d}$, by means of an equation similar to equation (21) on p. 84, namely:

$$\sigma = \overline{m}_{m.d}\,(1+r)+r\,.\,\overline{g-h} \dots\dots\dots\dots\dots\dots\dots (34)$$

We need, therefore, estimates for r and $\overline{g-h}$.

r is the ratio of imports of manufactures (including duty) to sales on

[1] Iron and steel, products of the metal-using industries, textiles, chemicals, paper and board, manufactures of wood, clothing, and leather and leather goods. Miscellaneous imports and sales were left out of the calculation since they included very different assortments of goods.

[2] See Chapter V, pp. 82–3.

the home market from home production at current prices. It was 0·16 in 1930 and 0·09 in 1935. For the reasons given on p. 84 we take the mean of these ratios, which is 0·12.

$g–h$ is the price elasticity of demand for manufactures with respect to changes in the prices of non-manufactures. There is not enough information to estimate this, but, since on general grounds one would expect it to be small, we shall assume that it lies between 0 and 1, with a most probable value of 0·5. This is little more than guesswork, but any plausible estimate would give much the same result.

From equations similar to (21), (19), (8), (9) and (13) in Chapter V we can now calculate all the parameters in the demand equations (32) and (33) except those referring to changes in the income-type variable. The results of these calculations are given below. Equation (32) becomes:

$$\Delta \log M = -6\!\cdot\!2\, \Delta \log \overline{MM}\!* + 5\!\cdot\!7\, \Delta \log \overline{P}_C + 0\!\cdot\!5\, \Delta \log \overline{G\!-\!H} + y\, \Delta \log \Upsilon.$$

And equation (33) becomes:

$$\Delta \log P_C = -1\!\cdot\!2\, \Delta \log \overline{P}_C + 0\!\cdot\!7\, \Delta \log \overline{MM}\!* + 0\!\cdot\!5\, \Delta \log \overline{G\!-\!H} + y\, \Delta \log \Upsilon.$$

The limits for $\overline{m}_{m.d}$, the price elasticity of demand for imports, are -4 and -13, given the above limits for σ and assuming $\overline{g\!-\!h}$ is 0 and 1 respectively. Similar limits for the price elasticity of demand for home-produced manufactures are $-0\!\cdot\!4$ and $-2\!\cdot\!4$.

No attempt is made here to estimate the parameter y for the income-type variable. From 1930 to 1935 industrial production rose by 21% (Table 42), but, for the reasons mentioned on p. 160, one cannot safely assume that this caused an increase in the demand for imported manufactures of 21%. The value of $y\, \Delta \log \Upsilon$ implied by the above equations is, in fact, 16%, which is not very different.

It must be stressed that these estimates are very uncertain. Two aspects of them which might be criticized—that the calculations are based on changes between only two years, 1930 and 1935, and that the interpretation of results based on the behaviour of large groups is doubtful—are commented on below. They might also be criticized for the number of simplifying assumptions on which they rest and for the inadequacy of the basic statistics. The rapidity of the fall in imports may have been partly due to the existence of a large amount of unused capacity in British manufacturing industry, which could therefore easily and quickly expand output to replace imports. In current circumstances, with much less idle capacity available, a similar rise in import prices might take appreciably longer to show its effects. Despite all these qualifications, the estimates are probably better than no estimates at all, and also better than some estimates previously made (see Section 4). It is difficult to see why they should exaggerate the *long*-term price elasticity of demand, and they may, indeed, understate it.

The reasons for concentrating attention on this period have already been discussed. It is one in which changes in relative prices, and only in relative prices, seem to have caused a substantial change in the demand for imported manufactures, and other periods in which the evidence is so clear are hard to find. In estimating the effects of these relative price changes, however, we only used the data for two years, 1930 and 1935, instead of attempting to make allowances for stock changes or lagged effects by using the data for a number of years on each side of 1932. The reasons for doing this were mainly those of convenience and the availability of data. There were Censuses of Production in both 1930 and 1935.[1] It seems unlikely that if more years were taken into account the results would be very different. As may be seen from Chart 7, the relation of imports to industrial production was relatively stable both in the years 1927–30 and in the years 1934–8, so that there seems little likelihood of error in taking 1930 as a representative year for the first period,[2] and 1935 as one for the second period.

One might argue that the large fall in imports which occurred in 1932 was in a sense fortuitous. The increases in duty might have been concentrated, for example, on a particular group of imports for which demand was highly elastic, and the increases in duty on other imports might have been relatively small. This could have led to a large drop in imports accompanied by only a small increase in their relative average price, and so to an apparently high elasticity of demand. Yet this would be a misleading guide to the normal reaction of imports to a more evenly spread price increase.

It is difficult to test the truth of this argument, since estimates of the elasticities of demand for individual imported manufactures are lacking. To judge by an arithmetical example given in Appendix I (pp. 203–4), however, it may not greatly matter whether the tariff changes were concentrated on imports for which there were close substitutes produced in this country or whether they were randomly distributed in relation

[1] There were also the Import Duties Act Inquiries in 1933 and 1934, which were not quite as comprehensive as the Censuses. Much less information on home production is available for other years.

[2] Mr Leak also regarded 1930 as a reasonable base-year from which to judge the effects of the import duties on imports. See 'Some Results of the Import Duties Act', *Journal of the Royal Statistical Society*, vol. 100, part 4, 1937, pp. 567–8. The results of the 1935 Census of Production were not available when he wrote.

to this characteristic. The elasticity of substitution estimated from the behaviour of imports in the one set of circumstances would be at least approximately applicable to their behaviour in the other. But what *would* make the results misleading would be, for example, a concentration of tariff increases on goods which formed a large proportion of imports but only a small proportion of home production of manufactures.

It is therefore important to see whether there was any unevenness of this kind in the impact of the factors affecting the demand for imports in this period; and so far as can be judged, there was not. There were, broadly speaking, three different kinds of factors involved. There were the shifts in demand or supply curves caused by the changes in exchange rates; there were the tariff changes in 1932; and there were other shifts in demand or supply curves due to changes in techniques and tastes, and the general course of industrial development—both secular and cyclical.

Changes in exchange rates by their very nature tend to affect a wide range of commodities, and there is no reason to suppose that their effects were concentrated on goods especially important in imports rather than in home-produced sales, or vice versa.

The changes in tariffs, although they certainly affected some commodities more than others, also seem to have been fairly evenly distributed as between imports and home sales. A calculation was made of the average rate of duty imposed under the Import Duties Act taking two different sets of weights: first, the values of imports of manufactures in 1930, and second, the values of the corresponding home-produced manufactures sold on the home market in 1930. The first calculation gave an average rate of duty of 17·2 % and the second one of 18·7 %, so that the difference is not substantial.[1]

Finally, there were the other changes mentioned above, and again (with one exception mentioned below) it is difficult to see why goods which had an especially high or low weight in imports *vis-à-vis* home-

[1] These calculations were based on the figures given by H. Leak in *Journal of the Royal Statistical Society*, 1937, pp. 575–7. These figures show the values of imports and sales on the home market from home production of manufactures in 1930 classified in accordance with the rates of duty imposed under the Import Duties Act and ruling at 1 January 1934. Specific rates were converted to *ad valorem* rates as closely as the available data permitted. Since imports from British countries (on which import duties were not imposed) are not distinguished in the figures, the classification is not exactly that required, but the error caused by this factor may be small. Non-ferrous metals were included, although they are not included in 'manufactures' in the rest of this study, and there are some other differences in classification. Only manufactures 'dutiable *only* under the Import Duties Act' or 'exempted from the general *ad valorem* duty' were included, and goods recorded by value only were omitted (pp. 568, 569).

produced sales should have been specially affected. Furthermore, since the big fall in imports was almost certainly caused by the first two groups of factors—the devaluation and tariff—and the changes caused by the third group were small in comparison, it would not greatly matter if their effects *were* somewhat unevenly distributed. The exception to this conclusion is the influence of the 'Buy British' campaign, but it seems doubtful whether this had any great effect on imports.[1]

(b) Demand with supply repercussions

In Chapter V, Section 3, there is a discussion of one possible supply equation for home-produced substitutes for imports and (Section 4) of the way in which a price elasticity of demand for imports can be defined which allows for changes in the price and quantity of home supply in response to changes in the price of imports. The estimates of the price elasticity of demand for imported manufactures which have just been given do not allow for these repercussions on home supply. They show what would happen to the quantity of imports demanded if there was a change in their average price *unaccompanied* by any change in the average price of home-produced manufactures for sale on the home market. One might try to estimate an elasticity of demand which allowed for supply repercussions in the way described in Chapter V, but, although this seemed feasible for food and materials, it does not seem either feasible or useful for manufactures. For manufactures, unlike food or materials, exports represent a substantial part of home production, and home production represents a substantial part of the whole economy. This makes the relatively simple supply equation discussed in Chapter V less useful, for the following reasons.

For food and materials, home supply was assumed to depend on three main factors: the price at which it was sold, the general price level and what were called 'trend factors'.[2] For manufactures sold on the home market we should have to add at least two important factors to this list: the price of exports and the price of imported raw materials. The price of exports is relevant because manufacturers are likely to switch their sales from home to export markets or vice versa in accordance with the relative profitabilities, and so prices, of sales in each market. The price of materials is relevant because they are so largely imported, and their prices can diverge so markedly from the general level of factor prices at home, that we cannot safely group them together with other factors of production used in manufacturing as described in Chapter V (pp. 86–7).

[1] Neither Mr Leak ('Some Results of the Import Duties Act', *Journal of the Royal Statistical Society*, 1937) nor any of the speakers in the ensuing discussion deemed it worth a mention in their consideration of the results of the Import Duties Act.

[2] See p. 85 for what this means in relation to agriculture.

This addition of two more factors in the supply function would make it appreciably more difficult to estimate the elasticity of supply, for well known reasons.

A further difficulty is that there may be only small changes in the prices of manufactures sold on the home market relative to those exported. From 1930 to 1935, for example, there was virtually no relative price change, although the quantity of home-produced sales on the home market rose by about 40 % while the quantity of exports fell by about 10 %. This suggests that manufacturing resources are very mobile as between exporting and selling on the home market, although there are other possible explanations as well.[1] If this were so, it would not only be difficult but also not very useful to measure the elasticity of supply of home-produced sales on the home market on the assumption that export prices were constant. For in practice, export prices would be bound to change more or less in line with the prices of sales on the home market.

An attempt was therefore made to measure the elasticity of supply assuming that the *demand curve* for exports was constant, and not the price of exports. This meant trying to answer the following sort of question. If the average price of manufactures sold on the home market rises by (say) 1%, and if the prices of factors of production used by manufacturing industry (labour and materials) remain constant, then, abstracting from changes in 'trend factors', and assuming that nothing affecting the demand for exported manufactures changes except their price, what will be the resultant increase in the supply of manufactures to the home market? The aim was to measure long-term elasticities, so that a distinction had to be drawn between changes in output and changes in capacity to produce output. It was the latter which were relevant, but they could not be directly measured. This, and the other difficulties mentioned,[2] meant that only widely spaced upper and lower limits to the value of the elasticity could be obtained, and because of their doubtful utility it does not seem worth reproducing the somewhat tedious process of estimation.[3]

[1] For example, the expansion of sales on the home market may have been largely due to a fuller utilization of manufacturing capacity normally devoted to that market, and there may have been little switching of capacity from producing for export to producing for the home market. Changes in the extent to which capacity is utilized are thus a further factor which should be taken into account in estimating elasticities of supply of manufactures (see below).

[2] One other difficulty not mentioned is that we need to know the price elasticity of demand for exports of manufactures in order to gauge the extent to which exports will change (and hence supplies of manufactures for the home market) in response to any given price change.

[3] For what they are worth, the upper and lower limits found for home-produced

Instead of attempting to measure the elasticity of supply directly, we can approach the problem of estimating the elasticity of demand for imports of manufactures—allowing for repercussions on home supply—from a different angle. Let us assume that we are trying to estimate the *long-term* change in the demand for imports accompanying a 1% rise, say, in their average price, this rise being due to a general rise in manufacturing prices abroad (and *not* to the imposition of a tariff on imports, which is discussed below). We shall assume no change in the general level of home factor prices, no change in raw material prices and no change in 'trend factors'. We shall also provisionally assume that the government regulates the level of demand in such a way as to maintain a constant level of output and employment in manufacturing.[1] In these circumstances there would be an increase in exports of manufactures (due to the rise in manufacturing prices abroad) and a reduction in imports. In order to maintain a constant level of manufacturing output, the government would have to cut the demand for manufactures for sale on the home market. Since export prices would tend to rise, the price of home-produced manufactures would have to fall so as to prevent an expansion of total manufacturing output. Consequently, the price of imports of manufactures would rise by *more* than 1% relative to the price of home-produced manufactures for sale on the home market. The drop in the demand for imported manufactures would therefore be *more* than seven times 1%[2] (to use the best estimate of the elasticity of substitution given on p. 161). Hence, on these assumptions, the price elasticity of demand for imports of manufactures would be (arithmetically) *more* than the elasticity of substitution, that is, on the estimate made above, arithmetically more than -7.

If the government stabilized the general level of employment in the whole economy, rather than just that in manufacturing industry, the fall in the demand for imports would not be so great. For some of the cuts in domestic demand would fall on other sectors of the economy, the home demand for manufactures would be cut by less, and the average

sales on the home market were 13 and 0, and for the supply of imports were infinity and 2.

[1] Some discussion of the value of making these assumptions is given below. It might be thought that some of them are in some way inconsistent with our aim of estimating *long-term* elasticities. 'Trend factors', for example, must by definition change in the long period. However, all we are really doing is abstracting from the effects of these other changes and concentrating attention on the effects of changes in import and export prices, etc.

[2] It would be more for two reasons. The *relative* quantity change would be a drop of more than 7% because of the more than 1% increase in the price of imports relative to home products. The *absolute* quantity decrease would be greater still, since there would be a fall in the sales of home products on the home market.

price of home-produced manufactures for sale on the home market would not fall so much. Even so, it seems likely that the elasticity of demand would be at least as big as the elasticity of substitution.

The effects of imposing an extra tariff on imports of manufactures averaging 1% *ad valorem* would not be so great as those just discussed. Let us first assume that the supply of imports is infinitely elastic, so that the domestic price would rise by the full 1% of the tariff. In this case there would be no stimulus to exports. Assuming that the government kept manufacturing output stable by cutting home demand for manufactures, it would have to cut to the point at which the average price of home-produced manufactures was unchanged at its original level.[1] The domestic price of imports would then be on average 1% higher than the average price of home products, and the fall in the demand for imports would be 7 %, taking the best estimate on p. 161.

But if the supply of imports were less than perfectly elastic, and if the government stabilized total employment and not just employment in manufacturing, the fall in the demand for imports would be less than 7 %. For the fall in the demand for imports would drive down their price so that the domestic price of imports would not rise by as much as 1%. Furthermore, the cuts in demand would fall partly on non-manufacturing sectors, so that manufacturing output and prices would rise somewhat (prices and output in other sectors of the economy falling in compensation). Hence imports would rise by less than 1% in price relative to home products and so the quantity demanded would fall by less than 7 %.[2]

In order to have some rough idea of the change in imports which

Table 43. *Percentage changes in various items, 1931–2*

Item

1	Volume of United Kingdom imports of manufactures	−44
2	Average value of United Kingdom imports of manufactures	−6
3	*Ad valorem* tariff on imports of manufactures	13
4	Wage rates in United Kingdom	−2
5	United Kingdom industrial production	1
6	Average of wage rates and raw materials prices in United Kingdom	−3
7	Volume of United Kingdom exports of manufactures	3
8	Average value of United Kingdom exports of manufactures	−8
9	Average of wage rates and raw material prices abroad (in £)	13
10	Index of manufacturing production abroad	−13

Sources: See p. 239.

[1] The cut in home demand would then equal the fall in imports.
[2] The two reasons given on p. 167, n. 2, apply here in reverse.

would result from a given change in the tariff, we look at the changes which took place between 1931 and 1932, as set out in Table 43.

The two main factors which might be held responsible for the 44 % fall in imports were the increase in tariffs and the devaluation of the pound. Now while the latter certainly led to a drop in manufacturing costs in the United Kingdom compared with abroad (compare lines 6 and 9 in the table) it may not have had a great effect on imports in the short period considered here. Furthermore, any effect it did have may have been largely offset by the large drop in manufacturing

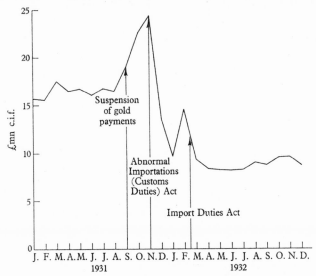

Chart 18. Monthly value of imports of manufactures, 1931–2

production abroad (line 10). This drop would tend to stimulate exports of manufactures to this country and to reduce the demand for imports from it. In fact, the prices of imported manufactures fell (excluding the tariff) in terms of sterling, despite the rise in the sterling costs of foreign manufacturers; also, United Kingdom exports scarcely increased. Hence it may be a fair estimate of the *long-term* effects of a tariff increase on imports, in the circumstances assumed in the previous paragraphs,[1] if we attribute the whole of the *short-term* change in imports from 1931 to 1932 to the increase in tariffs by an average *ad valorem* rate of 13 %. If we do so, the percentage change in imports accompanying an increase of 1 in the percentage *ad valorem* tariff works out at −4·3.[2]

[1] I.e. a constant level of employment at home, a small rise in prices of manufactures at home, a small fall in exports of manufactures, and a fall in import prices of manufactures, excluding the tariff.

[2] For this calculation the rather smaller drop in imports from 1930 to 1932 was

Some may feel that the assumptions on which the estimates in this section are based are unrealistic. If there is a general rise in manufacturing prices abroad, for instance, factor prices at home may be affected, and also raw material prices. Governments do not always maintain a constant level of employment. Nevertheless, it is thought that the estimates are useful. In any particular application of them it may be necessary to allow for the effects of changes in some of the assumptions, but at least a starting point has been given.

3. THE BEHAVIOUR OF TOTAL IMPORTS OF MANUFACTURES IN OTHER PERIODS

In this section we review the behaviour of total imports of manufactures since 1900, apart from the years 1930–5, to see whether it is consistent with there having been a high price elasticity of demand for them.

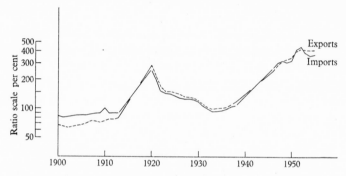

Chart 19. Prices of imports and exports of manufactures, 1900–55

Chart 7 shows the changes which occurred in the quantity of imports compared with the accompanying changes in industrial production.[1] This chart gives a rough indication of the relative movements of the quantities of imports and sales from home production on the home market (a more accurate picture being given by Chart 17, but for only

taken instead of the drop from 1931 to 1932, since the latter exaggerates the fall in imports on account of the rush of importers to beat the tariff at the end of 1931 (see Chart 18). The increase of 13 % in the tariff is that from 1930 to 1935, since the data for the change then are more readily available. The change from 1931 to 1932 is uncertain but was probably smaller, so that the estimated effect of a 1% change in tariffs is understated on this account. We have, then:

$$\Delta \log M, \quad 1930\text{–}2, \ = \ -0.2381$$
$$\Delta \log M^*, \quad 1930\text{–}5, \ = \quad 0.0549$$

$$\therefore \frac{\Delta \log M}{\Delta \log M^*} \ = \ -4.3.$$

[1] For some comments on these, see p. 153.

a part of imports and only since 1924). As well as the changes in relative quantities we need estimates of changes in the relative prices of imports and home sales, but the difficulty here is to find a suitable index of prices of home products. In default of a better one, a price index for exports of manufactures is compared with the price index for imports in Chart 19. No allowance is made for changes in import duties, but these were only substantial in 1932.

A comparison of the relative quantity and relative price changes shows that there were two peace-time periods, 1920–5 and 1946–55, when there were large changes in relative quantities unaccompanied by large changes in relative prices. In other peace-time periods, 1900–13, 1925–30, and 1933–8, both the relative quantity and relative price changes were fairly small (excluding year-to-year changes which might be due to stock changes or other temporary factors such as the strike in 1926). This is consistent with there having been a high price elasticity of substitution between imports and home products.

It is unfortunately impossible to estimate the elasticity of substitution from the data for these years. In the periods in which the relative quantity and price changes were small, the margin of error in the measurement of these changes is of the same order as the changes themselves.

For the period from 1920 to 1925 the only price index for home products is the export price index, and this seems too unreliable, given the small relative price change which occurred. Furthermore, at the start of this period there may have been some unsatisfied demand for imports of manufactures from countries affected by the war, so that the expansion of imports may have been partly due to the removal of this, and not merely to a fall in relative price. Table 44 shows the changing shares of different countries as sources of supply. The rise in the share of the United States, Canada and Japan (all relatively unaffected by the war) from 1913 to 1920 and the fall in the share of the war-affected countries in the same period was followed by a reverse movement from 1920 to 1924.

Table 44. *Percentages of retained imports of manufactures from different countries, 1913, 1920–4*

	1913	1920	1921	1922	1923	1924
Canada, Japan, United States	19	43	33	27	27	27
Austria-Hungary-Czechoslovakia, Belgium, France, Germany	56	22	33	36	39	39
All other countries	25	35	34	37	34	34

Note: The percentages refer to all goods included in Class III of the United Kingdom trade returns.
Source: Annual Statement of Trade.

For the period from 1946 to 1955 the expansion of imports was partly due to the relaxation of import controls. This was also a period in which the demand for imports was influenced by their relative availability. Buyers in this country were prepared to pay substantial premiums to secure steel and other manufactures which were in short supply at home. As a result, imports increased in some years, in both quantity and price, relatively to home products.[1]

Imports also fell sharply in relation to industrial production during the two war periods. The fall from 1938 to 1946 was largely due to import controls and the non-availability of supplies. The fall from 1913 to 1920 must also have been largely due to the non-availability of supplies (see Table 44). Such data as are available suggest that imports rose moderately in price relative to home products over the Second World War, but from Chart 17 it can be seen that there was an appreciable fall in import prices relative to export prices over the First World War. This is puzzling, since it is in the opposite direction to what one would have expected, given the relative fall in the quantity of imports. A possible explanation is that the large shifts in demand and supply which occurred as a result of the war affected particular commodities very differently and that the composition of imports and exports differed sufficiently to lead to the observed marked divergence in their average price movements.[2]

To sum up, although it has proved impossible to measure the price elasticity of demand for imports of manufactures from the data for other periods, our review supports the conclusion derived from the data for 1930–5 that the elasticity is high.

4. SOME OTHER ESTIMATES OF THE PRICE ELASTICITY OF DEMAND FOR IMPORTED MANUFACTURES[3]

In Section 2 we concluded that the price elasticity of demand for imported manufactures, *not* allowing for repercussions on home supply, may be about −6, with a range of possible values extending from −4

---

[1] For further details see pp. 54–5 and p. 183.

[2] See also Appendix I, pp. 203–4. If one reweights the average values for the separate letter groups of exports of manufactures by the values of imports, the following result is obtained for the index of average value in 1920 (1913 = 100)

Index of average value, Class III excluding IIIA, D, O:
United Kingdom exports (as published)   362
United Kingdom exports (reweighted)   314
United Kingdom imports   283

Clearly most of the difference between the changes in the average values of exports and imports from 1913 to 1920 was due to their different composition.

[3] This section discusses other estimates which are considerably smaller than those given in Section 2. Since it was written, J. Wemelsfelder has published estimates of

to −13. These estimates are considerably higher than those suggested by some other workers in this field. For the inter-war years, Chang[1] obtained an estimate of −1·12. Neisser and Modigliani[2] could obtain no satisfactory demand relation covering the whole of the inter-war period on account of the sharp break in 1931–2 which we have already noted. They obtained satisfactory relations for the period before and for that succeeding the introduction of the tariffs, and for these their estimated price elasticities were −1·29 (or −1·63 with a different 'income' variable) and −1·17, that is, they were of the same order as Chang's. Finally, the Federal Reserve Bank of New York's study[3] of United States imports gives estimates for the price elasticity of demand for imports of finished manufactures from Western Europe of the order of −2½. It seems unlikely that the behaviour of these imports should differ very greatly in this respect from that of the United Kingdom's.

In the three studies referred to the typical equation used to explain the demand for imports is of the form:

$$\text{Log (volume imports)} = a + b \log \text{(price index of imports divided by price index of home-produced manufactures)} + c \log \text{(some index of income or activity)}.$$

This is very similar to equation (32), p. 159, and so one would expect the value for b, the price elasticity of demand, to be similar to the value of the price elasticity given above. It is true that Chang and Neisser and Modigliani use somewhat different definitions of manufactures, but this can hardly account for much of the differences between their estimates and the ones given here.[4] What, then, *is* the explanation?

the price elasticity of Germany's demand for imported manufactures, based on a study of the lowering of import duties in Germany in 1956 and 1957. He concludes that 'the cut in import duties on industrial end-products appears to have had a highly stimulating effect on imports. The import [price] elasticity has even been estimated at 8 or 10'. See 'The Short-term Effect of the Lowering of Import Duties in Germany', *Economic Journal*, vol. 70, no. 277, March 1960, p. 102.

[1] Tse Chun Chang, *Cyclical Movements in the Balance of Payments* (Cambridge University Press, 1951), p. 113.

[2] H. Neisser and F. Modigliani, *National Incomes and International Trade* (University of Illinois Press, 1953), pp. 277–80 and p. 288.

[3] J. H. Adler, E. R. Schlesinger and E. van Westerborg, *The Pattern of United States Import Trade since 1923: some new Index Series and their Application* (Federal Reserve Bank of New York, 1952), p. 75.

[4] Chang includes all of Class III in his manufactures, and the value of Class III was about 40 % more in 1935 than that of the manufactured imports included in this study. Neisser and Modigliani's estimates refer to 'substitutable' imports, which exclude wood and timber, oils and fats, resins, and paper and cardboard (*National Incomes and International Trade*, p. 279).

As noted above, Neisser and Modigliani could obtain no satisfactory relation covering the whole period 1924–38. Their two sub-periods, 1924–31 and 1932–8, effectively omit the strongest evidence for a high price elasticity of demand, namely, the great fall in imports from 1931 to 1932. For their first sub-period they used an index of the average value of United Kingdom exports of manufactures as a measure of the price of home-produced manufactures. It is clear from Chart 17 that the divergences between import prices and export prices of manufactures were small over this period (as, indeed, over almost any period) and of the order of only 5 to 7 %. Errors of measurement could appreciably affect them, as also could a chance concentration of supply or demand shifts on particular groups of imports or exports.[1] There is therefore nothing inconsistent in the experience of these years with the view that the group price elasticity of demand is high for widely spread shifts in demand or supply such as would accompany a devaluation or general change in tariffs. But the apparent price elasticity as given by least squares regression does seem inconsistent with the experience of 1931–2. We may therefore dismiss it as due to a combination of special factors which occurred in the two sub-periods under review, and which have no general interest.[2]

Chang, unlike Neisser and Modigliani, appears to have obtained a satisfactory equation to explain the behaviour of imports over the whole period 1924–38. His equation is of the form described above (p. 173), his index of activity being home employment and his price index of home-produced manufactures being 'the index of wholesale prices of manufactured goods'.[3] His multiple correlation coefficient is high, being 0·975 'which means that only 5 per cent of the fluctuations in quantity of imports cannot be explained as connected with variations of employment and prices'.[4] The present writer confesses that this result is a mystery which he has been unable to resolve. In the first place, Neisser and Modigliani, using very similar data, could obtain no satisfactory equation for the whole period. In the second place, an application of Chang's own equation to the change from, say, 1930 to 1933, suggests that it is only consistent if there were an enormous increase in import

[1] See the arithmetical examples in Appendix I, pp. 203–4.

[2] Neisser and Modigliani do not themselves place much reliance on their estimates of the price elasticities. After some discussion they conclude 'Hence, for purely theoretical reasons, we cannot expect our approach (or any other thus far tried) to measure with any great reliability the effects of prices on imports.' (*National Incomes and International Trade*, p. 46.)

[3] Chang, *Cyclical Movements in the Balance of Payments*, p. 113. It is not clear what index Chang can have used for the period 1924–30.

[4] *Ibid.*

prices (inclusive of tariffs)[1] relative to British wholesale prices of manufactures. The new *ad valorem* tariffs imposed in 1932 would apparently have had to be of the order of 100 %, which is absurd.[2]

The estimates of the United States's price elasticity of demand for finished manufactures from Western Europe given in the Federal Reserve Bank of New York's study have been criticized by Liu,[3] who shows *inter alia* that the import price index and the two United States price index numbers for manufactured products used did not diverge significantly from each other during the period under review. The estimated price elasticity does not, therefore, give a reliable measure of the responsiveness of demand to changes in these relative prices.[4]

Liu presents estimates of his own which yield elasticities varying from −0·17 to −4·51.[5] These are short-period (year-to-year) elasticities, and hence probably lower than the long-period ones. Their magnitude is largely determined by the changes which occurred in the three years 1949–50–51. Changes in the ease or difficulty of buying goods were probably of the first importance in the years mentioned.

Upon examination it therefore appears that none of the cited estimates of the group price elasticity of demand for imports of manufactures is at all reliable, at least as an indicator of the medium- to long-run value

[1] Chang does not give his index of import prices inclusive of tariffs and so in the following test of his equation the change in this index is found as a residual.

[2] Chang's equation (*op. cit.*, p. 113) is:

log (quantity of imports of manufactures)
= 1·3942 + 1·4420 log (home employment) − 1·12 log (import prices corrected for tariffs divided by index of wholesale price of manufactured goods).

From 1930 to 1933 we have the following *changes* in the various logarithms:

Volume of retained imports, Class III	−0·3061
Home employment (Chang, p. 103)	−0·0208
Average value of imports, Class III, not corrected for tariffs	−0·1331
Board of Trade wholesale price index of manufactures	−0·0292

Inserting these values in the above equation yields the result that the change in the logarithm of import prices corrected for tariffs *minus* the change in the logarithm of import prices uncorrected = 0·3504. This implies that the tariff changes from 1930 to 1933 in effect multiplied the import index in 1933 (1930 = 100) by 2·24, thus corresponding to an average extra *ad valorem* tariff of over 100 %.

[3] Ta-Chung Liu, 'The Elasticity of U.S. Import Demand: a Theoretical and Empirical Reappraisal', International Monetary Fund *Staff Papers*, vol. 3, no. 3, February 1954, p. 416.

[4] Liu, *Elasticity of U.S. Import Demand*, p. 431.

[5] Liu, p. 441. The formula used by Liu makes the elasticity a function of the size of the change in import prices (which may be realistic) and also inversely proportional to imports. This last property seems a dubious one, since imported manufactures are very small in relation to total sales of manufactures in the United States (compare equation (21) on p. 84, which suggests that if σ is constant, and r is small, changes in r will not significantly affect $\bar{m}_M$, the price elasticity of demand for imports).

of the price elasticity of demand in our equation (32). The same difficulty occurred in all these empirical investigations (except that of Liu), namely, the relative movements of the two price series—the price of imported and of home-produced manufactures—were extremely small. This smallness *may* have been a coincidence, but seems far more likely to have been *due to the fact that the elasticity is really rather high*. Instead of regarding the data as inherently unsatisfactory, we can say that, on the contrary, they provide quite strong evidence of high elasticities. The least-squares technique is likely to be misleading in these circumstances, since small divergences in relative prices can easily occur on account of errors in measurement and chance concentrations of influences on particular types of goods. *These* divergences will accordingly *not* be accompanied by large quantity movements, and the 'best fit' will therefore not be given by an equation with a high price elasticity.[1]

5. SUBSTITUTION BETWEEN INDIVIDUAL IMPORTED AND HOME-PRODUCED MANUFACTURES

The main conclusion which it is the aim of this chapter to establish is that the price elasticity of demand for imported manufactures is high. This may appear to conflict with the well-known view that the market for an individual firm's manufactures is imperfect. It is argued elsewhere[2] that the elasticity of substitution between two large groups of goods is likely to be smaller than between the matched pairs of goods of which the groups are composed, so that the elasticity of substitution between total imports of manufactures and total home-produced sales on the home market is likely to be smaller than that between, say, imported cotton yarn and home-produced sales of cotton yarn on the home market. Hence, if the market for individual manufactures is imperfect, how much more so must be the market for all imports of manufactures! In this section our aim is to show that the elasticity of substitution between individual imported and home-produced manufactures is high, and generally much higher than our estimate for that between total imports and home-produced sales. Besides producing empirical evidence to support this conclusion, we call in the support of those economists who take the view that the market for manufactures is not very imperfect. We also attempt to reconcile our conclusions with the common view of the prevalence of imperfections.

[1] The classic statement of the case against the use of ordinary least-squares techniques to measure price elasticities in foreign trade is that of G. H. Orcutt, 'Measurement of Price Elasticities in International Trade', *Review of Economics and Statistics*, vol. 32, no. 2, May 1950, p. 117.

[2] See Chapter I, p. 6, and Appendix I.

There is a further reason for examining the behaviour of relative quantities and prices of individual manufactures. Our conclusions for the totals rest to a large extent on the experience of the years 1930–5 when a large drop in the quantity of imports was accompanied by only a small rise in their average relative price. This result might have been fortuitous. There might have been some peculiar combination of price movements which led to the *average* price changes in the two totals (imports and home sales) being about the same, even though there were large relative price changes amongst individual pairs of imported and home-produced goods. Hence it is worth examining some individual manufactures to see whether this was so.

The empirical evidence is summarized in Chart 20, showing the changes in relative quantities and relative prices of fifteen manufactures imported and produced at home between certain years. The vertical axis in each diagram shows, on a logarithmic scale, the result of dividing an index of the average value of the imports from foreign countries[1] of the good by an index of the average value of the home-produced good. The average value of imports has been adjusted so as to include tariffs, and thus represents the price to the buyer on the home market. The horizontal axis shows, again on a logarithmic scale, the result of dividing an index of the quantity of imports from foreign countries by an index of the quantity of sales from home production on the home market.[2] The figures are confined to the Census of Production years 1907, 1924, 1930, 1935, 1948, 1951 and 1954, and to the years of the inquiries undertaken under the Import Duties Act, 1933 and 1934. Data for home production for other years are not readily available. Further details of sources and methods used are in Appendix II, pp. 233–4.

The slope of the lines joining any two points in a diagram gives a measure of the apparent price elasticity of substitution between the imported and home-produced good.[3] Since the same scale has been used for the vertical as for the horizontal axis a 45° slope would corres-

[1] 'Foreign countries' here has the special significance given to it in the United Kingdom trade returns. It means, broadly speaking, countries outside the Commonwealth. Goods imported from Commonwealth countries largely escaped the duties imposed in 1932, hence the need for this distinction.

[2] More accurately, the figures for home sales are generally equal to production less exports. They therefore include 'sales' to stock by the producer.

[3] Some writers have pointed out that the slope of a line fitted to points such as those shown in the charts would only give a measure of the price elasticity of substitution in the demand functions under certain special assumptions. It seems probable that these assumptions are at least approximately satisfied for the data given in the charts. For further discussion of this point and references to the writers on it, see Chapter V, p. 83.

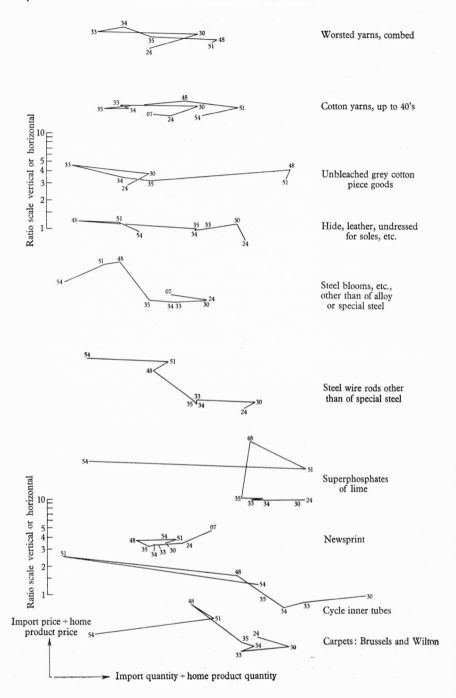

Worsted yarns, combed

Cotton yarns, up to 40's

Unbleached grey cotton
piece goods

Hide, leather, undressed
for soles, etc.

Steel blooms, etc.,
other than of alloy
or special steel

Steel wire rods other
than of special steel

Superphosphates
of lime

Newsprint

Cycle inner tubes

Carpets: Brussels and Wilton

Ratio scale vertical or horizontal

Import price ÷ home
product price

Import quantity ÷ home product quantity

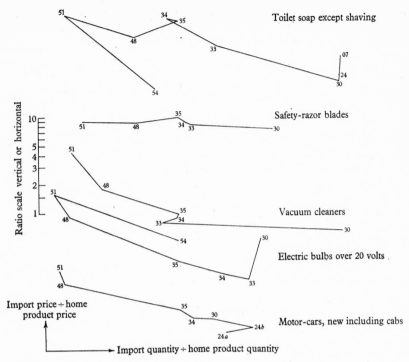

Chart 20. Relative quantities and prices of imports and home products sold on the
home market, census years

pond to an elasticity of 1. Since the relation between imports and home
sales from home production in any particular year could be influenced
on the demand side by erratic factors such as stock changes, and since
neither the quantity nor average value index numbers can claim to give
wholly accurate measurements of quantity and price, particularly
because of changes in quality, we cannot attach any importance to
small differences in the points. The general shape of the scatter of the
points is what matters. Even this, however, only gives us a measure of
the price elasticity of substitution if we can assume that the effects on
demand of changes in the ease or difficulty of buying goods have been
negligible. While this seems a reasonable enough assumption for 1935
and earlier years, it can hardly be true of the post-war years for all
products. In these years we have also to consider the effects of import
controls.

The main conclusion which can be drawn from this evidence is that
some extremely large changes in the relative quantities have occurred,
accompanied by relative price changes which were not nearly so large.

N 2

Some imports increased twenty-fold in relation to home production, for others the relative proportions fell to one-twentieth of what they were, yet relative prices (with some notable exceptions) did not change in anything like these proportions. Several different interpretations of this fact could be given, however, and we consider three which differ from the writer's own, which is that the price elasticity of substitution really is high.

It might be argued, in the first place, that all that these figures show is that foreign manufacturers selling in the United Kingdom market tend to base their prices on those charged by home manufacturers. Given this pricing rule, we must expect to find that relative quantities change much more than relative prices. But this does not mean that if the foreign manufacturer reduced his price by a small amount, and if home manufacturers left their prices unchanged, the foreign manufacturer could increase his sales by a large amount. On the contrary, he would find it difficult to increase his sales because the market is really very imperfect, and he would have to put on a lot of sales pressure to overcome these imperfections.

This view runs into several difficulties. In the first place, it is difficult to see why foreign manufacturers should continue to obey such a rule in the face of a tariff of 10 to $33\frac{1}{3}$ % and at a time when their share in the market was falling drastically. If the market really were very imperfect, the foreign suppliers should, in 1932, have been able to raise their prices by very large amounts[1] and still have been able to sell as much as they did. Nevertheless, they did not raise their prices to this extent, and the only explanation which the writer finds plausible is that they knew that if they did they would lose nearly all their sales. It seems implausible to believe that what governed their actions was a mere rule.

It is even more implausible when one discovers that foreign manufacturers did not in fact always keep their prices in line with those of home producers. For the standardized semi-manufactures, like cotton or woollen yarn, cotton cloth, steel blooms, billets and slabs, wire rods, undressed leather, superphosphate of lime, and newsprint (Chart 20) the relative price movements before the last war were extremely small. But for the less standardized manufactures such as vacuum cleaners,

---

[1] For example, the relative quantity of cotton yarn imported fell by 85 %. If the elasticity of substitution had been only, say, -3, it would have been possible nearly to double the price of imports in relation to the price of the home product. In fact, there was no significant change in the relative price at all. It is true that the 'Buy British' campaign may have been responsible for some of the drop in imports, and, in so far as this was so, the importer could not have raised his price. It seems doubtful whether this was an important factor, however (see also p. 165).

motor-cars and carpets, and for products sold more directly to consumers (cycle tubes, toilet soap and electric light bulbs—but not,
apparently, razor blades) some quite appreciable relative price movements did apparently occur, of the order of 20 to 50 % or even
more. It seems more plausible to believe that the explanation of the
difference between these two groups of products is that in the former
case the markets are more nearly perfect than the latter, rather than
that the former just happen to be served by foreigners who obey the
rule while the latter are supplied by cads who do not.

Instead of postulating a self-imposed pricing rule of the kind just
described, one might seek to explain the evidence in the charts by
reference to international cartels. In the case of electric lamp bulbs,
for instance, it is known that there was an international cartel in existence in 1930–5 which fixed quotas for sales in different markets, including that of the United Kingdom, and whose members sold at agreed
prices.[1] Various factors might have led to changes in the quotas, but
there would be little or no change in the relative prices charged by the
members in a particular market. If cartels were widespread, this might
account for the phenomenon observed of large changes in relative
quantities unaccompanied by large changes in relative prices. Yet this
need not imply that *demand* was sensitive to differences in relative prices.
It would merely show the existence of a well organized cartel.

In fact, however, such cartels often owed their origin to the sensitivity
of demand. Thus the Phoebus Agreement, which was the name given
to the international agreement to determine markets and prices for
electric bulbs, was a successor to previous agreements which had broken
down 'because there were always outside manufacturers to undercut
them', and itself was formed to put a stop 'to what all regarded as the
menace of cut-throat competition'.[2] Hence the existence of cartels
seems to show that demand is sensitive to price rather than the reverse.

A third possible interpretation of the much larger changes in relative
quantities compared with relative prices in Chart 20 is simply that
absolute changes in quantities are usually bigger than absolute changes
in prices. Hence *any* pair of commodities would tend to show the same
result. The relative quantity movements of, say, imported carpets and
imported steel billets would be much greater than their relative price
movements; but one would be foolish to conclude that there was a high
degree of substitutability in demand between carpets and steel billets.

In order to test this interpretation, estimates were made of the
average changes in relative quantity and relative price of every possible

---

[1] See Monopolies and Restrictive Practices Commission, *Report on the Supply of
Electric Lamps* (H.M.S.O. 1951).

[2] Monopolies Commission, *Report on the Supply of Electric Lamps*, p. 20.

pair of the thirty commodities (fifteen imported and fifteen home-produced) from 1930 to 1935. There are 435 such possible pairs. The average chosen (because it lends itself to easy computation) was the square root of the mean square relative quantity or relative price change, the measurements throughout being in logarithms to the base 10.[1] These averages were compared with similar averages for relative changes between imported and home-produced manufactures paired like with like (that is, the relative changes shown in Chart 20) of which there are only fifteen pairs. The results were as follows:

Table 45. *Analysis of relative quantity and price changes for 15 manufactures*

		Average relative quantity change (1)	Average relative price change (2)	Column (1) ÷ Column (2) (3)
		Logarithms to base 10		
1	All possible pairs of goods (435 pairs)	0·635	0·202	3·1
2	Imported and home-produced goods, paired like with like (15 pairs)	0·793	0·186	4·3
3	As for line 2, but only 'intermediate' goods* (8 pairs)	0·537	0·038	14·2
4	As for line 2, but only 'consumer' goods† (7 pairs)	1·008	0·269	3·7

* Unbleached grey cotton piece-goods, steel blooms, etc., hide leather, cotton yarn up to 40's, steel wire rods, newsprint, superphosphates of lime, worsted yarns.

† Cycle inner tubes, vacuum cleaners, electric light bulbs, motor-cars, carpets, safety-razor blades, toilet soap.

Source: Based on data given in S 78–137, described on pp. 233 ff.

The hypothesis is thus at least partially confirmed. Comparing the first and second columns of the table we find that the relative quantity changes were much larger than the relative price changes, no matter how we pair the goods. The ratio of the former to the latter, shown in the last column of the table, gives us a measure of the average elasticity of substitution. Although it is higher when we pair imported and home-

[1] If the logarithm of the quantity of commodity i in 1930 is Qi, its logarithm in 1935 being zero, while Pi is the corresponding logarithm for its price, then the average is:

$$Q_A = \sqrt{\frac{\overset{i,\,j\,=\,n}{\underset{i,\,j\,=\,1}{\Sigma}} (Qi - Qj)^2,\ (i \neq j).}{{}^nC_2}}$$

The expression for P_A is similar. $n = 30$, and ${}^nC_2 = 435$.

produced goods like with like than when we pair them in every con-
ceivable way, it is not much higher (4·3 compared with 3·1). Yet it *is*
considerably higher if we take only the standard 'intermediate' goods
(line 3 of the table). For them, the relative price movements were
comparatively small, and on average the relative quantity movements
were fourteen times as big. It seems fair to conclude that this substantial
difference in behaviour is evidence of a high degree of substitutability
between similar imported and home-produced intermediate products.
As regards the other goods in the sample, it must be admitted that the
evidence is rather inconclusive.[1]

Let us provisionally accept the conclusion that demand is highly
sensitive to changes in relative prices, and see whether this can be
reconciled with all the evidence in Chart 20. The principal apparent
exceptions are the post-war figures for steel blooms, etc., steel wire rods
and superphosphates, and the odd behaviour of electric light bulbs from
1930 to 1933. There are some other cases of odd behaviour, but they are
small enough to be attributed to changes in quality, stock changes and
the like.

The two steel manufactures are interesting since they seem to be clear
examples of the influence of shortages on demand. In the post-war years
home steel prices were controlled. Imports, as the charts show, had
become considerably more expensive than the home products. Nevertheless they were obtainable, whereas at the controlled prices only an
insufficient amount of home-produced supplies could be obtained,
particularly in 1948 and 1951. Consequently, steel consumers were
willing, whether collectively or individually, to pay substantially higher
prices for imported supplies than for home-produced supplies.[2] Im-

---

[1] The relative price changes for toilet soap seem to have been particularly large.
If it is excluded, the average elasticity of substitution for the remaining five 'consumer' goods works out at 6·0, which is quite high. It must also be remembered
that the average values of imports and home products are inadequate measures of
their prices. Errors here would tend to exaggerate the relative price movements for
similar goods (and toilet soap may be an example). If these errors could be removed,
all the ratios in column (3), lines 2, 3 and 4, might be appreciably greater.

[2] The way in which the imports were financed seems to have varied in different
years and for different products. At least up to the middle of 1951 the higher cost of
imported semi-finished steel seems to have been collectively borne by the whole
iron and steel industry, rather than by the individual importer of it. Imported finished
steel was resold at the lower domestic price, the loss being borne by the Exchequer.
In the middle of 1951, however, the Government decided to make the steel industry
bear this second loss, but it, in turn, seems to have been prepared to pass it on, at
least in part, to the individual buyer (see 'The Increase in Steel Prices', British Iron
and Steel Federation, *Monthly Statistical Bulletin*, vol. 26, no. 7, July 1951, p. 1).
However, some steel consumers imported steel on their own account. 'A number of
firms bought steel in Germany, France, Belgium and even Italy. They have got the

ported superphosphates also became more costly after the war in relation to the home product. In this case, consumers of the product
(mainly the farmers) did not have to bear the cost of importing. Indeed,
they received a subsidy even on the home price. The loss from imports
was borne by the Exchequer. An inquiry into the peculiar behaviour of
imports of electric light bulbs from 1930 to 1933 revealed the existence
of two markets for this apparently rather homogeneous commodity in
this country. Competition between these markets does indeed seem to
have been rather imperfect. The first market was that of the chain-store
customer, and bulbs here seem to have sold at substantially lower prices
than elsewhere, though the quality difference is uncertain.[1] The large
relative drop in the price of imports from 1930 to 1933–5 and the
reduction in quantity concealed two very different movements. There
was little change in the relative price of imports from foreign countries
other than Japan, accompanied by a large fall in imports from these
countries (since the tariff and devaluation made sales here less profitable). On the other hand, there was a very large proportionate increase
in imports of cheap Japanese bulbs for sale in the chain stores. This
increase was eventually reversed in 1935 by competition in the same
market from home producers.[2] Within the chain store market, at all
events, competition was not very imperfect.

On the whole, it seems fair to conclude that the evidence in Chart 20
is consistent with the view that the demand for imports of manufactures
is very sensitive with respect to differences in their prices relative to the
prices of similar goods produced in this country. The size of the price
elasticity of substitution depends on the nature of the product. For
standard semi-manufactures like textile yarns and steel it is large,
perhaps −15 or even larger. For more complicated manufactures, or
for goods sold more directly to private persons where branding and
advertising may be more important, the elasticity may be around −5,
but the slopes in the charts for these kinds of products often suggest

steel, though they had to pay two or three times the official British price for it',
Manchester Guardian Review of Industry, Commerce and Finance for 1952, p. 9.
[1] The reader can make the experiment for himself, or else refer to the Monopolies
Commission, *Report on the Supply of Electric Lamps* (1951), p. 42. It is shown there that
the difference between the chain store price and the 'normal' price has narrowed
considerably since before the war. In 1939 some chain store prices were only a third
of the 'normal' prices, and in 1950 about three-quarters as much. On the question
of the quality difference, the report states (p. 63), 'Representatives of one chain store
have told us that in their view the former difference in price did not reflect a corresponding difference in the quality of the lamps and that the price gap between the
two markets was largely artificial. On the other hand E.L.M.A. has stressed to us the
superior quality of its members' lamps.'
[2] Monopolies Commission, *Report on the Supply of Electric Lamps*, pp. 42, 43.

larger elasticities than this. Indeed, most of the steeper slopes, suggesting lower elasticities, occur in the changes over the war years, or in the post-war period (see carpets, vacuum cleaners, electric light bulbs and motor-cars in Chart 20). But here we cannot neglect the effects of shortages and of import controls which (as in the case of steel, mentioned above) made buyers more willing to pay higher prices for marginal supplies.

Sir Donald MacDougall, in his study of British and American exports,[1] concludes that for about 100 manufactured products exported by the United Kingdom and the United States the (unweighted arithmetic) average long-run elasticity of substitution in the *world* market might be of the order -4 to $-4\frac{1}{2}$.[2] This is appreciably lower than the average elasticity of substitution of imported and home-produced manufactures in the United Kingdom market which is suggested by the evidence just considered. However, the two sets of estimates are not necessarily inconsistent. In the first place, MacDougall was concerned to show that earlier estimates of price elasticities of demand or substitution for manufactures in international trade were on the small side, and he tended to be conservative in allowing for possible bias downwards in his estimates so as not to overstate the argument.[3] In the second place, the substitutability of two countries' exports in the *world* market may very well be smaller than the substitutability of the same two countries' sales to a single relatively small and compact market such as the

[1] 'British and American Exports: a Study suggested by the Theory of Comparative Costs', Part I, *Economic Journal*, vol. 61, no. 244, December 1951, p. 697; Part II, *Economic Journal*, vol. 62, no. 247, September 1952, p. 487.

[2] 'British and American Exports,' Part I, *Economic Journal*, December 1951, pp. 720, 724.

[3] Thus MacDougall makes no allowance in his estimates for possible bias due to the fact that the product elasticities of substitution are different for different products. He discusses this source of bias ('British and American Exports', Part II, *Economic Journal*, September 1952, pp. 490–2 and Appendix B, pp. 512–13) and concludes that it would lead to his *under*-estimating the true average product elasticity of substitution provided the 'supply substitution curves' sloped upwards. If these supply substitution curves sloped downwards, the bias would be the other way. In the end he makes no adjustment to his estimates on this account. It seems to the present writer that the fact that the product elasticities of substitution differ for different products might well lead to under-estimation of the average product elasticity of substitution *whatever* the slope of the 'supply substitution curves'. To take an extreme case, suppose that for some products the elasticities of substitution were infinite. Suppose that for all other products there were finite product elasticities of substitution. Then, regardless of the slopes of the 'supply substitution curves', the average product elasticity of substitution as estimated by least squares would be finite. Yet the true arithmetic average product elasticity would be infinite. This argument does not depend on the existence of *infinite* product elasticities of substitution, but would hold so long as some were large.

United Kingdom. The existence of transport costs and specific tariffs would lead to this result; also, the larger and more varied the market, the greater would be the scope for different countries to adapt their exports to the varying demands of other parts of the world. Another contributing factor might be a less perfect knowledge of prices charged in different parts of the world compared with prices in one specific market.

We come now to the second line of argument mentioned above. The view that the markets for manufactured products are, in the main, imperfect has been disputed by several economists. Mr P. W. S. Andrews, after reviewing the nature of the market in which the typical manufacturer sells, and pointing out that his customers are typically businessmen who have a keen and lively interest in buying from the cheapest source (allowing for quality differences), concludes 'In the long run, then, demand is very sensitive to differences in prices, and even a well-established market will give no protection against the competition of those who are able to quote a lower price for the same quality product with the same level of associated services.'[1] Dr H. R. Edwards takes the same view,[2] and Professor Thomas Wilson also throws doubt on the assumption that imperfections are important.[3]

Yet, if the markets are in fact perfect rather than imperfect, how is one to account for the existence and importance of advertising? Or for the fact that firms are usually willing and eager to sell more goods at the existing prices? What is the meaning of 'goodwill'? Why do manufacturers talk about their share of the market, and regard it as something which has been acquired with difficulty? This brings us to the third line of argument, in which we seek to reconcile the undoubted existence of goodwill[4] with the view that markets are rather perfect. The answer seems to be that the 'imperfections' are sufficient to render small price differences ineffective, but not large ones. The fact that one producer's prices are 1 or 2 % lower than another's may lead to virtually no drain of customers from one to the other, while a 5 or 10 % price difference might make them all change after a certain period had elapsed. Now a 5 or 10 % price difference may seem small. In Chart 20 such differences would appear negligible, and the evidence there is certainly

---

[1] *Manufacturing Business* (London, Macmillan, 1949), p. 154.

[2] 'Price Formation in Manufacturing Industry and Excess Capacity', *Oxford Economic Papers* (New Series), vol. 7, no. 1, February 1955, pp. 96–9.

[3] 'The Inadequacy of the Theory of the Firm as a Branch of Welfare Economics', *Oxford Economic Papers*, vol. 4, no. 1, February 1952, pp. 24–6.

[4] None of the writers cited above denies the existence of goodwill. Indeed both Andrews and Edwards stress its importance. See Andrews, *Manufacturing Business*, for example pp. 151–2, and Edwards, 'Price Formation in Manufacturing Industry', *Oxford Economic Papers*, 1955, pp. 95–6.

consistent with the view that these or smaller differences in prices can occur without there being any effects on demand. But a 5 or 10 % reduction in price may be large in relation to a firm's profit margin.[1] Consequently, if the costs of two firms were roughly the same, either of them would probably be unable to afford a price-cut sufficiently large to attract custom away from the other. Hence the imperfections may seem a minor barrier when one is thinking in terms of devaluation or tariffs of 20 % or so, and yet, because they constitute a threshold which is large in relation to profit margins, they may seem an important barrier to the individual firm.

This is not the end of the story. Even if one firm's costs are, say, 5 % lower than another's so that it could cut its prices by enough to draw away all the other's custom, it may be reluctant to do so for fear that the other firm will follow suit and stand the losses long enough to make the ultimate gain to the price-cutting firm seem very uncertain. The writer does not wish to enter into the realms of monopolistic or oligopolistic competition theory here. It is sufficient to make the point that the firm is not just concerned with its demand curve *assuming all other prices are constant* (which is what we have been discussing). It must also take into account the reactions of its competitors and potential competitors to any price changes it may make.[2] This may partly explain price rigidity, the desire to acquire new customers at *existing* prices, and the resort to advertising as an alternative to price cutting.

We conclude, therefore, that there is neither empirical evidence, a consensus of opinion amongst economists, nor a general presumption from common experience to show that elasticities of substitution between individual manufactures are so low as to rule out the possibility that the *group* price elasticities are high.

[1] In 1951 in all manufacturing industries, the cost of materials, fuel, transport payments, wages and salaries accounted for 85 % of the value of gross output, leaving only 15 % to cover depreciation, rents, rates, selling costs, interest charges, and profits. Hence in the typical manufacturing firm, a 5 or 10 % price cut would probably swallow up all its net profits. The percentages given here are obtained by relating the value of net output *less* wages and salaries to the value of gross output for all manufacturing industries as given in the *Annual Abstract of Statistics*, no. 93, 1956, p. 128.

[2] In Triffin's terminology, what we are saying here is that manufacturers are engaged in approximately 'homogeneous competition', rather than in 'heterogeneous competition'. The former is quite compatible with oligopoly, and may be more important in manufacturing than heterogeneous competition and product differentiation, which are often emphasized in economic textbooks. See R. Triffin, *Monopolistic Competition and General Equilibrium Theory*, Harvard Economic Studies, 67 (Harvard University Press, 1947), ch. III.

THE PROBLEM OF GROUPING[1]

I. INTRODUCTION

This study is directly concerned with the behaviour of large groups of goods, and not of individual goods: the same is true of much applied economics. Economic theory, however, often deals with the behaviour of individual persons, goods or firms. There is a natural tendency to regard the behaviour of the individual as in some sense 'fundamental', and hence to seek to relate the behaviour of groups to the behaviour of individuals. It is not suggested that this is a foolish thing to attempt. On the contrary, one's understanding of group behaviour can be greatly increased by such a procedure. But the knowledge gained in this way about *groups* is more likely to be of a qualitative than a quantitative kind. One may hope to discover what kind of causal factors are likely to be important, and in which direction they are likely to work, but not *how large* the effect of a given change in any one of them is likely to be so far as *group* behaviour is concerned. The only practical way of discovering that, at least for large groups, is to study group behaviour. It is one purpose of this appendix to show why this is so, and thus to meet the criticism which might be made of this study—that it fails to consider the behaviour of separate commodities.

Another purpose here is to show why the price elasticities of demand or substitution for groups of goods are likely to be smaller than the average elasticities of the individual goods composing them. This fact makes it necessary to consider a group of imports and a group of home-produced goods as imperfect substitutes for each other, even though they may be composed of goods which are individually perfect substitutes for each other.

Finally, it is hoped to show that it is not unreasonable to treat group elasticities in many respects just as one would treat individual goods elasticities, but that in certain circumstances the group elasticities may change even though the individual elasticities remain constant.

We first of all make an assumption that all prices within any particular group move together, which enables us to attack the problem by simple mathematical methods. This is helpful, because some of the

[1] This is the 'aggregation problem' as it is often called. 'Grouping' saves two syllables.

conclusions we draw are probably more generally applicable. It is shown, however, that this assumption is not likely to be satisfied, so that the attempt to proceed by simple mathematics has to be abandoned. The rest of the argument relies on appeals to intuition and arithmetical examples. This is unsatisfactory, but, as far as the writer knows, satisfactory solutions to the problems raised in this appendix have not yet been found.[1] It is best to consider a concrete example, so most of what follows is concerned with the price elasticity of demand for manufactures. Many of the points made are more generally applicable.

2. GROUPING WHEN ALL PRICES WITHIN GROUPS CHANGE EQUI-PROPORTIONATELY[2]

Using the notation described in Chapter V, suppose that the demand for a particular imported manufactured commodity, q, is given by:

$$M_q = d(\overline{M}_q, \overline{P}_q, \overline{P}_s, \overline{G}, \Upsilon)\dots\dots\dots\dots\dots\dots\dots\dots\dots\dots\dots(A1)$$

Here, M_q and $\overline{M}_q$ are the quantity and price of the import, $\overline{P}_q$ is the price of the nearest substitute produced at home, $\overline{P}_s$ is the price of some other home-produced manufacture which is a fairly close substitute (there may be several), $\overline{G}$ stands for the price of all *non*-manufactures (we use it in this appendix in preference to $\overline{G-H}$ since it is shorter, and since we must use it frequently), and Υ is some income-type variable, such as the index of production. We have omitted taxes and subsidies, and also the effects of changes in the output capacity ratio, so as to simplify matters. For the same reason we ignore all problems raised by lagged effects. The equation is assumed to be of the linear logarithmic form described in Chapter V.

[1] See, for example, W. Leontief's remarks that 'The theoretical conditions for admissible aggregation thus far derived are so stringent that their consistent application would have put under ban most of the simple statistical general equilibrium models. The entire question is, however, still wide open' (p. 410 of 'Econometrics' in *A Survey of Contemporary Economics*, edited by H. S. Ellis, Philadelphia, Blakiston, 1948). Professor Leontief gives references to some theoretical discussions. When it comes to practice, econometricians such as L. R. Klein, J. Tinbergen and the various writers cited on pp. 173 and 175 in effect side-step the issues involved.

Professor R. G. D. Allen discusses the problems involved in his *Mathematical Economics* (London, Macmillan, 1956), ch. 20, basing his analysis on H. Theil's *Linear Aggregation of Economic Relations*, Contributions to Economic Analysis, 7 (Amsterdam, North-Holland Publishing Company, 1954). So far as the writer can judge, Professor Allen's conclusion seems to be that what he calls 'perfect aggregation' could only be achieved if all the changes in the micro-variables, and if all the micro-parameters, were known. And even then the necessary computations would be quite beyond the powers of any computers in existence. Clearly, 'perfect aggregation' is an impracticable ideal.

[2] The conclusions of this section are summarized on p. 195.

We have as many of these equations as there are different imported manufactures, and we also have similar equations for the demand for home-produced manufactures. Our aim is to obtain a single demand equation for imported manufactures as a group, and another for home-produced manufactures as a group. In this part of our argument we assume that all $\Delta \log \bar{M}_q$ are equal, and that all $\Delta \log \bar{P}_q$ are equal (although $\Delta \log \bar{M} \neq \Delta \log \bar{P}$).

Since $\Delta \log \bar{P}_q = \Delta \log \bar{P}_s$, we may combine these terms in (A1), and the corresponding combined elasticity, which we may call $\bar{p}'_{q \cdot Mq}$, is equal to the sum of the two elementary elasticities in (A1), i.e.

$$\bar{p}'_{q \cdot Mq} = \bar{p}_{q \cdot Mq} + \bar{p}_{s \cdot Mq} \cdots \cdots \cdots \cdots \cdots \cdots \cdots \cdots \cdots \cdots \cdots \cdots \cdots (A2)$$

Let us now define r_q and σ_q in the same way as in equations (20) and (18) of Chapter V, so that

$$r_q = \frac{M_q}{P_q},$$

$$\sigma_q = \frac{\Delta \log M_q - \Delta \log P_q}{\Delta \log \bar{M}_q - \Delta \log \bar{P}_q} \text{ (which is negative)}.$$

Merging the P's together as described above, and so treating all home-produced manufactures as effectively one good in equation (A1), alters the appropriate values for r_q and σ_q. We now have

$$r'_q = \frac{M_q}{\Sigma(P_q)}.$$

And, using the result established by equation (21) of Chapter V,

$$\sigma'_q = \bar{m}_{q \cdot Mq}(1 + r'_q) + r'_q \cdot \bar{g}_{Mq} \cdots \cdots \cdots \cdots \cdots \cdots \cdots \cdots (A3)$$

Now r'_q is clearly very small, and $\bar{g}_{Mq}$ is also probably small. Hence we may put

$$\sigma'_q \backsimeq \bar{m}_{q \cdot Mq}.$$

But, using the same result as before (equation (21)),

$$\sigma_q = \bar{m}_{q \cdot Mq}(1 + r_q) + r_q(\bar{g}_{Mq} + \bar{p}_{s \cdot Mq}) \cdots \cdots \cdots \cdots \cdots \cdots (A4)$$

Hence from the last two equations we have

$$\sigma'_q = \frac{\sigma_q}{1 + r_q} - \frac{r_q(\bar{g}_{Mq} + \bar{p}_{s \cdot Mq})}{1 + r_q} \cdots \cdots \cdots \cdots \cdots \cdots \cdots \cdots (A5)$$

Equation (A5) enables us to place limits on the value of σ'_q in terms of σ_q. First, σ'_q cannot be arithmetically greater than σ_q. For $\bar{g}_{Mq} + \bar{p}_{s \cdot Mq}$ must be positive so long as M_q is a substitute, and not a complement, of all goods taken together other than P_q. Furthermore, $\bar{g}_{Mq} + \bar{p}_{s \cdot Mq}$

cannot be arithmetically greater than σ_q.[1] Hence the right-hand side of (A5) may be re-written so that

$$\sigma'_q = \frac{\sigma_q}{1+r_q}\left\{1+r_q \cdot A\right\},$$

where A is positive and arithmetically no greater than one $(A = -(\bar{g}_{Mq} + \bar{p}_{s} \cdot {}_{Mq}) \div \sigma_q)$. From this it clearly follows that σ'_q cannot be arithmetically greater than σ_q.

σ'_q reaches its greatest arithmetic value, which is σ_q, either when r_q is very small, or when A in the above expression equals one. For the latter to occur, $\bar{p}_q \cdot {}_{Mq}$ must $= 0$ (see fn. 1 below). But A will approach one if $\bar{p}_{s} \cdot {}_{Mq}$ is large in relation to $\bar{p}_q \cdot {}_{Mq}$. The economic significance of this is that σ'_q will be nearly as big as σ_q either if imports are small in relation to their home-produced nearest substitutes, or if there are plenty of other close substitutes produced at home as well.

σ'_q has its smallest arithmetic value when $A = 0$, i.e. when $\bar{g}_{Mq} + \bar{p}_{s \cdot Mq} = 0$. In this event, all the pairs of imported and home-produced manufactures are completely distinct, having no substitutes amongst other goods (manufactures or non-manufactures). Hence, algebraically:

$$\frac{\sigma_q}{1+r_q} \geqslant \sigma'_q \geqslant \sigma_q \dots\dots\dots\dots\dots\dots \text{(A6)}$$

So far we have only considered the demand for a single imported commodity. To obtain an equation for all imports as a group, we may re-write equation (A1) in the form of logarithmic changes (e.g. as in equation (2) in Chapter V), multiply by M_q, sum the equations for all the different imports (q's), and finally divide by the sum of imports. This gives:

$$\frac{\Sigma(M_q \, \Delta \log M_q)}{\Sigma(M_q)} = \frac{\Sigma(M_q \cdot \bar{m}_q \cdot {}_{Mq})}{\Sigma(M_q)} \cdot \Delta \log \bar{M}$$

$$+ \frac{\Sigma(M_q \cdot \bar{p}'_q \cdot {}_{Mq})}{\Sigma(M_q)} \cdot \Delta \log \bar{P}$$

[1] We have (cf. equation (8) in Chapter V):

$$\bar{m}_{q \cdot Mq} + \bar{p}_{q \cdot Mq} + \bar{p}_{s \cdot Mq} + g_{Mq} = 0.$$

In this equation, $\bar{m}_{q \cdot Mq}$ is negative, and the other elasticities almost certainly all positive or zero. Hence $\bar{g}_{Mq} + \bar{p}_{s \cdot Mq} \leqslant -\bar{m}_{q \cdot Mq}$.

We also have (cf. equation (A4)):

$$\sigma_q = \bar{m}_{q \cdot Mq} + r_q(\bar{m}_{q \cdot Mq} + \bar{g}_{Mq} + \bar{p}_{s \cdot Mq}).$$

Hence $-\sigma_q \geqslant -\bar{m}_{q \cdot Mq}$.

Hence $-\sigma_q \geqslant \bar{g}_{Mq} + \bar{p}_{s \cdot Mq}$, which proves the proposition in the text.

$$+ \frac{\Sigma(M_q \cdot \bar{g}_{Mq})}{\Sigma(M_q)} \cdot \varDelta \log \bar{G}$$

$$+ \frac{\Sigma(M_q \cdot y_{Mq})}{\Sigma(M_q)} \cdot \varDelta \log \Upsilon \ldots\ldots\ldots\ldots\ldots \text{(A7)}$$

The term on the left-hand side of (A7) is approximately the same (if the changes are small) as the change in the logarithm of total imports at constant prices.

The first three terms on the right-hand side are three changes in the logarithms of prices multiplied by three weighted averages of elasticities, the weights being the M_q's. It is these weighted average elasticities which we are concerned to measure. Our task is to see how these elasticities of substitution or demand for a *group* of imports of manufactures are related to the individual elasticities of substitution, or demand.[1]

Our first weighted average price elasticity in equation (A7) is

$$\frac{\Sigma(M_q \cdot \bar{m}_q \cdot_{Mq})}{\Sigma(M_q)} = \frac{\Sigma(M_q \cdot \sigma'_q)}{\Sigma(M_q)}.$$

which we may call $\bar{m}_M^*$ (we denote all the *group* elasticities by asterisks in this fashion).

If we now write $\sigma = \dfrac{\Sigma(M_q \sigma_q)}{\Sigma(M_q)}$, as the weighted average elasticity of substitution between the individual imports and their home-produced nearest substitutes, then it is clear that the maximum arithmetic value for $\bar{m}_M^*$ is σ, and, as we have seen, this is approached either when all the imports are small in relation to the home-produced supplies of the nearest substitutes, or when there are plenty of other close substitutes produced at home.

It also follows from (A6) that the smallest arithmetic value for $\bar{m}_M^*$ is given by

$$\bar{m}_M^* \geqslant \frac{\Sigma\left\{\dfrac{M_q \sigma_q}{1+r_q}\right\}}{\Sigma(M_q)} \quad \text{which} = \frac{\sigma \cdot \Sigma\left\{\dfrac{M_q}{1+r_q}\right\}}{\Sigma(M_q)}$$

if we assume that σ_q is uncorrelated with either M_q or with $\dfrac{M_q}{1+r_q}$ (this assumption seems reasonable; it implies that σ is also the simple

[1] The following analysis owes much to that given by Sir Donald MacDougall in 'British and American Exports: a Study suggested by the Theory of Comparative Costs. Part II', *Economic Journal*, September 1952, pp. 513–15.

unweighted average of the σ_q's). This minimum value occurs when the various pairs of imported and home-produced goods have no substitutes amongst other goods at all. In order to relate $\overline{m}_M{}^*$ to the other group elasticities we need to assume that

$$\frac{\Sigma(M_q \cdot \overline{g}_{Mq} \cdot \varDelta \log \overline{G})}{\Sigma(M_q)} = \frac{\Sigma(P_q \cdot \overline{g}_{Pq} \cdot \varDelta \log \overline{G})}{\Sigma(P_q)}$$

and

$$\frac{\Sigma(M_q \cdot y_{Mq} \cdot \varDelta \log \varUpsilon)}{\Sigma(M_q)} = \frac{\Sigma(P_q \cdot y_{Pq} \cdot \varDelta \log \varUpsilon)}{\Sigma(P_q)}.$$

These assumptions amount to saying that neither the price changes of non-manufactures ($\varDelta \log \overline{G}$), nor the 'income' changes ($\varDelta \log \varUpsilon$) favour or disfavour imported as compared with home-produced manufactures. It is only if we make these assumptions that we can use the relation between the group elasticity of substitution and the group elasticity of demand similar to equation (A3). But granted these, and because of our assumption that the price changes are uniform within the groups, we can treat the groups just as if they were single goods,[1] so that equations similar to (8), (9), (19) and (21) all hold.

Defining

$$r^* = \frac{\Sigma(M_q)}{\Sigma(P_q)},$$

$$\sigma^* = \frac{\dfrac{\Sigma(M_q \varDelta \log M_q)}{\Sigma(M_q)} - \dfrac{\Sigma(P_q \varDelta \log P_q)}{\Sigma(P_q)}}{\dfrac{\Sigma(M_q \varDelta \log \overline{M}_q)}{\Sigma(M_q)} - \dfrac{\Sigma(P_q \varDelta \log \overline{P}_q)}{\Sigma(P_q)}},$$

$$\overline{g}_M{}^* = \frac{\Sigma(M_q \cdot \overline{g}_{Mq})}{\Sigma(M_q)},$$

we have

$$\sigma^* = \overline{m}_M{}^*(1+r^*)+r^*\overline{g}_M{}^*.$$

If we neglect $r^*\overline{g}_M{}^*$, which is likely to be very small, and using our maximum and minimum values for $\overline{m}_M{}^*$, we have

$$\sigma\left[\frac{\Sigma\left\{\dfrac{M_q}{1+r_q}\right\}\cdot(1+r^*)}{\Sigma(M_q)}\right] \geqslant \sigma^* \geqslant \sigma(1+r^*).$$

[1] See J. R. Hicks, *Value and Capital*, 2nd ed. (Oxford, The Clarendon Press, 1946), p. 33.

Since r^* is small, we may safely replace the right-hand side by σ alone. The term in the square brackets is the same as Sir Donald MacDougall's 'index of similarity'[1] and we may call it S. Hence we may re-write the above inequalities as

$$S \, \sigma \geqslant \sigma^* \geqslant \sigma \dots\dots\dots\dots\dots\dots\dots\dots\dots\dots\dots\dots\dots\dots (A8)$$

The value of S depends on the uniformity with which imports are distributed in relation to home sales. If imports were always the same proportion of home sales for each and every good, then $r_q = r^*$ and $S = 1$. Hence in this case σ^* must $= \sigma$. If there were *no* home-produced manufacture corresponding to imports, $r_q = \infty$, and the value of S becomes zero. In fact, the value of S depends on the definitions one uses for 'a commodity'. This may appear to lead to the absurd conclusion that $S\sigma$ is quite arbitrary since one could in principle call every import a different commodity from every home-produced good, and so make S zero, or else one could group them all together and call them 'manufactures', in which case $S = 1$. In fact, however, although S is arbitrary, $S\sigma$ is not. The finer the commodity detail, the smaller in general is S and the larger (arithmetically) is σ. The values for σ in Chart 20 were found using a certain degree of refinement of commodity classification (roughly speaking, the degree was as fine as was made possible by the Censuses of Production or the Trade and Navigation Accounts, whichever was the cruder). Using about the same degree of refinement, S in 1935 turns out to be about 0·7.[2]

A further point to remember is that the finer our commodity detail,

---

[1] 'British and American Exports', Part II, *Economic Journal*, September 1952, p. 515.

If we call MacDougall's $Va = M_q$ and his $V_b = P_q$, then his $A = \dfrac{r_q}{1+r_q}$ and his

$B = \dfrac{1}{1+r_q}$. Substituting in his formula for the index of similarity,

i.e.

$$\left[\frac{\Sigma V_a B}{\Sigma V_a} + \frac{\Sigma V_b A}{\Sigma V_b} \right],$$

we get

$$\left[\frac{\Sigma \left\{ \dfrac{M_q}{1+r_q} \right\}}{\Sigma(M_q)} + \frac{\Sigma \left\{ \dfrac{P_q r_q}{1+r_q} \right\}}{\Sigma(P_q)} \right].$$

But $P_q r_q = M_q$, and $\Sigma(P_q) \cdot r^* = \Sigma(M_q)$.

Substituting in the square brackets then gives us the result stated above.

[2] This calculation is based on Dr T. Barna's working sheets used in the construction of his input-output matrix (published in the *Journal of the Royal Statistical Society*, vol. 115, part 1, 1952, under the title 'The Interdependence of the British Economy'). Altogether some 450 different manufactured imports were distinguished. See also Table 41, p. 156.

the larger is $\bar{p}_s \cdot {}_{Mq}$ likely to be. If, for example, we distinguish between luminous watches and non-luminous watches, then the $\bar{p}_s \cdot {}_{Mq}$ for each of these (i.e. the price elasticity of demand for imports with respect to changes in the prices of goods other than its own kind) is likely to be higher than if we lump them together. But, as we saw above (p. 191), the larger is $\bar{p}_s \cdot {}_{Mq}$ the more nearly does σ' approach σ, and the further is it removed from its lower (arithmetic) limit which determines $S\sigma$. Hence, even if increasing commodity refinement reduces S, and $S\sigma$, it makes $S\sigma$ a less and less probable limit. This point has the corollary that the greater we believe the substitutability of one manufacture for another to be, the higher (arithmetically) must we put σ^*.

We may summarize the conclusions reached in this section as follows:

(1) We can relate the simple totals of imports and home-produced sales to price changes and 'income' changes by means of demand equations similar to (A1).

(2) In these equations, the elasticities for the groups are the weighted averages of the elasticities for the individual goods in the groups, the weights being the values of the goods.

(3) These group price elasticities are related to each other in the same way as the individual good elasticities, i.e. as in equations (8), (9), (19) and (21) in Chapter V.

(4) These group price elasticities are related to the individual ones in a way which depends on the uniformity with which imports are distributed, and also on the degree of substitutability of one manufacture for another. The more uniformly are imports distributed, and the more closely substitutable is one manufactured good for another, the larger (arithmetically) become the group price elasticities in relation to the individual ones. Nevertheless, the group price elasticities can never be greater (arithmetically) than the individual ones and they will generally be smaller.

(5) Some calculations based on 1935 data suggest that if the typical elasticity of substitution between an imported manufacture and the home-produced article is σ using a commodity classification about as fine as that in Chart 20, then the group elasticity of substitution between all imported manufactures taken together and all home-produced manufactures sold on the home market, σ^*, lies between σ and $0 \cdot 7 \ \sigma$.

In what follows we shall give reasons for rejecting the second of the above conclusions, and for modifying the first, fourth and fifth. For the most part, however, we shall assume that these conclusions still hold even though the assumptions on which they are based do not. We cannot justify this assumption except by appeals to intuition, and by some arithmetical examples.

3. IS THE ASSUMPTION ABOUT UNIFORM PRICE CHANGES JUSTIFIED?

We must now consider whether the assumption made above, that price changes within each particular commodity group are the same, can be justified. It is obviously true that in the past the price changes have not been the same. We might avoid the difficulty if we could assume that the actual price changes were not correlated with the various price elasticities. For example, if the price changes of different imports were different, we should have to write the first term in equation (A7) as

$$\frac{\Sigma(M_q \cdot \overline{m}_q \cdot {}_{Mq} \cdot \varDelta \log \overline{M}_q)}{\Sigma(M_q)}.$$

If we could make the assumption just mentioned, and if the change in the logarithm of the price index for imports is given by

$$\frac{\Sigma(M_q \cdot \varDelta \log \overline{M}_q)}{\Sigma(M_q)},$$

then we could simply replace $\varDelta \log \overline{M}$ in equation (A7) by this change in the price index, and proceed as before.

If, however, $\overline{m}_q \cdot {}_{Mq}$ and $\varDelta \log \overline{M}_q$ are correlated, then we cannot do this. Now in general it seems probable that they *will* be correlated. Suppose, for example, that the only change which occurs is that the supply curves of all imported manufactures shift to the right in the same proportion. Suppose further that σ_q is the same for all manufactured imports. Finally, suppose that the price elasticity of supply of home manufactures for sale on the home market is the same for all manufactures. It is probably clear, intuitively, that the prices of those manufactures will be furthest depressed for which imports provide the greatest share of total sales on the home market. In other words, $\varDelta \log \overline{M}_q$ will be greatest (arithmetically) where r_q is greatest. But from equation (A4) it follows that $\overline{m}_q \cdot {}_{Mq}$ is likely to be arithmetically smaller the greater is r_q. Hence, $\overline{m}_q \cdot {}_{Mq}$ and $\varDelta \log \overline{M}_q$ are likely to be inversely correlated. The greater price changes are likely to be associated with the smaller price elasticities.[1]

The effect of this inverse correlation is likely to be that the observed quantity change for the group which is thought to be due to an observed

[1] Cf. G. H. Orcutt, 'Measurement of Price Elasticities in International Trade', *Review of Economics and Statistics*, May 1950, p. 125.

change in the price index for the group will be *smaller* than the quantity change which we should get if we multiplied the observed price change by the weighted average of the price elasticities for the individual goods. This means that if we were to use an equation like (A7) to forecast the demand for imports, and if we were to calculate our price elasticities for the groups by taking the weighted averages of the individual price elasticities as is done there, then we might very well over-estimate the extent of the effect on the demand for total imports of a given change in the price *index* of imports.[1] This suggests that we should not use simple weighted averages of individual price elasticities for our group elasticities, but rather something smaller.[2]

The same conclusion is reached if we consider the following hypothetical example. Suppose that the individual σ's were all $-\infty$, so that each imported good had a perfect home-produced substitute (Chart 20 suggests that this is not far from the truth for some imported semi-manufactures). Suppose now that, as previously, all the import supply curves shift by the same proportionate amount to the right, and that the other assumptions made above also hold. Then, as before, where r_q is greatest the price fall will be greatest. Hence, although for each separate commodity the prices of the import and of the home-produced substitute change equally, for all imports taken together the price index will not generally change in the same proportion as the

[1] Orcutt, 'Measurement of Price Elasticities' (*Review of Economics and Statistics*, May 1950) suggests that if the price change were due to devaluation, and if supply elasticities were infinite, since all import prices would fall to the same extent, the above sort of calculation would *not* overstate the effect on the quantity demanded. This is true, but only if the assumption of perfectly elastic supply curves be granted.

[2] It also suggests that total elasticity of substitution, σ^*, may in fact be arithmetically *smaller* than the lower limit σ suggested on p. 194 and in conclusion 5 on p. 195. Sir Donald MacDougall, after showing that the total elasticity of substitution is related to the product elasticity via the index of similarity, S, on similar assumptions to those mentioned above (i.e. uniform price changes within groups, and $\overline{g}_{M_q} + \overline{p}_{s \cdot M_q} = 0$), and after showing that the total elasticity would be larger if $\overline{g}_{M_q} + \overline{p}_{s \cdot M_q} > 0$, says that allowances should be made for other factors, such as varying elasticities of substitution from product to product, and varying changes in price according to elasticity of supply. He concludes, 'Further adjustments of this kind might tend to increase or to decrease the value of the total elasticity, but the author has been unable to think of any obvious reasons for such bias'. (See 'British and American Exports', Part II, *Economic Journal*, September 1952, p. 496.) For the reasons given above it seems probable that further adjustment might in fact tend to *reduce* the total elasticity of substitution in relation to the typical product elasticity. On the other hand, Sir Donald MacDougall's estimates of the typical product elasticity are, in the writer's opinion, probably conservative (i.e. arithmetically on the small side) for the reasons given on p. 185. Hence his conclusions on the probable size of the total elasticity of substitution between British and American exports are not necessarily biased upwards.

price index of sales from home production. In fact, the import price index will generally *fall* relatively to the home sales price index, for the price fall is greatest where r_q, and therefore M_q in relation to P_q, is greatest. The quantity of imports will also rise but only by a finite amount, since home supply is not infinitely elastic and home producers match the importer's price cuts, albeit at a lower level of sales. Hence there will be a finite fall in the price index of imports accompanied by a finite increase in the quantity index. In short, there will be a finite *group* price elasticity of demand. Yet were we to take the weighted average of the individual price elasticities we should get an infinite price elasticity of demand.[1]

4. EFFECTIVE GROUP PRICE ELASTICITIES

There seems to be no help for it; we must abandon the assumption that price changes are uniform or not correlated with our other variables, and we must also abandon the weighted average price elasticities in equation (A7). It is clear that the actual group price elasticities will depend not only on the same factors as the weighted average ones, but also on the composition of the supply or demand shifts which occur at any particular time. There seems to be some presumption that they will be smaller than the weighted average price elasticities, but apart from that there is nothing much one can say about them *a priori*. Worst of all, there seems to be no reason why they should be constant, even if the individual price elasticities are, so that they may be quite useless concepts.

Some grounds for avoiding this gloomy conclusion are given by the arithmetical examples set out below. In these we try to produce a model which has some similarities to the conditions prevailing in 1930–5. There are only four different kinds of manufactures in this model, as opposed to the hundreds in reality. Inspection of the data used for Table 41 showed that in 1935 imports could be divided into two groups of roughly equal size: fairly homogeneous intermediate goods (such as steel or textile semi-manufactures, leather, some chemicals, paper, etc.) and other goods (such as machinery, instruments, clothing, vehicles) whose quality could not be easily specified, or which were sold more directly to final personal consumers. The first group are probably closer substitutes for their home-produced opposite numbers than are the second group (see Chart 20 and p. 182). Within each group in 1935 the distribution in relation to similar home-produced goods sold on the home market was very like that for total imports, as shown in Table 41

---

[1] The writer has made some calculations which suggest that on not implausible assumptions the effective group elasticity might be of the order of -10 even though the weighted average was $-\infty$.

on p. 156. This distribution was very crudely represented in our model by taking one high and one low value for r (the ratio of imports to home-produced sales on the home market), such that the average value of r_a for all imports taken together (i.e. $\Sigma(M) \div \Sigma(P) = r^*$, p. 193) was about the same as in 1935 and also the value of the index of similarity (see p. 194) was about the same.[1] The four kinds of manufactures were therefore assumed to be as follows in the notional year 1935:

Number	M	P	r	σ
1	40	800	0·05	−20
2	40	800	0·05	−5
3	40	40	1·00	−20
4	40	40	1·00	−5

For each of these manufactures there were the two demand equations set out in Chapter VIII (equations (32) and (33)).

Two supply equations were also assumed, so that the four equations determining the changes in the quantities demanded or supplied of any particular import (M) or its home-produced substitute (P) were as follows:

$$\Delta \log M = \overline{m_M} . \Delta \log \overline{M} . M^* + \overline{p_M} . \Delta \log \overline{P}$$
$$+ \overline{g\text{-}h_M} . \Delta \log \overline{G\text{-}H} + \overline{y_M} . \Delta \log \Upsilon \dots\dots\dots\dots\dots (\text{A}9)$$
$$\Delta \log P = \overline{p_P} . \Delta \log \overline{P} + \overline{m_P} . \Delta \log \overline{M} . M^*$$
$$+ \overline{g\text{-}h_P} . \Delta \log \overline{G\text{-}H} + \overline{y_P} . \Delta \log \Upsilon \dots\dots\dots\dots\dots (\text{A}10)$$
$$\Delta \log M = \overline{m_S} . \Delta \log \overline{M} + \overline{w_{M.S}} . \Delta \log \overline{W}_M$$
$$+ \Delta S_M \dots\dots\dots\dots\dots\dots\dots\dots\dots\dots\dots\dots\dots\dots (\text{A}11)$$
$$\Delta \log P = \overline{p_S} . \Delta \log \overline{P} + \overline{w_{P.S}} . \Delta \log \overline{W}_P + \Delta S_P \dots\dots\dots\dots (\text{A}12)$$

In the two demand equations, (A9) and (A10), the symbols have the same meanings as in Section 2(a) of Chapter VIII (except that P is used instead of P_C). In the two supply equations, (A11) and (A12), $\overline{W}_M$ and $\overline{W}_P$ are index numbers of costs (wages and raw materials) of factors similar to those used by foreign and domestic manufacturers respectively. S_M and S_P stand simply for factors shifting the supply curves of imports and home-produced manufactures for sale on the home market respectively. The various parameters in the demand equations were assumed to be related to each other in the ways described in Chapter V, Section 2. For the supply equations, it was assumed that

$$\overline{w_{M.S}} < -\overline{m_S}$$
$$\overline{w_{P.S}} < -\overline{p_S}.$$

The reason for assuming these inequalities, instead of equalities (so that

[1] In fact, the value for r^* was 0·095 in the model as compared with 0·085 actual, and the value of S was 0·80 as compared with 0·73.

the two price elasticities would sum to zero in each equation, as in equation (23) p. 87), is briefly this. The assumption implies, for instance, that an equal proportionate increase in the price of imports and in manufacturing costs abroad, *ceteris paribus*, will lead to an increase (instead of no change) in the supply of imports. This seems plausible, because the increase in manufacturing costs abroad will tend to reduce the demand for and sales of manufactures produced abroad, other than those produced for sale in the United Kingdom. Resources will then tend to flow into production for export to the United Kingdom, that is, the supply of imports will tend to rise. Likewise, an equal proportionate increase in the prices of manufactures sold from home production in the home market and in home manufacturing costs will tend to stimulate such sales, since exports of manufactures will tend to fall and so the resources will be re-directed to producing for the home market.

One of the simplifications made in the model departs significantly from reality; this is the assumption that each type of manufacture is independent of all others (thus, for example, there is no term in equation (A9) to show that the demand for imports of one manufacture is affected by changes in the price of any other, apart from the home-produced substitute). It would have made the model very complex if we had allowed for interdependence; but as it is, without this allowance the behaviour of different goods is made to appear more varied than it would in fact be. In reality, substitution on both the demand and supply sides would tend to prevent divergent movements in prices and quantities.

The values for those parameters which were not directly related to r or σ were assumed to be the same for each good, and were within the ranges estimated in Chapter VIII. They may therefore be described as plausible values for those parameters and at least consistent with the experience of 1930–5. They were as follows:

$$\overline{g-h_M} = \overline{g-h_P} = \quad 0 \cdot 5 \quad \text{(price elasticity of demand with respect to non-manufactures),}$$

$$\overline{p_S} \qquad\qquad = \quad 1 \quad \text{(price elasticity of supply of home manufactures),}$$

$$\overline{w_{P.S}} \qquad\qquad = -0 \cdot 8 \quad \text{(elasticity of supply with respect to changes in home costs),}$$

$$\overline{m_S} \qquad\qquad = \quad 5 \quad \text{(price elasticity of supply of imports),}$$

$$\overline{w_{M.S}} \qquad\qquad = -4 \quad \text{(elasticity of supply of imports with respect to changes in foreign costs).}$$

All the other parameters were either regarded as exogenous factors or else could be calculated from the assumed values for r, σ and $\overline{g-h}$, e.g. by using equation (A4).

Our first trial run for the model was to insert values for the various changes in the exogenous factors (home factor costs, shifts in demand and supply curves) calculated by applying the above model and parameters to the change from 1930 to 1935. These exogenous changes were as follows:

$$\Delta \log M^* = 0\cdot0487^1$$
$$\Delta \log \overline{G\text{-}H} = -\ 0\cdot0132$$
$$y\ .\ \Delta \log \Upsilon = 0\cdot0607$$
$$\Delta \log \overline{W}_P = -\ 0\cdot0320$$
$$\Delta S_P = 0\cdot1906$$
$$\Delta \log \overline{W}_M = 0\cdot0434$$
$$\Delta S_M = 0\cdot4836$$

Most of these values are taken directly from Table 42. $y\ .\ \Delta \log \Upsilon$ is 15 % [2] ΔS_P and ΔS_M were calculated from the estimates referred to on p. 166.

Given all these parameters and exogenous changes, the changes in the quantity and price of imports and home-produced sales on the home market for each of the four goods could be calculated.[3] Consequently, the index numbers of quantity and average value for the four imports as a group, and the four home-produced sales as a group, could also be calculated. From these it was possible to calculate an 'observed' or 'effective' σ^*, which was simply the relative change in the index numbers of quantities for the two groups divided by the relative change in the corresponding index numbers of average values. This effective σ^* worked out at $-4\cdot9$, and taken in conjunction with the (mean) value of r^* gave a value of $-4\cdot4$ for $\overline{m}_M{}^*$ for the group.[4] It is interesting to

[1] In Table 42 the corresponding value for $\Delta \log M^*$ is $-0\cdot0414+0\cdot0964$ (line 4 minus line 3) which $= 0\cdot0550$, instead of the $0\cdot0487$ taken here, which was from an earlier, unrevised, version of the table.

[2] Compare the implied 16 % effect of the change in the income-type variable from 1930 to 1935, on p. 162.

[3] In these calculations, it was desirable for the reasons given on p. 84 to use the *average* values for r over the period, and not the values in '1935' or '1930'. It was necessary, therefore, to proceed by successive approximations. In fact, only two trials were sufficient to get very close approximations.

[4] This is a lower price elasticity than the best guess of -6 on p. 162 of Chapter VIII. The actual fall in the volume of imports from 1930 to 1935 was 33 % (Table 42), whereas in our model it works out at only 27 %. One reason for these differences may be that the actual σ's are higher than assumed in the model. The fact that in reality M is more smoothly distributed in relation to P than we have supposed and that there is substitution between the different M's (both on the demand and supply sides) may also lead to the real effective price elasticity being greater than in our model.

compare this with the weighted average value for $\overline{m_M}{}^*$ obtained by the formula given in equation (A7), and taking the mean values of imports as weights. This weighted average value is $-9\cdot6$, or considerably larger, thus confirming our conclusion that the effective price elasticity of demand is likely to be smaller than the weighted average of the individual price elasticities. The difference is probably exaggerated, however, by our assumed mutual independence of the four goods.

From the above values for r^*, σ^* and the various parameters, one can calculate what the changes in prices and quantities ought to have been if a set of four equations similar to that used above were to hold for the *groups*. In other words, $\varSigma(M)$ and $\varSigma(P)$ are treated in just the same way as the individual M's and P's, the only difference being in the values given to r and σ. The changes in the index numbers of quantities and prices calculated in this way agree very closely with those calculated as above, taking the four goods separately:

Percentage changes, '1930–5'

	4 goods separately	In groups
Imports, volume	-27	-26
Imports, average value	-8	-8
Home-produced sales, volume	34	33
Home-produced sales, average value	-19	-19

The close agreement is not particularly surprising, since the group elasticity of substitution was derived from the combined results of the four goods taken separately. In order to test whether this effective group elasticity was a useful concept, some different changes in the various exogenous factors were taken, and the two sets of calculations repeated. The exogenous price factors were chosen in such a way as to lead to a large *increase* instead of a large *decrease* in imports, as it was thought that this would provide a good test of the usefulness of the group elasticity. So $\varDelta \log M^*$, $\varDelta \log \overline{G\text{–}H}$, and $\varDelta \log \overline{W}_P$ were all put equal to zero, $\varDelta \log \overline{W}_M$ was put equal to $-0\cdot0434$ instead of plus the same quantity, and $\varDelta S_P$ and $\varDelta S_M$ were left as in the previous example. If we call the year by which all these changes had occurred '19XX', what they amount to is to suppose that in the United Kingdom prices of non-manufactures remained stable between '1935' and '19XX', whereas in other countries they fell. Tariffs were unchanged, and there was some growth in demand and supply due to the usual causes. It so happens that whether we calculate the resulting changes in the quantities and prices of the groups by taking the four goods separately, or by combining them and using the same σ^* as was found from our imaginary '1930–5' experience, we get virtually the same results:

Percentage changes, '1935–19XX'

	4 goods separately	In groups
Imports, volume	42	43
Imports, average value	−21	−21
Home-produced sales, volume	26	26
Home-produced sales, average value	−19	−19

In both of the examples described above the changes in the exogenous factors were assumed to be equal for each of the four kinds of goods. Thus the shifts in foreign costs in the last example were the same for each import. The next test to which the model was subjected was to assume that these shifts were different for the different imports. In order to simplify the computations the shifts for the individual goods were assumed to be the same as in the last model, but four alternative possibilities were studied:

1 The shifts affected only goods 1 and 3, i.e. those for which σ was large. Goods 2 and 4 were assumed to be quite unchanged.
2 The shifts affected only goods 2 and 4, i.e. those for which σ was small. Goods 1 and 3 were assumed to be quite unchanged.
3 The shifts affected only goods 1 and 2, i.e. those for which r was small. Goods 3 and 4 were assumed to be quite unchanged.
4 The shifts affected only goods 3 and 4, i.e. those for which r was large. Goods 1 and 2 were assumed to be quite unchanged.

In each case the changes in the groups were calculated in two different ways: by using the equations for the individual goods, and by using the equations for the groups (taking $\sigma^* = -4 \cdot 9$ as before). The former method gives the 'right' answers, the latter the ones we would get if we used our effective group elasticities. The results are compared below.

Percentage changes, '1935 to 19XX'

		Imports, volume		Imports, average value		Home-produced sales, volume		Home-produced sales, average value	
		S	G	S	G	S	G	S	G
1	σ large	23	24	−12	−13	13	13	−10	−11
2	σ small	20	24	−12	−13	13	13	−10	−11
3	r small	25	11	−12	−15	25	27	−18	−17
4	r large	18	44	−12	−10	1	−1	−1	−3

Note: S = changes calculated by taking goods separately.
G = changes calculated taking the goods in groups.

In none of these examples are the differences between the two methods of calculation large so far as either the volume or average value of home-produced sales are concerned. Nor are the differences in the average value of imports ever very large. In the first two examples the differences in the volume of imports are rather small. It is only for the volume of imports in the last two examples that we find appreciable differences. Here the use of the effective group elasticities appears to be seriously misleading.

Now in example 3 the changes are concentrated on the goods for which r is small. These are half of all the imports, but 95% of all the home-produced sales. For example 4 the changes are concentrated on the goods for which r is large. These are again half the imports, but now only 5% of all the home-produced sales. It is this *unequal weighting* of the exogenous changes as between imports and home sales which seems to cause the trouble. In both examples 1 and 2 the changes affect half of imports and half of home-produced sales, and even though the goods with high and low σ's are affected unequally, the resulting errors from using the group elasticities are not large.

All this suggests (although, of course, it does not *prove*) that the effective group elasticities may be fairly stable, and hence useful concepts, provided that they are *measured* in circumstances in which the shifts in exogenous factors are not distributed very differently in relation to imports as compared with home-produced sales, and provided that they are only *applied* in circumstances which also satisfy this requirement. It is noteworthy that the group elasticities of substitution which may be observed when this requirement is *not* satisfied can be very much smaller than the corresponding elasticities when it *is* satisfied. Thus in example 3 above the observed group elasticity of substitution works out at -0.1, and in example 4 it is -1.3, which may be compared with the previously obtained figure of -4.9.

The group price elasticities *may* be misleading, but, provided we are on our guard for the circumstances which are likely to make them so, they should be usable concepts. The examples may, indeed, exaggerate the extent to which they may mislead us on account of the assumed independence of the four kinds of goods (see pp. 200–1 above) and on account of the rather extreme degree of difference in the distribution of the changes assumed. In reality, we may generally hope for more random distributions. It is difficult in any case to see what can replace the group elasticities. It would be impossibly complicated to work with a model containing hundreds of different goods. We have already attempted, and failed, to relate the group elasticities to the individual ones by simple formulae. The conclusion must surely be that we must proceed on the assumption that history will repeat itself sufficiently closely to keep the group elasticities fairly stable. We must, therefore, measure these effective group elasticities directly. The usefulness of studying individual goods lies (so far as someone interested in *groups* is concerned) only in setting an upper limit to the group elasticity.

5. THE INDEX NUMBER PROBLEM

It is perhaps obvious that the index number problem is one aspect of the problem we have been discussing. Our measures of groups are all index numbers using some sort of weighting system, and the exact choice of a system would appear to be largely arbitrary, and yet to lead to appreciably different results. These differences may arise through the existence of correlation between the weights and the price or quantity relatives which compose the index number. It is well known, for example, that base-year weighted index numbers of volume of output are generally biased upwards in relation to end-year weighted index numbers, because output usually increases fastest where prices rise least.

Since our effective elasticities must be derived by direct measurement of groups, it is important to decide how these groups should be measured.

Index numbers of volume and price in 1935

(1930 = 100)

| | Base year for weights | |
Item	1930	1935
United Kingdom retained imports, Class III, manufactures		
Volume	82·0	74·7
Price	81·0	73·8
United Kingdom exports, Class III, manufactures		
Volume	92·3	87·9
Price	84·9	80·8
United Kingdom industrial production (net)		
Volume	124	114
Price	93·5	85·5

Note: In the 1930 column, the basic formula for the volume index is $\dfrac{p_{30}q_{35}}{p_{30}q_{30}}$, and for the price index is $\dfrac{p_{35}q_{30}}{p_{30}q_{30}}$.

In the 1935 column, the basic formula for the volume index is $\dfrac{p_{35}q_{35}}{p_{35}q_{30}}$, and for the price index is $\dfrac{p_{35}q_{35}}{p_{30}q_{35}}$.

The definitions of 'manufactures' used here are different from those used in Chapter VIII.

Sources: See footnote on p. 206.

The only practical solution is to take them very much as you find them,[1] but, if a choice is possible, there is something to be said for using similar weights for similar magnitudes throughout. The meaning of this is best illustrated by an example. In Chapter VIII the basic data are changes of index numbers of volume and average value from 1930 to 1935. Either of these years could be chosen to provide the weights, although it is rather more convenient to use 1930 values for the volume index numbers, and 1935 values for the price index numbers.[2] It is instructive to compare the differences in the results following from differences in the weights.

It is clear from the table that if, in Chapter VIII, we had used 1935 weights for the volume index numbers and 1930 weights for the price index numbers (with imports, for example,[3] this would mean using a volume index of 74·7 instead of 82·0, and a price index of 81·0 instead of 73·8) we should have had smaller increases (or bigger falls) in quantities accompanied by greater increases (or smaller falls) in prices. The differences are quite appreciable, and might have made some differences to our estimates of the various elasticities. It is true that the *relative* movements of the various price index numbers are not always much affected by the change of base year, and the same is true of the *relative* movements of the volume index numbers. Nevertheless, the relative movements of prices as compared with quantities *are* appreciably affected, and this could affect some of the estimates (though not, to any great extent, the price elasticity of substitution).

It will be recalled that the intercorrelation of prices and quantities is the essence of our problem. The existence of such intercorrelation is one important reason why the effective elasticities are smaller than the

[1] L. R. Klein has suggested that one should construct one's index numbers so that they satisfy one's theories of both micro- and macro-economics (see 'Macroeconomics and the Theory of Rational Behavior', *Econometrica*, vol. 14, no. 2, April 1946, p. 94). In practice, however, he seems to have abandoned this ideal, and used the available index numbers: see his *Economic Fluctuations in the United States, 1921–1941*, Cowles Commission Monographs, 11 (New York, Wiley; London, Chapman & Hall, 1950), especially pp. 13 and 14; and also *An Econometric Model of the United States, 1929–1952*, by L. R. Klein and A. S. Goldberger, Contributions to Economic Analysis, 9 (Amsterdam, North-Holland Publishing Company, 1955).

[2] The Board of Trade published estimates of the value of trade in 1935 at 1930 prices, and also in 1930 at 1935 prices (*Board of Trade Journal*, 23 January 1936, pp. 127–34 and 4 March 1937, pp. 295–303). Professor Bowley has also estimated index numbers of gross and net output of the industries covered by the Census of Production for these two years using alternately one and then the other to provide the weights. See his *Studies in the National Income, 1924–1938* (1944), pp. 149, 150. The index numbers of output used in Chapter VIII differ slightly from these, however, and the sources are given on p. 238.

[3] Apart from differences in classification.

weighted average ones. Our principal justification for using the effective elasticities at all is the belief that history repeats itself, so that the effective elasticity found on one occasion will also be found, at least approximately, to hold for others. Our consideration of 1930–5 index numbers shows that it may be important to use similar weighting systems when we come to make further applications. Thus, in Chapter VIII we use 1930 weights to measure volume changes from 1930 to 1935, and 1935 weights to measure price changes. If we wanted to use the elasticities given in Chapter VIII to estimate the probable effects of, let us say, the reduction of tariffs in 1962 on trade in 1965 as compared with 1960, then we should use 1960 weights for our volume index numbers and 1965 weights for our price index numbers—at least this is what we should aim at!

6. CONCLUSIONS ON THE PROBLEM OF GROUPING

In this study we have had to come to some practical conclusion as to the best methods to use. It cannot be pretended that we have solved the problems of grouping; we have given only a number of working assumptions which seem not unreasonable in themselves. These are set out below in the same order as our earlier conclusions based on the assumption of price uniformity within groups. We have retained these conclusions as far as possible, assuming that they still apply even when there is no price uniformity, unless there are strong reasons for rejecting them.

(1) We can relate the index numbers of volume of groups of imports and home sales to index numbers of their average value and of the average value of non-manufactures, and to index numbers measuring 'income' effects, by means of demand equations similar to those we have used for single goods.

(2) The elasticities in these equations are called 'effective' elasticities, since they are determined from direct measurement of historical changes in the groups and therefore take account of the various intercorrelations which do in fact occur. Provided that these elasticities are *measured* in circumstances in which the distribution of the external factors impinging on demand is roughly the same for imports as for home-produced sales and provided that they are then only used in circumstances which also satisfy this condition, it seems likely that their use will not give misleading results. A further condition which may be important is that the weighting systems of the index numbers used should be similar in the measurement and in the application of the elasticities.

(3) It is assumed that the various group price elasticities are related

to each other in the same way as are the individual good price elasticities (for example, that the reciprocity theorem, equation (19) p. 83, holds).

(4) The group price elasticities are generally arithmetically smaller than the weighted averages of the individual price elasticities. The effective group price elasticity of substitution is also less than the typical individual one by an amount which increases with the unevenness of distribution of imports in relation to home sales, and with a reduction in the substitutability of one manufacture for another.

(5) The possible range of values for the group price elasticity of substitution, σ^*, must be found by inspection of the behaviour of group index numbers, and this is done in Chapter VIII. However, the individual good σ's give a rough upper (arithmetical) limit to σ^*. In practice, since they are high (Chart 20) we can only say that they do not show that σ^* must be low.

APPENDIX II

STATISTICAL SOURCES AND METHODS

1. INTRODUCTION

This appendix contains the main statistical series estimated for this study, and a description of the sources and methods used. Series which were used in substantially the same form in which they were originally published are not repeated here. The series are numbered S1 to 137, listed on p. 242 and given on pp. 244–56. The sources and methods used in constructing them are given on pp. 209–34. There are some further notes to certain tables in the text on pp. 234–40, and notes to the charts on pp. 240–2.

Most of the estimates are shown to three significant figures, although for many the accuracy of the third figure is doubtful. Where the figures have been rounded, totals may differ slightly from the sum of the components.

1948 was chosen as the base year for most series because this was the base year in many official series for the post-war period.

The desirability of a common weighting system for all index numbers was discussed on pp. 205–7. In practice one must use the most readily available data, but as far as possible the years selected to provide the price weights for all index numbers of quantity were as follows:

For 1900–20   1913 prices
1920–30   1924 prices
1930–5   1930 prices
1935–55   1948 prices

A description of the formulae used for the index numbers of imports is given on p. 213, and similar formulae have been used elsewhere.

While it is hoped that the most important details of the methods used have been given, many details have been omitted. Attention is drawn in the notes to any particularly unreliable estimates.

2. NOTES TO THE MAIN SERIES, S1–137

(a) Retained imports 1900–55, S1–17, Charts 1, 4, 7, 11, 12, 19

The estimates of the value of all retained imports (i.e. total imports minus re-exports) and of the index numbers of quantity and price for the total and for various parts of the total were obtained by linking together estimates published for the most part in the *Board of Trade Journal*. There are four periods in which different classifications were used, and these are shown below. The current values of the various items are also given for 1948, to show their relative importance. The reasons for making the largest adjustments to the official classification are discussed in Parts I and II (pp. 4–6, 93, 120). Many of the smaller adjustments (for molasses, bismuth, iron pyrites and titanium ores) were originally made to collect materials for the chemicals industry into one group. This project was abandoned, but it seemed simplest to leave the figures as they were. The final classification is far from perfect. For example, a substantial part of the oils and seeds included in food should be in materials, alcoholic drink was not excluded from food before 1935 though it was excluded for later years, some of the materials (for example, iron scrap) might be better included in manufactures, since home production of close substitutes is large, and there are various small groups which do not fit in well where they are (for example, lubricants with fuels, live animals not for food and parcel post with manufactures).

(i) 1953–5 classification

Item	Composition of item
Food S4, 5	Class A, food, beverages and tobacco *plus* B2, oil-seeds, oil nuts and oil kernels *plus* B13, animal and vegetable oils, fats, greases, and derivatives *less* molasses (*ex* A7) *less* alcoholic beverages (*ex* A11) *less* A12, tobacco and tobacco manufactures
Materials S6, 7	Equals the sum of metal, textile and other materials, see below It also equals Class B, basic materials *plus* molasses (*ex* A7) *plus* D13, non-ferrous base metals *plus* jute yarn and manufactures (*ex* D9) *less* bismuth (*ex* D13)
Metal materials S12, 13	B11, metalliferous ores and metal scrap *plus* D13, non-ferrous base metals *less* titanium ores (*ex* B11) *less* bismuth (*ex* D13)
Textile materials S14, 15	B1, hides, skins and fur skins, undressed *plus* B6, silk *plus* B7, wool and other animal hair and tops *plus* B8, cotton *plus* B9, miscellaneous textile fibres and waste *plus* pulp for rayon (*ex* B5) *plus* jute yarn and manufactures (*ex* D9)

(i) *1953–5 classification* (contd.)

Item	Composition of item
Other materials S16, 17	B3, rubber, including synthetic and reclaimed *plus* B4, wood and cork *plus* B5, pulp and waste paper *plus* B10, crude fertilizers and crude minerals, excluding fuels *plus* B12, miscellaneous animal and vegetable crude materials *plus* molasses (*ex* A7) *plus* titanium ores (*ex* B11) *less* pulp for rayon (*ex* B5)
Fuels S8, 9	Class C, mineral fuels and lubricants
Manufactures S10, 11	Class D,[1] manufactured goods *plus* bismuth (*ex* D13) *plus* Class E, postal packages and live animals of a kind not normally used for food *less* jute yarns and manufactures (*ex* D9) *less* silver bullion (*ex* D11) *less* D13, non-ferrous base metals
Total S1–3	Total as published[1] *less* silver bullion (*ex* D11) This is equal to the sum of the above groups *plus* alcoholic beverages (*ex* A11) and tobacco, A12

(ii) *1935–8, 1946–53 classification*

Item	Composition of item	Value in 1948 £ million
Food S4, 5	Class I, food, drink and tobacco	874
	plus II J, seeds and nuts for oil, oils, fats, resins and gums	141
	less alcoholic drink (*ex* I G)	−23
	less molasses (*ex* I H)	−5
	less I I, tobacco	−42
	less crude petroleum (*ex* II J)	−31
	Total	913
Materials S6, 7	Equals the sum of metal, textile and other materials, see below	
	It also equals Class II, raw materials and articles mainly unmanufactured	641
	plus molasses (*ex* I H)	5
	plus III D non-ferrous metals and manufactures thereof	89
	plus jute yarns and manufactures (*ex* III L)	17
	less II A, coal	—
	less II J, seeds and nuts for oil, oils, fats, resins and gums	−141
	less bismuth (*ex* III D)	—
	Total	610

[1] In 1953 the gift of Canadian aircraft worth £35 million was excluded, and in 1954 a similar gift of £7 million was excluded.

(ii) 1935–8, 1946–53 classification (contd.)

Item	Composition of item	Value in 1948 £ million
Metal materials S12, 13	Class II C, iron ore and scrap	28
	plus II D, non-ferrous metalliferous ores and scrap	34
	plus III D, non-ferrous metals and manufactures thereof	89
	less iron pyrites and titanium ores (*ex* II D)	−1
	less bismuth (*ex* III D)	—
	Total	149
Textile materials S14, 15	Class II F, raw cotton and cotton waste	106
	plus II G, wool, raw and waste, and woollen rags	65
	plus II H, silk, raw and waste, and artificial silk waste	2
	plus II I, other textile materials	25
	plus II K, hides and skins, undressed	28
	plus pulp for rayon (*ex* II L)	7
	plus jute yarn and manufactures (*ex* III L)	17
	Total	251
Other materials S16, 17	Class II B, non-metalliferous mining and quarry products, other than coal	13
	plus II E, wood and timber	94
	plus II L, paper-making materials	52
	plus II M, rubber	25
	plus II N, miscellaneous raw materials and articles mainly unmanufactured	26
	plus molasses (*ex* I H)	5
	plus iron pyrites and titanium ores (*ex* II D)	1
	less pulp for rayon (*ex* II L)	−7
	Total	210
Fuels S8, 9	Class II A, coal	—
	plus crude petroleum (*ex* II J)	31
	plus III A, coke and manufactured fuel	—
	plus III P, oils, fats and resins, manufactured	127
	Total	159
Manufactures S10, 11	Class III,[1] articles wholly or mainly manufactured	475
	plus bismuth (*ex* III D)	—
	plus Class IV, animals not for food	8
	plus Class V, parcel post	16
	less III A, coke and manufactured fuel	—
	less III D, non-ferrous metals and manufactures thereof	−89
	less jute yarn and manufactures (*ex* III L)	−17
	less III P, oils, fats and resins, manufactured	−127
	Total	267
Total S1–3	Total as published[1]	2,014
	This also equals the total of the above groups *plus* alcoholic drink (*ex* I G) and tobacco, I I.	

[1] In 1953 the gift of Canadian aircraft worth £35 million was excluded.

(iii) 1913, 1920–35 classification

The same classification was adopted as for 1935–8 and 1946–53, with the following exceptions. Alcoholic drink was left with food; molasses were not transferred from food to materials; jute yarn and manufactures were not transferred from manufactures to materials, and bismuth was not transferred from materials to manufactures; iron pyrites and titanium ores were not transferred from metal to other materials; and pulp for rayon was not transferred from other to textile materials. In short, fewer adjustments were made to the published figures, but all the major adjustments were still made.

(iv) 1900–13 classification

The main source for the estimates for 1900–13 was *British Overseas Trade from 1700 to the 1930's*, by W. Schlote (Oxford, Blackwell, 1952). Hence the classification is based on his, which in turn follows the Brussels Register (Schlote, *British Overseas Trade*, p. 10). Schlote's estimates were adjusted so far as possible to make them conform to the classification adopted for 1913 and 1920–35. The remaining substantial difference was the inclusion of seeds and nuts for oil, oils, fats, resins and gums, other than crude petroleum, in other materials instead of in food.

The methods used to link the published series differed in the five periods just considered. In describing them we concentrate our attention on how estimates of imports at constant prices were obtained. These estimates were then linked together to obtain the index numbers of quantity with 1948 as the base year. The index numbers of price were 'average values', that is, they were obtained by dividing imports at current prices by imports at constant prices. The basic formulae were, therefore:

$$_{o}Q_{n} = \frac{\Sigma(p_{o}q_{n})}{\Sigma(p_{o}q_{o})}; \quad _{o}P_{n} = \frac{\Sigma(p_{n}q_{n})}{\Sigma(p_{o}q_{n})}$$

where $_{o}Q_{n}$ and $_{o}P_{n}$ are respectively the quantity and price index numbers for the year n, with the year o as base, and the p's and q's refer to the prices and quantities of imports in year n or year o. In general, whenever index numbers with different base years were linked together, this was done by simple proportion, and not by means of the Fisher 'ideal' index. For example, if an index of quantity based on year n prices was to be linked to an index based on year o prices to obtain an index for year m with year o as 100, the calculation would be as follows:

$$_{o}Q_{m} = (_{n}Q_{m} \div _{o}Q_{n}) \times 100.$$

In this calculation year n would be called the 'link year'.

The estimates of imports at constant prices were often obtained after numerous adjustments to the published classification. In obtaining the price index numbers, *all* these adjustments were not always made, so that the coverage was not always identical with the quantity index numbers, although there was broad agreement between them.

(v) 1935–8, 1946–53 sources and methods

A somewhat more laborious procedure was followed for the period 1935–8, 1946–53 than for earlier periods so as to produce estimates of imports at constant 1948 prices in which the weighting system was changed as little as possible. It was thought, for reasons given on pp. 205–7, that this would make comparisons with other statistical series (such as the index of industrial production, in which 1948 values were used as weights throughout) more meaningful. Ideally, one should weight an index of quantity for each commodity by its value in 1948 so as to obtain a fully 1948 weighted index of quantity, but this would have been too laborious and lengthy a task. As a second best, an index of quantity was obtained for each of the single letter groups in the official classification (such as I A, I B, I C, etc.) by linking together the index numbers of quantity published in various issues of the *Board of Trade Journal*. These published index numbers were based on successively 1935, 1938, 1947 and 1950 value weights and the link years were the last three. The resulting index numbers, converted to the base 1948 = 100, were weighted by the values of imports in 1948 and then combined as required. The estimates were therefore weighted by 1948 values as between the single-letter groups, but within the groups they were weighted by values of the years given above.

Imports of fuels at constant prices were obtained by multiplying quantities in each year by their prices (strictly, their average values) in 1948, so that the resulting index number is fully 1948 weighted. This procedure was necessary for the analysis in Chapter II and was practicable because of the relatively small number of different fuels. The statistics were obtained from the *Annual Statement of Trade*.

The revised valuation of parcel post was used from 1950 onwards in the estimates of the current value of total imports and of the relevant price index numbers.

(vi) 1953–5 sources and methods

The method used to estimate imports at constant 1948 prices for 1953–5 was similar to that just described, with a modification made necessary by the change in the official classification of the trade statistics. The current value of imports in 1953 in each of the divisions in the new classification in the published statistics (A1, A2, A3, etc.) was divided by a price index for 1953 with the base 1948 = 100. These price index numbers were obtained for each of the single letter groups in the old classification (I A, I B, I C, etc.) by dividing the current values in 1953 by the value at 1948 prices obtained as described above. The price index number used for any division was that of the letter group which corresponded most nearly to it. This gave estimates of imports of each division in 1953 at 1948 prices. The index numbers of quantity on the base 1954 = 100 published in the *Board of Trade Journal* were then used to obtain similar estimates for 1954 and 1955.

As before, imports of fuels at 1948 prices were estimated by multiplying quantities by the relevant prices in 1948.

(vii) *1913, 1920–35 sources and methods*

For the years 1913 and 1920–35 estimates of retained imports at constant prices of various years were published in the *Board of Trade Journal*. No attempt was made, as for later years, to weight these by the prices of a single year, but the weights used in the published estimates were, with one exception, accepted. All that was necessary, then, was to re-combine the published estimates so as to obtain the classification already described, and then to link together the various periods so as to obtain a continuous index. The exception was for the years 1926 and 1927. For the years 1924, 1925, 1928, 1929 and 1930, estimates at 1924 prices were published in the *Board of Trade Journal*, but for 1926 and 1927 only estimates at 1925 prices were published. Estimates for these years at 1924 prices were obtained by using the index numbers of quantity given by H. W. Macrosty,[1] with adjustments for some discrepancies they seemed to contain.

The base years in the published figures, and the link years, were as follows: 1913, 1922, 1923, 1924 and 1930.

As before, imports of fuels were obtained by direct multiplication of prices and quantities. The prices were those of the years 1913, 1924 and 1930, the link years being 1920 and 1930.

(viii) *1900–13 sources and methods*

For most retained imports the index numbers of quantity were derived from estimates of total imports and re-exports at constant 1913 prices given in Schlote's *British Overseas Trade*. As his classification was not exactly that required, additional estimates were made of total imports and re-exports of fuels and metal materials, of re-exports of textile and other materials, of retained imports of tobacco and of total imports of semi-finished iron and steel at 1913 prices, using the *Annual*

[1] 'The Overseas Trade of the United Kingdom, 1924–1931', *Journal of the Royal Statistical Society*, vol. 95, part 4, 1932, p. 607.

Statement of Trade, the *Statistical Abstract for the United Kingdom*, and a series of estimates of imports at constant 1900, 1910, 1911 and 1912 prices given in *Imports and Exports at Prices of 1900* for 1900–9, 1900–11, 1900–12, 1900–13 (Cd. 5160, 6314, 6782, 7432; 1910–14).

(ix) Current values for link years

To help the reader who may want to re-combine the index numbers in different ways the following table of retained imports at current prices in various years is given. These show the current values of imports included in the index numbers of quantity for the various periods mentioned above. The coverage therefore is not the same throughout these years. For convenience the figures for 1957 given in Parts I and II are also included, although they were not used in the construction of the index numbers.

Year	Total*	Food	Materials Total	Metals	Textiles	Fuels	£ million Manu-factures
1913†	659‡	268	236	41	107	12	139
1913†	659	295	204	41	107	13	139
1922	900	462	225	27	136	41	154
1923	979	506	240	43	123	37	181
1924	1,140	568	304	52	177	43	208
1930	958	465	207	44	86	48	224
1948	2,014	913	610	149	251	159	267
1957	3,937	1,472	1,185	389	386	463	704

* Includes alcoholic beverages and tobacco.

† Upper line for period 1900–13, lower line for 1913 and after.

‡ This is the correct total, but the total of the groups, plus 7 for unmanufactured tobacco, would be 661 owing to double counting, probably as between materials and manufactures.

(b) Price index of exports of manufactures, 1900–55, S18, Chart 19

The sources and methods used were the same as those used for the price of imports, with some minor modifications. For 1953–5 the index of the 'average value' of Class D, manufactured goods, with base 1954 = 100, was linked on at 1953. For the years 1913, 1920–38, 1946–53, the exports included were those in Class III, articles wholly or mainly manufactured. For the years 1900–13, the index was that given by Schlote in *British Overseas Trade*, appendix table 26, p. 177, for manufactured goods.

(c) Price index of national output, 1900–55, S19

The price index of national output was obtained in a similar manner to the price index numbers of imports, that is, by dividing estimates of the current value of output by estimates of its value at constant prices, the prices being those of different periods which were then linked together to obtain a continuous series with 1948 = 100.

For the years 1946–55 the current value of the gross domestic product at factor cost, given in the Central Statistical Office's *National Income and Expenditure 1956*, table 1, was divided by the index of the gross domestic product at 1948 factor cost given in the same source, table 13.

A link with 1938 was provided by the current value of the gross domestic product at factor cost given in *National Income and Expenditure 1956*, table 1, in conjunction with the estimates of the gross domestic product at 1948 factor cost for the years 1935–8 given in S24 and described on p. 220. The link for the latter was taken with the average of the four years 1935–8, since the estimate for 1938 above was thought unreliable (p. 221).

For the years 1900–13 and 1920–38 estimates were obtained of the values at current and constant prices of consumers' expenditure at market prices, public authorities' current expenditure on goods and services, gross domestic fixed capital formation, exports, net invisibles and retained imports. The sum of these items other than retained imports, less retained imports, gave an approximation to gross national output at market prices. The price index was then obtained by dividing an index of the current value series by an index of the constant price series.

For the years 1900–13 and 1920–38 estimates of the current value of public authorities' current expenditure on goods and services and gross domestic capital formation were obtained from J. B. Jefferys and Dorothy Walters, 'National Income and Expenditure of the United Kingdom, 1870–1952',[1] tables I and XV. The current value of consumers' expenditure and also its value at constant 1938 prices were obtained in the main from figures kindly supplied by Mr D. A. Rowe. The current values of exports and retained imports and their values at constant 1913 prices for the years 1900–13, 1920–33 were obtained from Schlote's *British Overseas Trade*, and for later years from the *Board of Trade Journal*. The current value of net invisibles was obtained for the years 1900–13 from A. K. Cairncross, *Home and Foreign Investment, 1870–1913* (Cambridge University Press, 1953) and for the years 1920–38 from the *Board of Trade Journal*. The current values of public authorities' expenditure and of net invisibles were deflated by the consumer goods and services price index given in Jefferys and Walters, 'National Income and Expenditure of the United Kingdom, 1870–1952,' tables XVI and XVIA, to obtain estimates at constant prices.

[1] In *Income and Wealth, Series V*, International Association for Research in Income and Wealth (London, Bowes and Bowes, 1955), pp. 1–40.

The current value of gross domestic fixed capital formation was deflated by their price index for capital goods (Jefferys and Walters, tables XVI and XVIA).

(d) Index of industrial production 1900–55, S20, 21, Chart 12

The series used for total industrial production is not given here, since it is simply the same as that given by T. M. Ridley in 'Industrial Production in the United Kingdom, 1900–1953' (*Economica*, New Series, vol. 22, no. 82, February 1955, p. 1) except that for the years after 1948 the estimates in the *Annual Abstract of Statistics*, no. 93, 1956, were taken. The output included is that of the mining, manufacturing, building, gas, electricity and water industries.

The series for 'metals' production in principle includes the output of the metals, engineering, shipbuilding, electrical goods and vehicles industries. For the years 1948–55 the estimates in the *Annual Abstract* for 1956 were taken, and for 1946 and 1947 those in the *Annual Abstract* for 1954. The years 1935–8 and the link with 1948 were obtained as described on p. 221. The years 1901–13 and 1920–35 were obtained by combining the index numbers for the basic metal and the metal products industries given in *Industrial Statistics 1900–1955*, Organisation for European Economic Co-operation (Paris, 1955), pp. 8, 9. The weights used to combine them were those on p. 152 of the same work. A check showed close agreement between the resulting index and one for the above group of industries based on the Censuses of Production for 1907, 1924, 1930 and 1935. (Using the geometric average of 1907 and 1924 weighted index numbers for the change from 1907 to 1924, and a 1930 weighted index number for the period 1924–35.) For 1900 an estimate was obtained from the data given in W. G. Hoffmann's *British Industry 1700–1950* (Oxford, Blackwell, 1955), tables 2 and 54B.

The series for 'textiles' production in principle includes the output of the textiles, leather, leather goods and fur and clothing industries. For the years 1935–8 and 1946–55 the sources are the same as for 'metals'. The estimates for 1907, 1924, 1930, 1933, 1934 and 1935 were based on the various Censuses of Production, using the following works: for 1924 and later years, C. F. Carter, W. B. Reddaway and R. Stone, *The Measurement of Production Movements* (Cambridge University Press, 1948), p. 125, with weights for 1930 from Bowley, *Studies in the National Income*, p. 150; for 1907 and 1924, A. Maddison, 'Output, Employment and Productivity in British Manufacturing in the last Half Century', *Bulletin of the Oxford University Institute of Statistics*, vol. 17, no. 4, November 1955, p. 363, taking the geometric average of 1907 and 1924 weights. The intervening years were obtained by interpolation using the index of production for the textile industry given by the

O.E.E.C.'s *Industrial Statistics 1900–1955*, p. 10, and the same index was used to extrapolate for the years 1901–6. An estimate for 1900 was obtained from Hoffmann's *British Industry 1700–1950*.

Since the above estimates were made, K. S. Lomax has published estimates for the years 1900–38 which are the result of a thorough re-working of the field. See 'New Index-numbers of Industrial Production 1900–1938', *London and Cambridge Economic Bulletin*, no. 26, June 1958, p. v and *Journal of the Royal Statistical Society*, Series A (General), vol. 122, part 2, 1959, p. 185, 'Production and Productivity Movements in the United Kingdom since 1900'.

Adjustments for weighting bias

For the reasons given on pp. 134–6 it was thought desirable for some purposes to adjust the index of total industrial production in 1935–8 so that the change from 1935–8 to the post-war years should be the same as an index which was weighted throughout by 1948 prices. The index numbers of metals and textiles production, S20 and 21, were already approximately fully 1948 price-weighted, but the index of total industrial production for this period was the geometric average of 1935 and 1946 weighted index numbers (Ridley, 'Industrial Production in the United Kingdom, 1900–1953', *Economica*, February 1955, p. 1). An index which is more or less fully 1948 price-weighted is that given in S29. Comparing it with Ridley's index for the period 1935 to 1948 we get for 1935, 1948 = 100:

$$\begin{array}{ll} \text{S 29} & 81 \cdot 6 \\ \text{Ridley} & 79 \cdot 5 \end{array}$$

1935–8 was therefore adjusted by multiplying by $1 \cdot 027 = \left(\dfrac{81 \cdot 6}{79 \cdot 5} \right)$. This adjustment was only made in Tables 5, 6 and 36, and not in Charts 4, 7 and 11, nor (through error) in the regression analysis of Section 5 of Chapter VII.

(e) Price index numbers of imported materials and national output, war years and before 1900, S22, 23

In order to estimate the lagged effects of relative price changes on the demand for imported materials (see Chapter VII, Section 5) it was necessary to estimate price index numbers of imported materials and national output for the war years 1914–19 and 1939–45, and also for some years before 1900. The coverage of these estimates is often different from that of the series S7 and 19, and they are more unreliable. Only the estimates for the war years are given in S22 and 23.

The price index of imported materials for 1914–19 was obtained by interpolating between 1913 and 1920, as in S7, using the price index for imported raw materials and semi-manufactured goods given in Schlote, *British Overseas Trade*, appendix table 26, pp. 177, 178. That for 1939–45 was also interpolated, using the 'average value' index for imports of raw materials, class III, given in the *Statistical Digest of the War*, History of the Second World War, U.K. Civil Series (H.M.S.O. and Longmans Green, 1951). The price index for the years prior to 1900 was obtained by linking the series from Schlote to S7 at 1900.

The price index numbers of national output for 1914–19 and 1939–45 were obtained by taking a weighted average of three price index numbers: for consumers' expenditure, exports and imports. The weights used were respectively the values of consumers' expenditure, of the rest of final expenditure and of imports in 1913 and 1938. The weight for imports was negative. The three price index numbers for 1914–19 were obtained from Mr D. A. Rowe and from Schlote's *British Overseas Trade*. For 1939–45 they were obtained from the *London and Cambridge Economic Bulletin*, no. 17, March 1956. The price index of national output for the years before 1900 was obtained in a similar way to that used for the years 1900–13 (see above, S19).

(f) Gross domestic product at 1948 factor cost, 1935–8 and 1948, S24–29

The estimates of the gross domestic product at 1948 factor cost for 1935–8 were made by estimating the change in the output of various sectors of industry between one or more pre-war years and 1948, and also between the four pre-war years. The various outputs were weighted by the contributions to the gross domestic product at factor cost in 1948 of their respective industries in a manner similar to that used in the official estimates of gross domestic product at 1948 factor cost—see the Central Statistical Office's *National Income Statistics: Sources and Methods* (H.M.S.O. 1956), pp. 37–44 and appendix IV. The relative weights were virtually the same as in appendix IV, although the money value given in S24–29 differs slightly from the most recent estimates on account of later revisions.

The main sources used for the index numbers of output were as follows.

For agriculture, forestry and fishing the change from before the war to 1948 was based on H. T. Williams, 'Changes in the Productivity of Labour in British Agriculture', a paper read to the Agricultural Economics Society in July 1953. His index of net output at 1945–6 prices was taken. It differs from the official index of 'net' agricultural output used in S36 in subtracting all the principal inputs into agriculture from other industries, and not merely imported feeding stuffs, animals and seeds. It therefore shows an appreciably smaller increase from the pre-war to the post-war period. The changes between the pre-war years were estimated by using the London and Cambridge Economic Service's index of agricultural production.

For all industries included in the official index of industrial production with the exception of building and contracting, and engineering, shipbuilding and electrical goods the change from 1935 to 1948 using 1948 net outputs as weights was taken from B. C. Brown, 'Industrial Production in 1935 and 1948', *London and Cambridge Economic Bulletin*, December 1954, p. v. Brown gave no estimates for building and contracting, and his estimates for engineering, shipbuilding and electrical goods were not taken since it was thought that they understated the increase in production appreciably. Instead, the estimates of the Central Statistical Office for the change from 1935 to 1946, with 1946 weights, published in Studies in Official Statistics no. 1, *The Interim Index of Industrial Production* (H.M.S.O. 1948), were taken, coupled with their estimate for the change from 1946 to 1948 published in the *Annual Abstract of Statistics*. The same sources were used to obtain the change in the output of building and contracting from 1935 to 1948. The changes in output between the four pre-war years were estimated mainly by using the Board of Trade's index numbers of output published in its *Journal*, supplemented by the London and Cambridge Economic Service's index numbers and by employment statistics. It seems probable that the estimates for 1938 are appreciably too low (see R. and W. M. Stone, 'Indices of Industrial Output', *Economic Journal*, September 1939, and also K. S. Lomax, 'Production and Productivity Movements in the United Kingdom since 1900', *Journal of the Royal Statistical Society*, vol. 122, part 2, 1959). The industries included in 'metals' and 'textiles', S27 and 28, are the same as in S20 and 21.

Estimates of the change in the output of the service industries from 1937 to 1948 were taken from M. Robson and C. F. Carter, 'Changes in the Real Product since 1937', *London and Cambridge Economic Bulletin*, no. 4, December 1952, p. vi. Their estimate of the change in the whole of the gross domestic product from 1937 to 1948 agreed closely with that given here. For the changes in the output of services between the pre-war years the very approximate estimates of A. L. Bowley (*Studies in the National Income*, p. 195, table B) were used. These relied mainly on employment statistics.

(g) *Food at farm or dock gate prices, 1935–8, 1946–55, S30–35 and Table 3*

The estimates of food output, imports, change in stocks and exports were first obtained for 1948 and then extrapolated by various means over the other years. The estimates of consumption were simply output plus imports minus the increase (or plus the decrease) in stocks minus exports. These estimates are particularly uncertain because they do not appear to be consistent with the official estimates of food consumption at retail prices. Some discussion of the apparent inconsistency is given at the end of this section (p. 223).

Food output at 1948 market prices was estimated as follows, the aim being to get a total which, when added to food imports as defined on p. 211, would give food consumption at farm or dock gate market prices.

		£ million
1	'Net' output, including allotments, etc.	774*
2	*Plus* rough estimate of value of items deducted from 'gross' output to get 'net' output, *other than* imported items at their c.i.f. values	36
3	*Less* non-food items included in output	−30*
4	*Plus* value of landings of fish of British taking in Great Britain	47
5	*Less* rough estimate of subsidies included in value of net output	−170
6	Equals estimated value of output at farm gate market prices	657

* Averages for 1947–8 and 1948–9.

The reference to 'gross' and 'net' outputs are to the definitions used in, for example, *Agricultural Statistics, United Kingdom—Part II* (H.M.S.O. 1953). The Ministry of Agriculture, Fisheries and Food kindly helped in obtaining some of the above estimates, but are in no way responsible for the final figures taken.

To obtain imports of food at market prices, the estimates described above (p. 211 and S4) were taken with the addition of customs duties on food (estimated at £62 million from the *Annual Statement of Trade*, 1950, supplement to vol. II) and less the estimated value of subsidies on imports (£217 million)—this being a particularly uncertain estimate.

Changes in stocks of food were obtained by multiplying the estimates given in the writer's 'Changes in Stocks of mainly Imported Goods in the United Kingdom '(*Bulletin of the Oxford University Institute of Statistics*, February 1958) by 0·822. This is the ratio of food imports at market prices to their c.i.f. value in 1948 obtained in the way just described, and it was assumed that the same ratio held for changes in stocks of food.

Exports of food were obtained as the sum of Class I, food, drink and tobacco, *less* I I, tobacco, *plus* II J, seeds and nuts, etc., this sum being divided by 2 to obtain a rough estimate of the food content of exports valued at farm or dock gate prices.

The resulting estimate of food consumption has the following defects besides those already mentioned: some imported manufactured food is included; imported and home-produced foodstuffs used for brewing or distilling (such as barley) are included (although imported alcoholic beverages are not); all changes in stocks of crude food are not allowed for and some oils and seeds used for industrial purposes (for example, for making soap or paint) are included in imports. Some may be puzzled by the inclusion of imported feeding stuffs in imports, but, since they are deducted in arriving at 'net' output of home agriculture, they do not appear in the final estimate of consumption. While the allocation of subsidies between home output and imports is very uncertain, the total to be deducted in arriving at consumption at market prices is reasonably sure.

To project the estimates forwards and backwards from 1948, the following series were used. For output, there was taken the index of agricultural net output, including production from holdings of less than an acre, given in Cmnd. 390, *Annual Review and Determination of Guarantees, 1958*, the estimates for calendar years being the averages of those given for farm years. This index is weighted by 1945–6 prices. For imports, the series S4 was taken. For the change in stocks the *Annual Review of Guarantees, 1958*, was taken. For exports, estimates at constant 1948 prices were constructed from the data given in the *Board of Trade Journal* in the same way as for imports.

The index of the price of food consumption at farm or dock gate market prices, S35, was obtained by estimating the current value of consumption and then dividing it by its estimated value at constant 1948 prices. The current values of imports, exports and stock changes were obtained from sources already mentioned. The current value of net output was kindly supplied by the Ministry of Agriculture, Fisheries and Food. Customs duties on food were then added (as obtained from the Supplements to volume II of the *Annual Statements of Trade*) and subsidies subtracted. The latter were, in principle, the total of subsidies to agriculture and food, as given in the various Blue Books on *National Income and Expenditure*, *less* subsidies not included in the value of agri- cultural net output. These were the various 'production grants', fertilizer subsidies and feeding stuffs subsidies, estimates of which were obtained from a variety of sources.

If the estimates of food consumption at farm or dock gate prices described here are compared with estimates of food consumption at retail derived mainly from official sources as described on p. 238, they seem inconsistent with one another. The apparent inconsistency is most easily seen if one subtracts the former estimates from the latter, and so arrives at an estimate of the cost (at current and constant 1948 prices) of the processing and distribution of food. One can then calculate a quantity and price index for processing and distribution, and the resulting series show rather implausible movements. These calculations are shown below. All prices are market prices.

Average for years	Consumption of food				Implied processing and distribution costs	
	Farm or dock gate		Retail		£ million	
	Current prices	1948 prices	Current prices	1948 prices	Current prices	1948 prices
1935–8	616	1,422	1,227	2,172	611	750
1946–9	1,323	1,354	2,164	2,243	841	889
1954–5	2,226	1,618	3,976	2,598	1,750	980

			1946–9 = 100			
	Price	Quantity	Price	Quantity	Price	Quantity
1935–8	44·3	105	58·6	96·8	86·1	84·4
1946–9	100	100	100	100	100	100
1954–5	141	119	159	116	189	110

			1935–8 = 100			
1935–8	100	100	100	100	100	100
1946–9	226	95·2	171	103	116	119
1954–5	318	114	271	120	219	131

It can be seen that the implied rise in the price of processing and distribution of food from 1935–8 to 1946–9 is implausibly small, and the rise in its volume implausibly large. From 1946–9 to 1954–5 the reverse is true: the rise in the price is implausibly large and that of the volume implausibly small. From 1935–8 to 1954–5, however, the changes are not implausible. The rise in the price of processing and distribution of 119% compares with one of 153% in the index of the price of national output (S19). It may be on the low side, but it is probably not very much out. The rise of 31% in the volume of processing and distribution compares with a rise of 20% in the volume of food consumption at retail. This is not implausible, because, with rising food consumption, one would normally expect the pattern to change in favour of more highly processed products (see p. 18). Hence what this comparison suggests is that it is the estimates for 1946–9 which are most dubious. Some sources of error have been referred to. One possibility not mentioned is that the official index of net output of agricultural production understates the increase in output from 1935–8 to 1946–9 and overstates it thereafter. Another possibility is that the estimates of consumption of food at retail overstate the increase in the volume of consumption from 1935–8 to 1946–9 and understate the rise thereafter.[1]

[1] The writer had the advantage of seeing an unpublished study by Mr G. F. Ray in which a similar comparison was made of food consumption at retail and food imports and home food production for the years 1950 to 1958. Mr Ray made numerous adjustments to the figures in an attempt to reconcile them, including several not made

(h) Food output at factor cost, 1870–1955, S36, 37, Chart 2

As for S30, food output was defined, as far as possible, so as to yield a series which, when added to imports of food (and feeding stuffs) would give a measure of food available for consumption or export. It was the response of *this* food output (and not, for example, net value added by farming) to changes in relative prices which it was desired to estimate (as in Section 4 of Chapter VI).

For the period 1935–9 to 1951–5 the official index of net output, as in S30, was taken.

For the period up to 1935–9 the estimates were based on those made by Dr E. M. Ojala in *Agriculture and Economic Progress* (Oxford University Press, for the Oxford University Agricultural Economics Research Institute, 1952). Using the estimates of inputs given by him in table XIX of the appendix, estimates of the current value and value at 1911–13 prices of inputs of imported feeding stuffs, imported animals and seeds were constructed. These were valued as far as possible at import prices, exclusive of margins of distribution, since it was desired to construct an index of net output in which only imported agricultural goods were netted out, and not payments to home distributors. In this last respect the index differs from the official net output index used above. The estimated values of these inputs were then subtracted from Dr Ojala's estimates for the current values and values at 1911–13 prices of the gross output of agriculture given in tables XVI and XVII of the appendix, and so an index of the volume of net output was obtained.

For the change from 1930–4 to 1935–9 there was some doubt as to the best estimate to take. Dr Ojala's estimate shows virtually no change in the volume of gross output (table XVII of the appendix). However, other estimates suggest that there was probably an increase. Those given by Professor Bowley, for example, in *Studies in the National Income* (p. 194) show an increase of over 7% between 1930–4 and 1935–8. For this and other reasons it was thought best to estimate the change in the volume of gross output from 1930–4 to 1935–9 by the process of deflation of current values derived from official estimates. This gave an estimate of gross output in 1935–9 at 1911–13 prices, from which the inputs could be subtracted to obtain net output in the manner described above.

In Dr Ojala's estimates, the agricultural production of Southern

in the estimates given above. Nevertheless, the inconsistency which remained was so large that he concluded that part of the explanation might lie in the two possible sources of error mentioned above. Mr Ray also made estimates of the changes in food consumption, production and imports from 1938 to 1950, which were broadly in agreement with those given here.

Ireland is included up to 1923 and excluded afterwards. An attempt was made to remove this discontinuity in the series by the following adjustment. The net output of agricultural production in Eire and Great Britain valued at international prices and for an average of years about the period 1933–5 is estimated at $173 million and $761 million per annum respectively by Mr Colin Clark (*The Conditions of Economic Progress*, 2nd ed., London, Macmillan, 1951, table facing p. 201). The concept of net output is not exactly the same as that used here, and Northern Ireland is omitted. However, no allowance was made for these differences, nor for the difference in the period referred to, and the procedure adopted was simply to multiply the estimates for the years prior to 1923 by a factor equal to $\dfrac{761}{761+173}$.

The price index of output at factor cost, S37, was obtained for the period 1935–9 to 1951–5 by dividing an index of the current value of net output (see p. 223) by the index of quantity, and for the years before 1939 by dividing the estimates of net output at current prices by those at 1911–13 prices described above, subsidies to farmers being included in the value of output in 1930–4 and 1935–9.

The above estimates refer only to groups of years, but for applying the lagging system described on p. 107 it was desirable to have annual estimates. These were obtained by interpolation between the estimates for groups of years. Up to 1924 the average value of United Kingdom imports of food (from Schlote's *British Overseas Trade*, appendix table 26) was used as a guide. From 1925 to 1939 the index of prices paid to farmers was used (from the *London and Cambridge Economic Bulletin*, March 1956). These interpolations were originally made using the average value of *gross* output of agriculture for the groups of years. This agrees closely with the average value of *net* output up to 1920–2. Hence, up to that period the calculations were not revised. After 1920–2, however, the average value of *net* output was used for the groups of years.

Although the series S36 and 37 are described as 'food' output they in fact include a small proportion of non-food agricultural commodities (such as wool).

(*i*) *Food imports and output at market prices, 1870–1955, S38–40, Chart 8*

In Chart 8 a comparison is given of the relative changes in quantity and price of food imports and output. The index numbers of quantity used were S39 and S36, and were strictly speaking weighted by factor costs and not market prices. S39 is basically the same series as S4, the figures for 1870–99 coming from the same source as those for 1900–13.

The market price of food output, S38, is the same series as its factor cost price, S37, up to 1924–9, it being assumed that net indirect taxes and subsidies on farm output were negligible until then. For 1930–4 and 1935–9, £5 million per annum and £10 million per annum respectively were subtracted from the current values of output on account of subsidies (see Ojala, *Agriculture and Economic Progress*, p. 215, table XX), before dividing these by the values at 1911–13 prices as described above. The estimate for 1935–8 was obtained by multiplying the 1935–9 estimate by a factor derived from the official index of prices paid to farmers, including exchequer grants and acreage payments, in *Agricultural Statistics 1940–1944, England and Wales, Part II* (H.M.S.O. 1948). The change from 1935–8 to 1954–5 was obtained by division of the same current and constant price series used for S30 and in S35 after subtracting £8 million per annum for subsidies in 1935–8 and £185 million per annum in 1954–5.

In estimating the market price of food imports, S40, the same methods and sources were used as for S5 except that customs duties were added to the current values of imports for 1913 (used as a link year) and subsequent years, and an estimate of £25 million per annum (i.e. about three-quarters of the bread subsidy) was subtracted in 1954–5.

(j) Materials at 1948 import prices, 1935–8, 1946–55, S41–62 and Tables 5, 36, 37 and 39

In making the estimates of output, change in stocks, exports and consumption of materials the aim was to include all the principal materials included in imports (as defined for S6) and their close substitutes (such as scrap metal for imported new metal). Generally speaking, consumption was obtained as a residual equal to output plus retained imports minus any increase or plus any decrease in stocks and minus exports. Exports include the crude content of some semi-manufactured exports, and for textiles (and so for the total also) the crude content of some imported semi-manufactures was also estimated and included in consumption.

The estimates of output (S41, 47, 52 and 58) were mainly obtained by multiplying data expressed in physical units by the average value of the corresponding import in 1948. In some cases average values were obtained from the 1948 Census of Production or from the Trade Returns for exports. Most of the data came from various issues of the *Annual Abstract of Statistics* and *Monthly Digest of Statistics* supplemented, especially for before the war, by the Census of Production Reports and by estimates made for T. Barna's 'The Interdependence of the British Economy', *Journal of the Royal Statistical Society*, vol. 115, part 1, 1952, and by C. T. Saunders, 'Consumption of Raw Materials in the United

Kingdom: 1851–1950', *Journal of the Royal Statistical Society*, Series A (General), vol. 115, part 3, 1952. The following were included:

Metals: Iron ore, output of copper, zinc, lead, tin, aluminium and nickel metal, both virgin metal and scrap, *less* imports of metallic ores, concentrates and scrap.

Textiles: Cotton waste, man-made fibres, virgin wool, mungo and shoddy, net value added in production of jute yarn and cloth (multiplied by an index of output of these products), cattle hides, calf skins, and sheep and lamb pelts.

Other: Softwood, hardwood, pitwood, reclaimed rubber, molasses, straw for paper, rags, etc., and waste paper.

The estimates of imports (S42, 48, 53 and 59) are the same as those in S6, 7, and 12 to 17.

The estimates of the changes in stocks (S43, 49, 54 and 60) were mainly obtained by multiplying data expressed in physical units by the average value of the corresponding import in 1948. In some cases, and especially in the later years for which statistics of changes in government stocks have not been published, the change in stocks was obtained as a residual from published estimates of consumption, production, imports and exports. In principle, therefore, changes in government stocks are included throughout. The sources used were similar to those for output described above. Further details, and a list of the thirty-eight items included, are given in the writer's 'Changes in Stocks of Mainly Imported Goods in the United Kingdom', *Bulletin of the Oxford University Institute of Statistics*, February 1958, pp. 53–4 and 213–14.

The estimates of exports (S44, 50, 55 and 61) were for the most part made in either of two ways. First, where the whole of any letter group in the old trade classification consisted of crude materials similar to imports, exports at constant 1948 prices were obtained in the same way as imports, that is, by linking together the Board of Trade's published index numbers of quantity. Second, where the export value included an appreciable amount of processing in this country, the crude material content was estimated, generally by multiplying physical units of the item in question by an average value per unit corresponding to the imported crude material (with allowance for wastage in processing in some cases). An example of the first method is group II L, paper-making materials, which are included in exports of 'other' materials at their full 1948 export values. An example of the second method is exports of cotton yarns, *ex* III I, where the weight of the exports (in lb.) was multiplied by the average value of raw cotton imports per lb. in 1948 (after increasing the weight of exports by 15% to allow for wastage). The following were included:

Metals: II C, iron ore and scrap, II D, non-ferrous metalliferous ores and scrap, and, *ex* III D, aluminium and alloys, brass and copper alloys, copper, lead, nickel and alloys, tin and zinc valued at *import* average values per ton.

Textiles: II F, raw cotton and cotton waste, II G, wool raw and waste, and woollen rags, II H, silk raw and waste, and artificial silk waste, II K, hides and skins, *ex* III I, cotton yarns, grey unbleached cotton piece-goods, *ex* III J, wool tops, *ex* III L, jute yarns and manufactures.

Other: II L, paper-making materials, II M, rubber.

The estimates of the crude content of imported textile semi-manufactures (S45 and 56) were made in the same way as the second method described above for exports. Only the crude content of imported cotton yarns and grey unbleached cotton piece-goods was included.

(*k*) *Expenditure on fuels at constant prices, 1924–38, 1946–55, S63–65, Charts 5 and 6*

Estimates of the physical quantities of various fuels purchased by three groups of consumers—domestic and commercial, manufacturing industry and transport (defined below)—were made for each of the years 1924–38, 1946–55. These were multiplied by the approximate average prices paid in the following years: for 1924 to 1930, the prices of 1924; for 1930 to 1935, the prices of 1930; for 1935 to 1955, the prices of 1948. This gave, for each group, a series of expenditure at constant prices for three periods, which were then linked together at 1930 and 1935. The resulting index numbers are therefore similar in weighting and construction to those used for imports (S2, 4, 6, 8 and 10).

'Domestic and commercial' includes domestic consumers, shops, offices, hospitals, schools, and street lighting. It excludes petrol for motoring, which is included in 'transport'.

'Manufacturing industry' includes in principle all the industries included in the index of industrial production except for coal mines, coke ovens, oil refineries and the manufactured fuel trade, and gas and electricity undertakings.

'Transport' includes railways, road transport including private motoring, coastal shipping and marine craft (but not bunkers for ocean-going vessels), and aircraft.

The main source used was the *Ministry of Fuel and Power Statistical Digest, 1955*, supplemented, especially for before the war, by R. Stone, *The Measurement of Consumers' Expenditure and Behaviour in the United Kingdom, 1920–1938, Vol. I* (Cambridge University Press, 1954); PEP (Political and Economic Planning), *The British Fuel and Power Industries* (London, 1947); the working sheets for T. Barna, 'The Interdependence of the British Economy', *Journal of the Royal Statistical*

Society, Series A, vol. 115, 1952; and various Census of Production Reports, the *Annual Statement of Trade* and earlier issues of the *Ministry of Fuel and Power Statistical Digest*.

The available figures do not match the above three categories of consumption exactly, and it is not always clear where certain consumers (for example, agriculture) are included and how far others (for example, the Armed Forces) are included at all. In what follows, the items included in each group are listed in accordance with their description in the *Ministry of Fuel and Power Statistical Digest, 1955*, except where otherwise stated.

(i) *Domestic and commercial*

Coal (1953 *Digest*) = Table 90, consumption of domestic, miners, miscellaneous (including Service Departments) and non-industrial establishments.

Coke and manufactured fuels (1953 *Digest*) = Table 4, net disposals to shops, offices, hospitals, etc., and domestic.

Oil = Table 153, deliveries of kerosene burning oil for inland consumption *plus*, Table 154, deliveries of gas/diesel and fuel oils for central heating (private houses and other premises).

Electricity = Table 109, sales to domestic and farm premises, shops, offices and other commercial premises and public lighting *plus*, Table 113 (p. 148), sales by railways and transport undertakings to similar consumers.

Gas = Table 116, sales for public lighting, and to domestic, commercial and other (excluding industrial) consumers.

(ii) *Manufacturing industry*

Coal = Table 5, adjusted inland coal consumption *less* Table 72 consumption by gas and electricity works, coke ovens, and collieries, and *less*, Table 143, consumption by the manufactured fuel trade and *less* estimated consumption by oil refineries (see 1953 *Digest* Table 4) and *less* consumption by domestic and commercial and transport, derived as explained above and below.

Coke and manufactured fuels (1953 *Digest*) = Table 4, net disposals to agriculture, industry and transport. Of these, industry is far the biggest, and the other two were included for convenience.

Oil = Table 153, deliveries of kerosene vaporizing oil, gas/diesel oil and fuel oil for inland consumption *less* consumption of oil by the electric power industry (Tables 91 and 98) and *less* deliveries of oil for gas manufacture, central heating, marine craft, rail traction and diesel-engined road vehicles (Table 154).

Electricity = Table 109, sales to factories and other industrial premises *plus*, Table 113 (p. 148), sales by railway and transport undertakings to factories and other industrial premises *less*, Table 40, electricity consumed by coal mines minus electricity produced by them, *less,* Table 160, purchased electricity used by oil refineries, *less,* 1953 *Digest* Table 4, electricity used or lost by the carbonization industries minus electricity produced by them.

Gas = Table 116, sales to industrial consumers *plus,* Table 137, coke ovens disposals of gas to steel works and industrial consumers (excluding collieries, gas works and electricity stations).

(iii) Transport

Coal = Table 72 consumption by railways and coastwise bunkers.

Coke and manufactured fuel assumed to be negligible, and included under 'industry' (see above).

Oil = Table 153, deliveries for inland consumption of aviation spirit and wide-cut gasoline, motor spirit, kerosene aviation turbine fuel, *plus,* Table 154, inland deliveries for marine craft, rail traction and diesel-engined road vehicles.

Electricity = Table 109, sales for traction *plus,* Table 113 (p. 148), sales of railway and transport undertakings for traction.

Gas = assumed negligible.

The sources just listed sometimes provide a run of figures covering much of the period. For the rest, the series were extrapolated backwards or forwards by linking on the most nearly comparable estimates which could be derived from the works cited.

The average prices used to multiply the physical units of the various fuels were mostly obtained from the same sources. In principle, the prices are meant to be those paid by the purchaser inclusive of taxes and distribution costs, but for coke-oven gas used by industry, where the transaction is often within a single firm, the price used was that of gas purchased from gas undertakings, also all fuels purchased by transport were valued, so far as possible, at their wholesale and not retail prices. Fuels purchased by domestic and commercial consumers were valued at retail prices, as far as possible.

(l) Sales on the home market and imports of five groups of manufactures, 1924–38, 1946–55, S66–77, Chart 17

Sales on the home market are defined as gross output plus retained imports minus exports of the products concerned. Changes in stocks are not allowed for, so that 'sales' include 'sales to stock' (which may be positive or negative). Gross output is defined as in the Censuses of Production, so that sales from one establishment to another within any trade are included as well as sales to establishments outside the trade.

The index numbers of sales at constant prices were obtained by estimating gross output, retained imports and exports at constant prices.

The prices used were those of 1924 for the period 1924 to 1930, those of 1930 for the period 1930 to 1935 and those of 1948 for the period 1935 to 1938 and 1946 to 1955. These are the same price weights as were used in constructing the index numbers of the quantity of retained imports (S2, 4, 6, 8 and 10), and the estimates of imports and exports for each of the five groups of manufactures were obtained using, in the main, the methods and sources already described (pp. 209 ff.). Exports were deducted at their estimated factory value, this being 6% less than their f.o.b. value as given in the Trade Returns.

The estimates of gross output at constant prices were obtained by multiplying the values of gross output in each of the base years, 1924, 1930 and 1948, by index numbers of *net* output at constant prices. This was done since index numbers of gross output for broad industry groups are not generally available. It is not thought that this was a serious source of error, however. The published index numbers of net output are themselves usually based on index numbers of gross output for the individual census trades, and it is only in combining these that net output weights are used. A comparison of changes in output between 1924 and 1930, and between 1930 and 1935, using first gross output weights and then net output weights, shows generally little difference between the two (see Bowley, *Studies in the National Income*, pp. 147–50). The estimates of gross output in the base years were obtained from the *Annual Abstract of Statistics for 1956*, Bowley, *op. cit.*, and various Censuses of Production. The index numbers of net output were obtained mainly from the sources mentioned on p. 218 and used for S20 and 21.

The coverage of the series is not exactly uniform throughout the period. The items included in 1948 are listed below, and a table showing the current values in the three base years is appended.

Retained imports and exports

Iron and steel = III C, iron and steel and manufactures thereof.
Engineering products = III F, electrical goods and apparatus, *plus* III G, machinery, *plus* III S, vehicles.
Textiles = III I, cotton yarns and manufactures, *plus* III J, woollen and worsted yarns and manufactures, *plus* III K, silk and artificial silk yarns and manufactures, *plus* III L, manufactures of other textile materials.
Chemicals = D 1 (on the current trade classification), chemicals.
Paper and board = III R paper, cardboard, etc.

Gross output

Iron and steel = Part of Order V, blast furnaces, iron and steel smelting and rolling, sheets, tinplate, iron and steel tubes and iron foundries.

Engineering products = All Orders VI and VII, i.e. engineering, ship-building and electrical goods and vehicles.

Textiles = All Order X, textiles.

Chemicals = All Order IV, chemicals and allied trades, *less* mineral oil refining.

Paper and board = Part of Order XV, paper and board, wallpaper, cardboard boxes, cartons and fibre-board packing cases, stationery and paper bags.

Current values in the base years

| | \multicolumn{3}{c}{Sales on home market} | \multicolumn{3}{c}{£ million Retained imports} |
Item	1924	1930	1948	1924	1930	1948
Iron and steel	245	212	636	28	29	20
Engineering products	345	387	1,866	23	29	56
Textiles	539	340	1,028	55	45	69
Chemicals	183	174	636	13	13	48
Paper and board	62	76	235	14	18	24
Total	1,374	1,189	4,402	134	134	217

(m) *Imported and home-produced supplies of fifteen manufactures, census years, 1907–54, S78–137, Chart 20*

Index numbers of the quantities and prices of fifteen manufactures imported and produced in this country were estimated and used in the construction of Chart 20. The index numbers of quantity were obtained from data expressed in physical units. The index numbers of price were obtained by dividing values by quantities, i.e. by obtaining 'average values', and not price quotations.

The main sources were the Census of Production Reports for 1907, 1924, 1930, 1935, 1948 and 1954, the Import Duties Act Inquiries of 1933 and 1934, and the *Annual Statement of Trade*. Not all the results of the 1954 Census of Production were available when the work was done.

'Imports' refer in all cases to imports from 'foreign countries' as defined in the *Annual Statement of Trade*, that is, broadly speaking, from countries outside the Commonwealth and excluding Ireland. The reason for confining attention to imports from these countries is that the tariffs enforced in 1932 were mostly confined to imports from them. The 'price' of imports includes tariffs, which were estimated from data in the supplements to Vol. II of the *Annual Statement of Trade* and in the Customs Tariffs valid on various dates. These estimates were un-certain in some cases since the composition of the individual items in the Annual Statements was not known.

'Home' in the tables means all supplies of the good in question sold on the home market other than imports from foreign countries. The quantity of 'home' supplies was measured by production (as total sales by home producers in some cases) plus retained imports from all sources *less* total imports from foreign countries and *less* exports to all countries. Strictly speaking, re-exports out of imports from foreign countries should be added to this figure, but the adjustment would be small. More important, changes in stocks were ignored. The 'price' of 'home' supplies was for simplicity of calculation assumed to be the same as that of home production, being obtained by dividing the value of output (or sales in some cases) by the quantity of output (or sales). This short-cut is justified as long as imports from British countries were small (as they generally were) and the price of exports did not diverge appreciably from that of sales by home producers on the home market (or else exports were small).

The descriptions of the individual items are those given in the Censuses of Production. In some cases the same description does not apply throughout the series; for example, shaving soap was included with other toilet soap in the *Annual Statement of Trade* for 1907, so that the quantities and prices for the change in imports from 1907 to 1924 are based on series which include shaving soap. This fact, together with the fact that even where the description is unchanged it refers to a heterogeneous collection of goods, means that the index numbers of both price and quantity are unsatisfactory. This is especially so where imports were very small, as they often were. Consequently, the differences in the changes in prices of the imported and home-produced manufactures, which were marked in some periods and for some goods, may have been partly or mainly due to changes in their composition, and not to any difference in the relative price movements of identical products.

Two sets of estimates, A and B, are given for imports of motor-cars in 1924 (S134 and 135, see also Chart 20). A is based on annual rates for the first seven months of 1924, when a duty of $33\frac{1}{3}\%$ on imported cars was in force. B is based on annual rates for the last five months of 1924, when there was no duty.

3. NOTES TO SOME TABLES IN THE TEXT

(a) Adjustments for weighting bias in Tables 5, 6, 36, 37 and 39

The estimates of imports of materials at constant prices (S42, 48, 53 and 59) were obtained by linking together series weighted by the prices of various years (see p. 214). For reasons given on pp. 134–6, it was thought desirable to adjust these estimates so as to obtain some corresponding as nearly as possible to fully 1948 price weighted estimates. Only the figures for 1935–8 were adjusted, since the difference between the actual estimates and fully 1948 weighted ones was probably only substantial for the change from 1935–8 to after the war, and relatively small for later changes. The adjustments consisted in multiplying the 1935–8 import estimates by the following factors:

Metal materials	1·111
Textile materials	1·053
Other materials	1·075
All materials	1·071

These adjustment factors were estimated mainly by comparing the estimates of imports obtained as already described with estimates using 1948 price weights for the individual commodities for the years 1935 and 1948. This comparison was only made for a sample, but it showed that the linked estimates were appreciably biased relative to the direct and fully 1948 price weighted estimates.

Exports of materials in 1935–8 were, for simplicity of calculation, adjusted by the same factor as imports, although they were not all estimated by the same method of linking as imports. Production was not adjusted, since it was already fully 1948 price weighted. Consumption, being the residual, was adjusted by the same absolute amount as imports minus exports.

These adjustments were only made to the estimates in Tables 5, 6, 36, 37 and 39, and to the estimates used in the regression analysis described in Chapter VII, Section 5. The figures given in S41–62 and Charts 4, 11 and 12 are not adjusted for weighting bias.

(b) Imports and consumption of fuels, pre-war and post-war, Table 7

Estimates of production, retained imports, exports and bunkers and inland consumption of coal and of five kinds of petroleum products (crude oil, motor and aviation spirit, kerosene, gas/diesel oil and fuel oil) in tons were made for the averages of 1935–8, 1946–9 and 1954–5. Changes in stocks and errors and omissions were obtained as a residual. These estimates were then multiplied by the average value of the corresponding import in 1948 (c.i.f. values, exclusive of duty) to obtain the figures in Table 7, p. 33. The remaining imports of petroleum products (industrial spirits, lubricating oils, etc.) shown in line 15 of the table were estimated in the same way.

The main source was the *Ministry of Fuel and Power Statistical Digest, 1955*, supplemented by the other works cited on p. 229. In what follows, the references are to the 1955 *Digest* unless otherwise stated. For some years estimates were obtained by linking on the most nearly comparable series to the ones mentioned below.

Coal

Production = Table 4, column (1), coal production, *less*, Table 72, collieries' consumption of coal.

Retained imports, exports and bunkers were obtained from the *Annual Statement of Trade*.

Inland consumption = Table 5, gross inland coal consumption, *less*, Table 72, collieries' consumption of coal.

Oil (crude and refined)

Production = for crude oil, Table 4, production of crude shale oil and crude petroleum; for refined oil, *Annual Abstract of Statistics*, no. 94, 1957, Table 173, production from petroleum refineries and distillation plants.

Retained imports, exports and bunkers = Tables 148 and 149, total imports, exports and re-exports and bunkers, *less* re-exports obtained from the *Annual Statement of Trade* after converting gallons to tons.

Inland consumption = for crude oil, this is a residual and so includes changes in stocks (thought to be small). It is simply production *plus* imports *less* exports. For refined oil, Table 153, deliveries of petroleum products for inland consumption.

(c) Distribution and purchases of fuels in 1954, Tables 8 and 9

Table 8, p. 34, shows the percentage distribution of each of five fuels (coal, refined oil, electricity, gas and coke) amongst each of seven consuming sectors, three 'final' (domestic and commercial, manufacturing industry and transport) and four 'intermediate' (coal, oil refining, electricity and gas and coke). The percentages were derived from estimates of physical quantities (tons for coal, oil and coke, kilowatt-hours for electricity and therms for gas), and these in turn were obtained using the same methods and sources as for S63–65, described on pp. 229 ff. Since the items included in the consumption of the three 'final' sectors are listed there, it only remains to give the items included in the consumption of the four 'intermediate' sectors. As on p. 235, the references are to the *Ministry of Fuel and Power Statistical Digest, 1955*, unless otherwise stated.

Consumption by:	Consumption of:	
Coal	Coal	= zero, since coal output is defined so as to exclude colliery consumption.
	Refined oil, coke, and gas	= assumed negligible.
	Electricity	= Table 40, consumption *less* production.

Consumption by:	Consumption of:	
Oil refining	Coal	= 1953 *Digest*, Table 4, coal used by the petroleum industry.
	Refined oil	= zero, since refinery output is defined so as to exclude refinery oil consumption.
	Electricity	= 1953 *Digest*, Table 4, electricity used by the petroleum industry *less* electricity produced by it.
	Gas and coke	= assumed negligible.
Electricity	Coal	= Table 72, consumption by electricity works.
	Refined oil	= Table 91, columns (3) and (4), oil used for firing and engines *plus*, Table 98, column (3), oil for firing used by railway and transport authorities generating electricity.
	Electricity	= zero, since electricity output is defined so as to exclude losses in generation and transmission.
	Gas and coke	= assumed negligible.
Gas and coke	Coal	= Table 72, consumption by gas works and coke ovens *plus*, Table 143, coal used by the manufactured fuel trade.
	Refined oil	= Table 154, inland deliveries of gas/diesel and fuel oils for gas manufacture.
	Electricity	= 1953 *Digest*, Table 4, electricity used by the carbonization industries *less* electricity produced by them.
	Gas and coke	= zero, since output is defined so as to exclude consumption of gas and coke by the carbonization industries.

Table 9, p. 35, shows the percentage distribution of each of five consuming sectors' purchases of fuels amongst each of five fuels. These percentages were derived from estimates of *values*, and not physical quantities as in Table 8. The basic data of physical quantities were, however, the same as in Table 8, the values being found by multiplying the quantities by the estimated average price of the relevant fuel in 1954, these being, in the main, prices paid by the purchaser inclusive of duty and distribution costs. For transport, however, wholesale and not retail prices were used throughout.

(d) Data used in estimating the changes in the demand for food, 1935–8 to 1946–9 and 1954–5, Table 19

The estimates of the quantity and price of food consumption at farm or dock gate market prices are given in S34 and 35, and described on p. 221.

The price index of non-food consumer goods was estimated by dividing an index of the current value of consumers' expenditure on goods and services other than food by an index of the same expenditure at 1948 market prices. To obtain this it was necessary to estimate the current value and value at 1948 market prices of consumers' expenditure on all goods and services and similarly for expenditure on food.

Estimates of the current value and value at 1948 market prices of all consumers' expenditure and of expenditure on food at *retail* prices were obtained for the years 1938, 1946–55 from the Blue Book on *National Income and Expenditure, 1957*, Tables 19 and 20. For the years 1935–7 they were linked on at 1938 using estimates for total consumers' expenditure kindly supplied by Mr D. A. Rowe, and estimates for expenditure on food at retail given in R. Stone, *The Measurement of Consumers' Expenditure and Behaviour in the United Kingdom, 1920–1938, Vol. I*, p. 174, table 66.

To obtain the price index of non-food consumer goods under 'Food measured at farm gate' in Table 19, expenditure on food at farm or dock gate prices was subtracted from total consumers' expenditure. For the corresponding index under 'Food measured at retail' in Table 19, expenditure on food at retail prices was subtracted.

The estimates of population for the years 1935–8 and 1948–55 were obtained from the *London and Cambridge Economic Bulletin*, no. 26, June 1958. They refer to the *de facto* population. For 1946 and 1947, estimates of the *de facto* population are not available in the standard sources and so the numbers of the armed forces stationed in the United Kingdom in these years were roughly estimated and added to the estimates of the civilian population given in the *Bulletin*.

(e) Data for 1930–5, Table 42

The sources used for imports and exports (Table 42, lines 1–3, 10 and 12–14) were the same as those described on p. 215 and used for S7, 10 and 11.

The average value of imports corrected for the change in tariffs, line 4, was obtained by multiplying the uncorrected average value, as in line 3, by an index of 1 plus the *ad valorem* rate per unit of duty in 1935, with 1930 = 1. The duties in 1930 amounted to £10 million and in 1935 to £22·3 million (Supplement to vol. II of the *Annual Statement of Trade*). 1 plus the *ad valorem* rate per unit of duty was

1·045 in 1930 and 1·185 in 1935, and the index of this in 1935, with 1930 = 1, was 1·134.

Sales of manufactures from United Kingdom production on the home market, lines 5–7, were derived in a similar way to S66–71, described on pp. 231 ff.

The index numbers of United Kingdom wage rates, line 8, and of wage rates abroad, line 15, were obtained from data in the *Statistical Year-book of the League of Nations, 1940–41* (Geneva, 1941), pp. 76, 77. The index numbers for Canada, the United States, Germany, Belgium, France, the Netherlands, Sweden, Switzerland and Czecho-Slovakia given there were used together with estimates for Japan, Italy, Norway and India. For the last four countries, it was assumed that wage rates in domestic currency fell 3%, that is by the same amount as in the United Kingdom. This is a doubtful assumption, and even the published index numbers are of doubtful comparability, some referring to hourly rates or earnings, whereas the United Kingdom index refers to weekly rates. However, it is hoped that the combined index is not seriously misleading. This was obtained by first correcting the domestic index numbers for changes in exchange rates (given in the same source) and then weighting them in proportion to the value of United Kingdom imports of manufactures (Class III) from the various countries in 1930. The first nine countries listed above accounted for about 75% of United Kingdom imports of manufactures in 1930, and the last four for about 8%.

The index of the average value of the national product of the United Kingdom, excluding manufacturing, line 8, was derived from the price index of national output, S19, and index numbers of the volume and price of manufacturing net output based on data from A. Maddison's 'Output, Employment and Productivity in British Manufacturing', *Bulletin of the Oxford University Institute of Statistics*, November 1955.

The source for the index of industrial production, line 9, is given on p. 218.

United Kingdom factor prices, line 11, and factor prices abroad, line 16, were obtained by combining the index of material prices in line 10 (assumed to be common to both) with the respective index numbers of wage rates, lines 8 and 15. The weights used were 1 for materials to 4 for wages.

(f) Percentage changes in various items, 1931–2, Table 43

The sources used for Table 43 were the same as for Table 42 with the following exceptions: for exports of manufactures the whole of Class III was taken, instead of Class III excluding IIIA, D and O (coke, non-ferrous metals and manufactured oils), but the difference is not substantial; for the index of wage rates abroad, only the first nine countries (for which index numbers were published) listed on p. 239 were taken, no estimates for Japan, Italy, Norway and India being included. The change in the index of 1 plus the *ad valorem* rate of tariff on imports of manufactures from 1931 to 1932, line 3, is that from 1930 to 1935 calculated as described on p. 238. This was taken because of the difficulty of estimating the change from 1931 to 1932 and because of doubts as to its significance (see p. 169, n. 2). Manufacturing production abroad, line 10, was obtained from *Industrialization and Foreign Trade* (Geneva, League of Nations, 1945), pp. 128 and 140.

4. NOTES TO THE CHARTS

Chart 1. The series for imports are S2, 4, 6, 8 and 10, and industrial production is from the source given on p. 218.

Chart 2. For agricultural output and price see pp. 225 ff., 336 and 37; for the price of national output see pp. 216 ff., S19 and 23; and for unemployment, see Table 18, p. 105. The regression analysis is discussed on pp. 101 ff.

Chart 3. The index numbers of manufacturing production for the United States and the rest of the world came from MacDougall, *The World Dollar Problem* (1957), p. 485, table D2.

The index of materials consumption in the rest of the world came from the same source, Table B4, p. 468, the sum of the consumption of metals (excluding gold), industrial wood, natural rubber and natural textile fibres.

The index of materials consumption in the United States came from *Raw Materials in the United States Economy, 1900–1952*, United States Bureau of the Census, Working Paper no. 1 Preliminary (Washington, 1954), table A5, physical structure materials *less* tobacco.

Chart 4. For the quantity and price of imports of materials, see pp. 209 ff. and S6, 7 and 22; for the index of industrial production, see p. 218; and for the index of the general price level see pp. 216 ff. and S19 and 23.

Chart 5. For domestic and commercial expenditure on fuels, see pp. 229 ff. and S63. Consumers' total expenditure was obtained by linking the estimates of expenditure at 1948 market prices for 1938, 1946–55 in *National Income and Expenditure, 1957*, Table 20 to estimates for the years 1924–38 at 1938 prices kindly supplied by Mr D. A. Rowe. Consumers' expenditure on fuels was obtained by linking the estimates of expenditure at 1948 market prices for 1938, 1946–55 in the source first mentioned to estimates for the years 1924–38 at 1938 prices given in R. Stone, *The Measurement of Consumers' Expenditure and Behaviour in the United Kingdom, 1920–1938, Vol. I*, p. 237, table 103.

For manufacturing industry's expenditure on fuels, see pp. 229 ff.

and S64. The index of manufacturing production was derived as follows:

1924–38 from K. S. Lomax, 'New Index-numbers of Industrial Production 1900–1938', *London and Cambridge Economic Bulletin,* June 1958.

1935 and 1948, S26, see p. 221.

1946–8 *Annual Abstract of Statistics,* no. 90, 1953, table 137.

1948–55 *Annual Abstract of Statistics,* no. 94, 1957, table 151.

For transportation expenditure on fuels, see pp. 229 ff. and S65.

Chart 6. The sources and methods used were the same as those described on pp. 229 ff. for S63 and 64. The estimates themselves are given below. The original estimates were expressed in logarithms, and the averages are accordingly geometric averages for 1935–8 or 1943–55. Some of the estimates are most uncertain, in particular those for prices of oil, gas and coke for industry, and for quantities of domestic and commercial and manufacturing industry's oil and coke.

1935–8 = 100

	1954–5 Quantity	1954–5 Price*
Domestic and commercial		
Coal	87·7	249
Oil	146	244
Electricity	411	80·5
Gas	144	207
Coke	143	319
'Manufacturing' industry		
Coal	101	353
Oil	522	265
Electricity	352	152
Gas	290	207
Coke	165	483

* The price index numbers are lagged, the index for any year being the geometric average for the five years ending in that year.

Chart 7. For imports of manufactures, see pp. 209 ff. and S10. For industrial production, see p. 218.

Chart 8. See pp. 225 ff. and S36 and S38–40.

Chart 9. From estimates made by W. E. G. Salter in 'A Consideration of Technological Change with particular Reference to Labour Productivity', a University of Cambridge Ph.D. dissertation, 1955 (see also p. 127, n. 2).

Chart 10. Estimates made from the series used in Chart 3.

Charts 11, 12. For imports of materials, see pp. 209 ff. and S6, 12, 14 and 16. For industrial production, see pp. 218 ff. and S20 and 21.

Charts 13–16. The basic series for the quantity of imports and industrial production are the same as for Charts 11, 12. The index numbers of the price of imports are from S7, 13, 15, 17 and 22, and the general price level from S19 and 23. These series were adjusted in various ways before making the regression analysis as described on pp. 133 ff.

Chart 17. See pp. 231 ff. and S66–77.

Chart 18. Imports of manufactures from the Trade and Navigation Accounts. The imports included are Class III, articles wholly or mainly manufactured, less III A, coke and manufactured fuel, III D, non-ferrous metals and manufactures thereof, and III O, oils, fats and resins manufactured.

Chart 19. For imports of manufactures, see pp. 209 ff. and S11; for exports, see p. 216 and S18.

Chart 20. See pp. 233 ff. and S78–137.

5. LIST OF THE MAIN STATISTICAL SERIES, S1–137

Retained imports, value, £ million, 1900–55	S 1
Retained imports, index numbers of quantity and price, 1900–55	
total	S 2, 3
food	S 4, 5
materials	S 6, 7
fuels	S 8, 9
manufactures	S 10, 11
metal materials	S 12, 13
textile materials	S 14, 15
other materials	S 16, 17
Exports of manufactures, index numbers of price, 1900–55	S 18
National output, index numbers of price, 1900–55	S 19
Industrial production, metals and metal-using industries, 1900–55	S 20
Industrial production, textiles, clothing and leather industries, 1900–55	S 21
Imports of materials and national output, price index numbers for the war years	S 22, 23
Gross domestic product at 1948 factor cost, 1935, 1936, 1937, 1938 and 1948, total, agriculture, etc., total manufactures, metals and metal-using, textiles, clothing and leather, total industrial	S 24–29

Index numbers 1948 = 100

Year	Value £ million S1	Retained imports Total Quantity S2	Price S3	Food Quantity S4	Price S5
1900	460	79·4	28·7	85·1	27·7
1901	454	81·1	27·7	87·2	28·4
1902	463	82·6	27·7	85·8	28·7
1903	473	82·4	28·4	89·4	28·7
1904	481	83·3	28·6	88·9	28·4
1905	487	83·8	28·8	86·3	29·4
1906	523	86·3	30·0	88·7	29·4
1907	554	87·5	31·4	88·3	30·7
1908	513	84·0	30·3	85·3	31·4
1909	533	86·2	30·6	86·7	32·4
1910	575	87·5	32·5	86·5	33·1
1911	577	90·0	31·8	89·1	32·8
1912	633	96·9	32·4	89·6	34·4
1913	659	99·0	33·0	93·3	33·8
1920	1,714	87·1	97·4	82·1	98·8
1921	980	72·8	66·6	84·7	69·0
1922	900	85·6	52·1	92·8	53·2
1923	979	95·9	50·6	107	50·2
1924	1,140	108	52·4	118	51·3
1925	1,167	112	51·7	116	52·0
1926	1,116	117	47·3	114	48·7
1927	1,095	120	45·4	119	47·2
1928	1,077	116	45·9	119	47·1
1929	1,112	123	44·9	123	46·1
1930	958	120	39·6	123	40·3
1931	798	123	32·1	134	32·4
1932	652	108	29·8	130	30·4
1933	627	110	28·3	126	28·4
1934	681	116	29·0	127	28·2
1935	701	117	29·7	126	29·5
1936	787	126	31·0	129	31·1
1937	953	133	35·5	130	35·3
1938	859	126	33·9	134	33·8
1946	1,251	81·0	76·6	84·0	77·2
1947	1,735	95·0	90·6	98·8	91·8
1948	2,014	100	100	100	100
1949	2,217	109	101	109	102
1950	2,528	109	115	107	109
1951	3,781	125	150	116	126
1952	3,342	111	150	107	131
1953	3,193	120	132	117	124
1954	3,264	125	130	114	126
1955	3,758	139	134	121	127

For notes see Section 2 (a), p. 209.

Index numbers 1948 = 100

Retained imports

	Materials*		Fuels		Manufactures	
Year	Quantity	Price	Quantity	Price	Quantity	Price
	S6	S7	S8	S9	S10	S11
1900	82·2	27·0	6·11	72·5	124	26·6
1901	83·9	24·6	5·90	64·2	127	25·5
1902	85·7	24·2	6·75	58·1	135	25·8
1903	80·0	26·1	6·53	61·9	136	26·3
1904	84·9	26·6	6·75	63·8	129	26·9
1905	88·2	26·1	6·85	59·1	134	27·5
1906	89·9	29·4	7·27	59·2	141	27·5
1907	97·0	31·1	7·59	60·1	132	28·1
1908	92·2	27·4	8·33	58·6	126	28·4
1909	94·7	27·8	8·85	51·5	130	28·7
1910	96·3	32·1	8·75	48·5	139	32·2
1911	96·9	30·7	9·38	43·1	149	28·7
1912	109	30·3	11·1	48·1	168	28·7
1913	107	31·9	12·4	60·9	174	29·3
1920	97·0	94·5	20·1	207	134	82·7
1921	59·1	53·8	26·1	164	87·8	63·7
1922	78·7	47·7	25·0	96·7	117	48·4
1923	78·1	51·4	27·1	78·6	145	45·9
1924	89·7	56·8	33·0	78·2	168	45·4
1925	96·6	54·8	32·6	74·8	191	43·7
1926	93·6	47·6	75·0	79·3	192	41·4
1927	97·9	44·7	47·2	68·4	215	40·3
1928	92·5	46·3	47·7	52·4	212	41·2
1929	103	44·8	48·6	55·3	222	40·3
1930	93·8	36·8	55·3	52·6	214	38·2
1931	87·4	27·5	51·9	35·4	220	34·3
1932	87·1	25·4	52·6	37·4	124	32·3
1933	97·0	25·7	57·9	33·3	120	30·5
1934	107	28·4	63·4	31·9	138	30·3
1935	109	28·1	65·7	32·2	144	30·6
1936	123	29·3	69·4	33·5	163	31·3
1937	135	35·8	72·4	41·6	183	33·7
1938	115	32·3	74·8	39·2	156	34·3
1946	80·8	72·0	83·9	65·3	60·0	83·8
1947	94·5	86·8	78·7	82·3	90·7	96·8
1948	100	100	100	100	100	100
1949	108	103	100	93·9	117	97·8
1950	108	131	107	116	122	101
1951	120	202	145	138	156	130
1952	97·9	187	145	149	142	141
1953	113	150	159	125	127	123
1954	120	145	178	117	149	114
1955	127	157	215	120	192	117

* See S22 and p. 219 for estimates of the price index of materials imports for the war years.

For notes see Section 2 (a), p. 209.

Year	Metal materials		Retained imports Textile materials		Other materials	
	Quantity S12	Price S13	Quantity S14	Price S15	Quantity S16	Price S17
1900	42·6	43·6	101	25·8	80·1	24·1
1901	41·8	40·3	110	22·9	77·0	22·9
1902	45·6	36·0	107	23·1	81·3	22·5
1903	44·6	37·1	95·8	26·4	78·2	23·3
1904	46·6	38·6	106	28·5	79·6	21·9
1905	48·1	39·7	117	26·2	75·9	22·7
1906	50·0	47·2	115	30·0	81·0	24·3
1907	52·0	49·2	130	31·7	83·6	25·9
1908	53·5	39·3	117	28·1	81·9	23·8
1909	53·2	39·0	123	28·6	83·4	24·3
1910	52·6	40·3	120	34·4	90·7	28·1
1911	53·2	41·2	126	32·3	85·8	26·8
1912	54·4	45·2	152	30·0	90·7	27·3
1913	59·1	45·7	131	33·5	102	26·9
1920	48·5	94·6	122	111	95·1	77·0
1921	28·7	61·6	72·7	57·2	60·8	49·8
1922	34·7	52·2	109	51·0	67·1	44·8
1923	49·8	56·8	86·8	58·3	82·6	43·9
1924	57·0	61·1	106	68·6	85·8	43·0
1925	58·9	62·1	118	63·7	87·6	43·7
1926	56·0	60·5	113	48·7	88·3	45·1
1927	60·7	56·1	111	45·2	103	41·6
1928	62·9	54·0	108	52·6	85·8	37·8
1929	66·9	55·3	113	48·9	114	37·0
1930	64·8	44·8	95·8	36·9	112	33·4
1931	58·4	33·3	97·2	25·6	95·9	27·3
1932	45·0	31·4	107	24·6	94·9	24·1
1933	48·0	33·3	120	25·5	107	23·1
1934	68·6	33·8	111	28·3	131	26·2
1935	74·6	35·7	113	28·0	127	25·0
1936	81·8	38·4	137	29·9	135	24·4
1937	97·4	49·8	139	33·5	155	31·7
1938	89·1	43·3	119	28·2	129	30·9
1946	75·8	72·0	85·3	57·3	78·9	90·0
1947	90·5	90·7	90·7	75·7	102	95·7
1948	100	100	100	100	100	100
1949	100	110	114	107	105	93·7
1950	99·3	132	113	146	108	110
1951	105	183	108	232	144	187
1952	111	214	85·5	175	103	177
1953	105	184	111	152	121	124
1954	118	175	107	148	136	121
1955	132	200	101	143	155	137

For notes see Section 2 (a), p. 209.

Index numbers 1948 = 100

Year	Exports of manufactures Price S18	National output Price* S19	Industrial production Metals Quantity S20	Textiles Quantity S21
1900	21·6	25·0	21·7	78·8
1901	21·3	24·7	21·1	77·5
1902	20·3	24·5	21·7	79·5
1903	20·8	24·8	22·5	77·5
1904	21·3	25·0	21·8	73·6
1905	21·6	25·2	25·7	85·5
1906	22·6	25·4	25·8	87·5
1907	23·9	25·9	25·2	95·4
1908	23·6	25·9	21·1	83·5
1909	22·9	26·1	23·4	98·4
1910	23·6	26·3	26·2	92·4
1911	24·4	26·7	26·8	109
1912	24·6	27·6	28·1	122
1913	25·4	28·0	32·4	126
1920	89·9	78·7	41·3	87·5
1921	71·2	73·0	16·6	67·0
1922	52·6	61·8	27·3	99·4
1923	48·5	57·6	40·1	86·5
1924	48·3	57·4	39·8	97·4
1925	47·4	56·7	37·8	105
1926	44·7	57·0	29·0	99·4
1927	42·1	55·4	44·6	108
1928	41·9	54·9	43·9	105
1929	40·9	54·5	46·7	106
1930	39·2	54·2	43·3	86·9
1931	34·9	53·5	35·0	90·0
1932	32·1	51·8	33·9	95·1
1933	31·6	50·8	39·2	102
1934	31·7	50·7	47·1	104
1935	31·7	51·0	56·0	113
1936	32·3	51·5	65·5	118
1937	35·3	52·7	72·6	120
1938	37·8	54·3	65·2	108
1946	79·1	90·6	84·0	83·4
1947	91·6	95·1	92·0	89·7
1948	100	100	100	100
1949	103	102	106	108
1950	107	102	114	117
1951	126	111	122	115
1952	133	122	122	98·4
1953	130	124	125	113
1954	129	126	137	115
1955	131	129	150	115

* See S23 and p. 219 for estimates of the price index of national output for the war years.

For notes see: (for S18) Section 2 (b), p. 216.

(for S19) Section 2 (c), p. 216.

(for S20, 21) Section 2 (d), p. 218.

Index numbers 1948 = 100

Year	Imports of materials Price S22	National output Price S23
1914	30·4	27·3
1915	32·1	29·8
1916	46·7	34·9
1917	62·9	42·1
1918	78·4	54·5
1919	78·3	65·0
1939	32·7	55·9
1940	46·0	68·9
1941	53·7	75·8
1942	55·5	78·5
1943	65·9	83·4
1944	67·6	84·0
1945	68·7	86·8

For notes see Section 2 (e), p. 219.

£ million

Gross domestic product at 1948 factor cost

Year	Total S24	Agriculture, etc. S25	Manufacturing Total S26	Manufacturing Metals S27	Manufacturing Textiles S28	Total industrial S29
1935	8,720	530	2,650	930	710	3,890
1936	9,150	540	2,900	1,090	740	4,210
1937	9,220	540	3,050	1,210	750	4,380
1938	9,030*	540	2,810*	1,090*	680*	4,080*
1948	10,020	620	3,570	1,670	630	4,760

* These estimates are probably too low. See p. 221.

For notes see Section 2 (f), p. 220.

£ million (1948 market prices)
Food at farm or dock gate prices

Index numbers 1948 = 100

Year	Output S30	Retained imports S31	Change in stocks S32	Exports S33	Consumption S34	Consumption Price S35
1935–8 av.	490	974	..	42	1,422	43·3
1946	623	631	−69	29	1,294	85·7
1947	618	742	−11	25	1,346	98·0
1948	657	751	33	40	1,335	100
1949	696	817	33	41	1,439	106
1950	708	801	−53	51	1,511	111
1951	721	874	10	53	1,532	127
1952	740	800	21	50	1,469	138
1953	758	879	35	54	1,548	137
1954	755	857	−54	60	1,606	134
1955	755	911	−25	62	1,629	142

For notes see Section 2 (g), p. 221.

Index numbers 1911–13 = 100

Yearly averages for	Food output Quantity S36	Factor cost price S37	Market price S38	Food imports Quantity S39	Market price S40
1870–6	100	118	118	37·3	127
1877–85	94·4	107	107	52·4	115
1886–93	97·3	89·4	89·4	63·8	93·4
1894–1903	94·9	86·5	86·5	89·2	82·5
1904–10	99·1	92·3	92·3	96·1	91·4
1911–13	100	100	100	100	100
1920–2	96·4	239	239	95·4	230
1924–9	91·6	160	160	124	146
1930–4	91·8	142	139	134	97·4
1935–9	93·5	154	..	..	..
1946–50	126	416	..	..	..
1951–5	142	476	..	..	..
1935–8	93·5	152	145	136	102
1954–5	144	481	383	123	368

For notes see Sections 2 (h) and (i), pp. 225 and 226.

£ million (1948 c.i.f. prices)

Total materials

Year	Output S41	Retained imports S42	Change in stocks S43	Exports S44	Crude content imported semis S45	Consumption S46
1935–8 av.	133	733	..	108	1	759
1946	173	493	−54	66	1	654
1947	169	576	1	60	8	691
1948	177	610	−32	65	10	764
1949	183	657	1	79	11	771
1950	188	660	−52	88	11	823
1951	196	730	35	63	17	846
1952	185	597	2	66	9	724
1953	198	689	10	74	3	806
1954	207	728	−7	73	11	880
1955	213	774	2	83	12	913

Metal materials

Year	Output S47	Retained imports S48	Change in stocks S49	Exports S50	Consumption S51
1935–8 av.	38	128	..	31	135
1946	72	113	−22	36	171
1947	75	135	−4	33	180
1948	76	149	3	29	194
1949	77	150	9	32	185
1950	74	148	−10	33	198
1951	78	157	3	19	212
1952	83	166	7	24	219
1953	81	156	11	27	199
1954	79	175	1	24	230
1955	87	196	−1	28	256

Textile materials

Year	Output S52	Retained imports S53	Change in stocks S54	Exports S55	Crude content imported semis S56	Consumption S57
1935–8 av.	70	319	..	72	1	317
1946	55	215	−28	28	1	270
1947	54	228	−18	26	8	281
1948	57	251	−40	36	10	322
1949	62	287	0	46	11	315
1950	73	285	−22	53	11	339
1951	75	272	−9	42	17	331
1952	64	215	−7	41	9	254
1953	78	278	−4	45	3	318
1954	86	268	−8	46	11	326
1955	84	253	−14	52	12	311

For notes see Section 2 (j), p. 227.

£ million (1948 c.i.f. prices)

Year	Output S58	Retained imports S59	Other materials Change in stocks S60	Exports S61	Consumption S62
1935–8 av.	26	287	..	5	307
1946	46	165	−4	2	213
1947	41	213	23	1	230
1948	44	210	5	1	248
1949	44	220	−9	1	271
1950	41	227	−20	2	286
1951	43	302	41	1	303
1952	38	216	2	1	251
1953	39	255	3	2	288
1954	42	285	0	3	325
1955	42	325	18	3	346

For notes see Section 2 (j), p. 227.

Index numbers 1948 = 100

Year	Expenditure on fuels at constant prices by Domestic and commercial S63	Manufacturing* S64	Transport† S65
1924	63·3	59·8	41·6
1925	62·9	55·9	39·1
1926	52·7	41·0	46·7
1927	70·2	60·7	49·9
1928	67·3	56·8	56·1
1929	74·4	59·2	58·7
1930	74·3	56·1	67·6
1931	73·6	51·8	64·9
1932	74·2	51·7	68·8
1933	74·0	55·3	74·4
1934	79·3	62·3	77·1
1935	83·4	66·4	82·4
1936	87·2	72·0	87·1
1937	90·5	75·1	91·6
1938	85·6	73·0	96·8
1946	95·5	88·1	95·0
1947	99·0	89·4	102
1948	100	100	100
1949	102	102	108
1950	107	108	117
1951	115	113	124
1952	114	114	128
1953	116	119	138
1954	122	125	146
1955	126	131	153

* Including building and contracting.
† Including private motoring.

For notes see Section 2 (k), p. 229.

Index numbers 1948 = 100

Sales of manufactures on the home market at constant prices

Year	Total of five groups S66	Iron and steel S67	Engineering products, etc. S68	Textiles S69	Chemicals S70	Paper and board S71
1924	51·5	50·9	38·7	73·8	46·4	60·7
1925	51·7	46·1	36·2	82·4	43·4	59·8
1926	42·7	19·7	29·8	77·8	36·6	64·8
1927	57·5	59·0	43·4	82·7	46·7	73·1
1928	54·3	51·1	41·2	78·4	49·7	67·1
1929	58·0	58·7	43·6	79·7	53·0	82·3
1930	52·6	54·5	40·6	68·4	50·5	77·6
1931	49·9	40·8	36·2	79·2	45·7	75·1
1932	48·5	37·2	34·3	76·0	48·6	82·2
1933	55·8	53·2	37·6	83·8	57·0	85·8
1934	63·2	64·8	45·6	87·4	61·8	98·6
1935	70·0	69·1	56·8	92·7	61·2	102
1936	79·9	86·0	68·1	100	63·8	112
1937	85·5	95·9	75·6	104	68·9	102
1938	76·8	75·0	69·2	94·0	67·8	90·1
1946	85·4	80·5	89·1	79·9	87·2	88·9
1947	92·7	87·2	95·6	88·6	94·8	97·2
1948	100	100	100	100	100	100
1949	107	105	107	109	107	113
1950	116	105	113	120	120	132
1951	123	112	123	124	128	146
1952	118	123	125	97·8	121	118
1953	129	120	134	116	140	133
1954	140	123	149	124	151	159
1955	151	140	166	123	158	176

For notes see Section 2 (l), p. 231.

Index numbers 1948 = 100

Retained imports of five groups of manufactures at constant prices

Year	Total of five groups S72	Iron and steel S73	Engineering products, etc. S74	Textiles S75	Chemicals S76	Paper and board S77
1924	145	257	99·3	197	94·9	125
1925	168	308	134	221	97·7	133
1926	168	356	121	203	108	147
1927	192	430	138	230	108	163
1928	179	335	132	226	106	181
1929	192	340	164	225	126	194
1930	178	330	137	216	101	197
1931	177	322	115	236	103	198
1932	94·7	170	64·9	88·4	69·7	168
1933	89·2	138	56·9	84·4	73·0	176
1934	108	184	80·9	82·7	96·2	202
1935	111	179	91·1	80·4	102	209
1936	128	221	118	87·1	111	228
1937	155	281	159	98·7	132	251
1938	136	189	121	94·9	154	204
1946	52·1	58·4	45·0	40·0	67·6	67·5
1947	83·2	79·2	65·8	74·6	110	100
1948	100	100	100	100	100	100
1949	117	187	118	126	89·7	86·8
1950	121	119	94·9	136	126	128
1951	162	148	103	182	191	202
1952	148	372	175	88·0	126	117
1953	126	224	142	79·7	136	123
1954	145	113	137	125	175	189
1955	192	412	173	134	187	230

For notes see Section 2 (l), p. 231.

Index numbers 1935 = 100

Year	Worsted yarns, combed Import Quantity S78	Price S79	Home Quantity S80	Price S81	Cotton yarns, up to 40's Import Quantity S82	Price S83	Home Quantity S84	Price S85
1907	..	..	..	..	435	90·4	129	103
1924	85·0	125	87·3	167	530	194	102	233
1930	215	127	67·1	120	804	130	81·3	123
1933	25·5	107	96·5	96·7	141	101	94·2	93·8
1934	46·9	131	92·4	105	177	103	98·0	98·6
1935	100	100	100	100	100	100	100	100
1948	457	291	89·5	309	543	496	74·3	405
1951	445	595	98·5	667	2,200	738	81·0	707
1954	..	..	..	..	721	449	63·1	528

Index numbers 1935 = 100

	Unbleached grey cotton piece goods				Hide, leather, undressed for soles, etc.			
	Import		Home		Import		Home	
Year	Quantity S86	Price S87	Quantity S88	Price S89	Quantity S90	Price S91	Quantity S92	Price S93
1907	..	..	..	..	..	..	..	..
1924	73·9	190	132	214	352	110	104	142
1930	90·0	150	93·2	125	270	151	100	132
1933	14·7	141	103	97·5	126	112	91·7	108
1934	53·2	107	100	101	90·5	93·9	91·6	97·6
1935	100	100	100	100	100	100	100	100
1948	2,410	487	76·1	371	6·44	344	117	289
1951	2,610	660	92·5	611	14·1	545	97·7	474
1954	..	..	..	..	22·1	320	91·5	346

	Steel blooms, billets and slabs				Steel wire rods			
	Import		Home		Import		Home	
Year	Quantity S94	Price S95	Quantity S96	Price S97	Quantity S98	Price S99	Quantity S100	Price S101
1907	108	107	64·5	91·9	..	..	..	..
1924	320	145	78·3	139	146	134	44·6	151
1930	257	120	65·2	119	180	108	40·6	108
1933	104	94·8	58·4	95·3	82·8	101	81·9	95·4
1934	137	99·9	82·8	102	97·1	100	94·6	101
1935	100	100	100	100	100	100	100	100
1948	64·4	630	137	251	53·1	530	155	245
1951	46·6	809	142	338	85·0	841	166	318
1954	22·0	716	179	456	12·7	1,177	186	406

	Superphosphates of lime				Newsprint			
	Import		Home		Import		Home	
Year	Quantity S102	Price S103	Quantity S104	Price S105	Quantity S106	Price S107	Quantity S108	Price S109
1907	..	..	..	..	117	165	25·2	114
1924	371	113	77·8	117	105	211	45·2	195
1930	341	103	79·7	105	116	156	76·3	148
1933	109	95·6	86·1	99·6	107	109	84·9	106
1934	165	94·3	97·5	98·0	111	101	98·7	97·7
1935	100	100	100	100	100	100	100	100
1948	300	732	241	186	25·7	529	35·2	458
1951	967	551	197	267	97·8	687	47·2	571
1954	5·15	1,160	230	480	99·7	581	66·5	548

For notes see Section 2 (m), p. 233.

Index numbers 1935 = 100

	Cycle inner tubes				Carpets: Brussels and Wilton			
	Import		Home		Import		Home	
Year	Quantity S110	Price S111	Quantity S112	Price S113	Quantity S114	Price S115	Quantity S116	Price S117
1907	..	..	..	..	..	..	..	..
1924	..	..	..	..	68·8	205	46·7	176
1930	678	149	56·6	152	170	140	53·2	156
1933	237	83·1	92·6	102	75·0	86·4	77·6	109
1934	172	68·5	108	95·4	113	95·2	82·8	105
1935	100	100	100	100	100	100	100	100
1948	80·1	370	156	238	47·6	677	167	272
1951	1·00	955	152	383	82·9	836	166	476
1954	126	391	150	303	3·82	531	143	434

	Toilet soap, except shaving				Safety-razor blades			
	Import		Home		Import		Home	
Year	Quantity S118	Price S119	Quantity S120	Price S121	Quantity S122	Price S123	Quantity S124	Price S125
1907	1,930	44·4	34·9	101	..	..	..	..
1924	3,740	50·5	69·8	185	..	..	..	..
1930	2,890	39·1	54·9	164	262	211	23·6	281
1933	229	60·3	88·8	108	92·0	105	67·2	123
1934	76·2	103	97·7	95·9	91·0	100	76·8	111
1935	100	100	100	100	100	100	100	100
1948	42·4	149	127	214	42·9	156	123	176
1951	10·4	278	173	234	17·1	164	186	177
1954	110	105	198	210	..	..	..	..

	Vacuum cleaners				Electric bulbs over 20 volts			
	Import		Home		Import		Home	
Year	Quantity S126	Price S127	Quantity S128	Price S129	Quantity S130	Price S131	Quantity S132	Price S133
1907	..	..	..	..	..	..	..	..
1924	..	..	..	..	..	..	..	..
1930	1,000	114	17·8	174	384	229	52·7	133
1933	42·3	85·1	64·5	106	362	74·4	68·2	115
1934	73·9	90·1	79·3	99·5	251	74·7	82·2	103
1935	100	100	100	100	100	100	100	100
1948	20·5	203	137	114	10·9	352	167	118
1951	13·3	552	188	124	8·77	609	200	119
1954	..	..	..	..	216	220	224	132

For notes see Section 2 (m), p. 233.

Index numbers 1935 = 100

Motor-cars, new, including cabs

Year	Import Quantity S134	Price S135	Home Quantity S136	Price S137
1924A	104*	102*	} 33·7	179
1924B	197†	114†		
1930	108	109	48·8	139
1933	28·9	96·2	..	..
1934	103	88·8	73·8	109
1935	100	100	100	100
1948	2·28	392	39·3	209
1951	2·79	611	54·4	245
1954	..	..	..	..

* First seven months of 1924, annual rate, see p. 234.
† Last five months of 1924, annual rate, see p. 234.

For notes see Section 2 (m), p. 233.

LIST OF WORKS CITED

I. BOOKS, ARTICLES AND SERIAL PUBLICATIONS

ADLER, J. H., SCHLESINGER, E. R. and VAN WESTERBORG, E. *The Pattern of United States Import Trade since 1923: some New Index Series and their Application* (Federal Reserve Bank of New York, 1952).

ALLEN, R. G. D. *Mathematical Economics* (London, Macmillan, 1956).

ANDREWS, P. W. S. *Manufacturing Business* (London, Macmillan, 1949).

BARNA, T. 'The Interdependence of the British Economy', *Journal of the Royal Statistical Society*, Series A (General), vol. 115, part 1, 1952, p. 29.

BELLERBY, J. R. *Agriculture and Industry: Relative Income* (London, Macmillan, 1956).

BEVERIDGE, WILLIAM H. *Full Employment in a Free Society* (London, Allen and Unwin, 1944).

BOWLEY, A. L. (ed.). *Studies in the National Income, 1924–1938*, National Institute of Economic and Social Research, Economic and Social Studies, 1 (Cambridge University Press, 1944).

BRITISH IRON AND STEEL FEDERATION. 'The Increase in Steel Prices', B.I.S.F. *Monthly Statistical Bulletin*, vol. 26, no. 7, July 1951, p. 1.

BROWN, B. C. 'Industrial Production in 1935 and 1948', *London and Cambridge Economic Bulletin*, December 1954, p. v.

CAIRNCROSS, A. K. *Home and Foreign Investment, 1870–1913: Studies in Capital Accumulation* (Cambridge University Press, 1953).

CARTER, C. F., REDDAWAY, W. B. and STONE, R. *The Measurement of Production Movements*, University of Cambridge Department of Applied Economics, Monographs, 1 (Cambridge University Press, 1948).

CHANG, TSE CHUN. *Cyclical Movements in the Balance of Payments* (Cambridge University Press, 1951).

CLARK, COLIN. *The Conditions of Economic Progress*, 2nd ed. (London, Macmillan, 1951).

CLARK, K. R. 'Some Indicators of General Price and Cost Movements affecting Agriculture in the United Kingdom', *Farm Economist*, vol. 8, no. 10, 1957, p. 58.

CORDEN, W. M. 'The Control of Imports: a Case Study', *Manchester School of Economic and Social Studies*, vol. 26, no. 3, September 1958, p. 181.

DANIEL, G. H. 'Britain's Energy Prospects', *Institution of Production Engineers Journal*, vol. 36, no. 2, February 1956, p. 76.

DOW, J. C. R. and DICKS-MIREAUX, L. A. 'The Excess Demand for Labour: a Study of Conditions in Great Britain, 1946–56', *Oxford Economic Papers* (New Series), vol. 10, no. 1, February 1958, p. 1.

EDWARDS, H. R. 'Price Formation in Manufacturing Industry and Excess Capacity', *Oxford Economic Papers* (New Series), vol. 7, no. 1, February 1955, p. 94.

The Financial Times, 7 October 1959.

HEMMING, M. F. W. and CORDEN, W. M. 'Import Restriction as an Instrument of Balance-of-Payments Policy', *Economic Journal*, vol. 68, no. 271, September 1959, p. 483.

HEMMING, M. F. W., MILES, C. M. and RAY, G. F. 'A Statistical Summary of the Extent of Import Control in the United Kingdom since the War', *Review of Economic Studies*, vol. 26, no. 70, February 1959, p. 75.

HICKS, J. R. *A Revision of Demand Theory* (Oxford, The Clarendon Press, 1956).

HICKS, J. R. *Value and Capital*, 2nd ed. (Oxford, The Clarendon Press, 1946).

HOFFMANN, W. G. *British Industry 1700–1950* (Oxford, Blackwell, 1955).

JEFFERYS, J. B. and WALTERS, DOROTHY. 'National Income and Expenditure of the United Kingdom, 1870–1952' in *Income and Wealth, Series V*, International Association for Research in Income and Wealth (London, Bowes and Bowes, 1955).

JOHNSON, D. GALE. 'The Nature of the Supply Function for Agricultural Products', *American Economic Review*, vol. 40, no. 4, September 1950, p. 539.

JURÉEN, L. 'Long-term Trends in Food Consumption: a Multi-Country Study', *Econometrica*, vol. 24, no. 1, January 1956, p. 1.

KEYNES, J. M. assisted by R. B. LEWIS. *Stocks of Staple Commodities*, London and Cambridge Economic Service, Special Memoranda, 1 (April 1923).

KEYNES, J. M. and ROWE, J. W. F. *Stocks of Staple Commodities*, London and Cambridge Economic Service, Special Memoranda, 16 (February 1926).

KLEIN, L. R. and GOLDBERGER, A. S. *An Econometric Model of the United States, 1929–1952*, Contributions to Economic Analysis, 9 (Amsterdam, North-Holland Publishing Company, 1955).

KLEIN, L. R. *Economic Fluctuations in the United States, 1921–1941*, Cowles Commission Monographs, 11 (New York, Wiley; London, Chapman & Hall, 1950).

KLEIN, L. R. 'Macroeconomics and the Theory of Rational Behavior', *Econometrica*, vol. 14, no. 2, April 1946, p. 93.

LEAK, H. 'Some Results of the Import Duties Act', *Journal of the Royal Statistical Society*, vol. 100, part 4, 1937, p. 558.

LEONTIEF, W. 'Econometrics' in *A Survey of Contemporary Economics*, ed. by H. S. Ellis (Philadelphia, Blakiston, for The American Economic Association, 1948), pp. 388–411.

LEWIS, W. A. 'World Production, Prices and Trade, 1870–1960', *Manchester School of Economic and Social Studies*, vol. 20, no. 2, May 1952, p. 105.

LIU, TA-CHUNG. 'The Elasticity of U.S. Import Demand: a Theoretical and Empirical Reappraisal', International Monetary Fund *Staff Papers*, vol. 3, no. 3, February 1954, p. 416.

LOMAX, K. S. 'New Index-numbers of Industrial Production, 1900–1938', *London and Cambridge Economic Bulletin*, no. 26, June 1958, p. v.

LOMAX, K. S. 'Production and Productivity Movements in the United Kingdom since 1900', *Journal of the Royal Statistical Society*, Series A (General), vol. 122, part 2, 1959, p. 185.

London and Cambridge Economic Bulletin, no. 17, March 1956.

London and Cambridge Economic Bulletin, no. 26, June 1958.

LUTTRELL, W. F. 'Britain's Fuel and Power Budget', I and II, *Times Review of Industry*, March 1958, p. 37 and April 1958, p. 36.

LUTTRELL, W. F. 'Realities of the National Fuel Position', *Times Review of Industry*, February 1958, p. 11.

MacDOUGALL, SIR DONALD. 'British and American Exports: a Study suggested by the Theory of Comparative Costs.' Part I, *Economic Journal*, vol. 61, no. 244, December 1951, p. 697. Part II, *Economic Journal*, vol. 62, no. 247, September 1952, p. 487.

MacDOUGALL, SIR DONALD. 'The Use of Home Resources to Save Imports: a Comment', *Economic Journal*, vol. 60, no. 239, September 1950, p. 629.

MacDOUGALL, SIR DONALD. *The World Dollar Problem: a Study in International Economics* (London, Macmillan, 1957).

MACROSTY, H. W. 'The Overseas Trade of the United Kingdom, 1924–1931', *Journal of the Royal Statistical Society*, vol. 95, part 4, 1932, p. 607.

MADDISON, A. 'Output, Employment and Productivity in British Manufacturing in the Last Half Century', *Bulletin of the Oxford University Institute of Statistics*, vol. 17, no. 4, November 1955, p. 363.

Manchester Guardian Review of Industry, Commerce and Finance, 1952.

Manchester Guardian Survey of Industry, Trade and Finance, 1955.

MEINKEN, K. W., ROJKO, A. S. and KING, G. A. 'Measurement of Substitution in Demand from Time Series Data—a Synthesis of Three Approaches', *Journal of Farm Economics*, vol. 38, no. 3, August 1956, p. 711.

MORRISSETT, I. 'Some recent Uses of Elasticity of Substitution: a Survey', *Econometrica*, vol. 21, no. 1, January 1953, p. 41.

National Institute Economic Review, no. 1, January 1959.

National Institute Economic Review, no. 6, November 1959.

NEISSER, H. and MODIGLIANI, F. *National Incomes and International Trade: a Quantitative Analysis* (Urbana, University of Illinois Press, 1953).

NICHOLSON, R. J. '"Product-Elasticities of Substitution" in International Trade', *Economic Journal*, vol. 65, no. 259, September 1955, p. 441.

OJALA, E. M. *Agriculture and Economic Progress* (Oxford University Press, for The Oxford University Agricultural Economics Research Institute, 1952).

ORCUTT, G. H. 'Measurement of Price Elasticities in International Trade', *Review of Economics and Statistics*, vol. 32, no. 2, May 1950, p. 117.

PEP (Political and Economic Planning). *The British Fuel and Power Industries* (London, PEP, 1947).

RAY, G. F. *Trends in Food Consumption*, National Institute of Economic and Social Research, unpublished mimeographed paper (London, 1959).

RIDLEY, T. M. 'Industrial Production in the United Kingdom, 1900–1953', *Economica*, New Series, vol. 22, no. 82, February 1955, p. 1.

ROBINSON, E. A. G. 'The Cost of Agricultural Import-Saving', *Three Banks Review*, no. 40, December 1958, p. 3.

ROBINSON, E. A. G. 'The Problem of Living within our Foreign Earnings further Considered', *Three Banks Review*, no. 38, June 1958, p. 3.

ROBINSON, E. A. G. and MARRIS, R. L. 'The Use of Home Resources to Save Imports', *Economic Journal*, vol. 60, no. 237, March 1950, p. 177.

ROBINSON, E. A. G. and MARRIS, R. L. 'The Use of Home Resources to Save Imports: a Rejoinder', *Economic Journal*, vol. 61, no. 241, March 1951, p. 176.

ROBSON, M. and CARTER, C. F. 'Changes in the Real Product since 1937', *London and Cambridge Economic Bulletin*, no. 4, December 1952, p. vi.

ROMANIS, ANNE. 'The Shipping Bill for British Imports', *Bulletin of the Oxford University Institute of Statistics*, vol. 16, nos. 9–10, September–October 1954, p. 329.

SALTER, W. E. G. *A Consideration of Technological Change with particular Reference to Labour Productivity*, University of Cambridge Ph.D. Dissertation, 1955.

SALTER, W. E. G. *Productivity and Technical Change*, University of Cambridge Department of Applied Economics, Monographs, 6 (Cambridge University Press, 1960).

SAUNDERS, C. T. 'Consumption of Raw Materials in the United Kingdom: 1851–1950', *Journal of the Royal Statistical Society*, Series A (General), vol. 115, part 3, 1952, p. 313.

SCHLOTE, W. *British Overseas Trade from 1700 to the 1930's*, translated by W. O. Henderson and W. H. Chaloner (Oxford, Blackwell, 1952).

SCHULTZ, T. W. *The Economic Organization of Agriculture* (New York, McGraw-Hill, 1953).

SCOTT, M. FG. 'Changes in Stocks of mainly Imported Goods in the United Kingdom', *Bulletin of the Oxford University Institute of Statistics*, vol. 20, no. 1, February 1958, p. 53.

SCOTT, M. FG. 'Interdependence and Foreign Trade', *Oxford Economic Papers* (New Series), vol. 9, no. 1, February 1957, p. 88.

SCOTT, M. FG. 'The Problem of Living within our Foreign Earnings', *Three Banks Review*, no. 26, June 1955, p. 3.

STONE, R. and STONE, WINIFRED. 'Indices of Industrial Output', *Economic Journal*, vol. 49, no. 195, September 1939, p. 476.

STONE, RICHARD. *The Measurement of Consumers' Expenditure and Behaviour in the United Kingdom, 1920–1938, Vol. I*, Studies in the National Income and Expenditure of the United Kingdom, 1 (Cambridge University Press, 1954).

THEIL, H. *Linear Aggregation of Economic Relations*, Contributions to Economic Analysis, 7 (Amsterdam, North-Holland Publishing Company, 1954).

TRIFFIN, R. *Monopolistic Competition and General Equilibrium Theory*, Harvard Economic Studies, 67 (Harvard University Press, 1947).

WEMELSFELDER, J. 'The Short-term Effect of the Lowering of Import Duties in Germany', *Economic Journal*, vol. 70, no. 277, March 1960, p. 94.

WILLIAMS, H. T. 'Changes in the Productivity of Labour in British Agriculture', paper read to the Agricultural Economics Society, July 1953.

WILSON, T. 'The Inadequacy of the Theory of the Firm as a Branch of Welfare Economics', *Oxford Economic Papers* (New Series), vol. 4, no. 1, February 1952, p. 18.

II. OFFICIAL PUBLICATIONS

(1) UNITED KINGDOM

Note: H.M.S.O. = Her Majesty's Stationery Office, London.

Ministry of Agriculture, Fisheries and Food. *Agricultural Statistics 1940–1944, England and Wales, Part II* (H.M.S.O. 1948).

Ministry of Agriculture, Fisheries and Food. *Agricultural Statistics, United Kingdom, Part II* (H.M.S.O. 1953).

Central Statistical Office. *Annual Abstract of Statistics* (H.M.S.O.).

Central Statistical Office. *The Interim Index of Industrial Production*, Studies in Official Statistics, 1 (H.M.S.O. 1948).

Central Statistical Office. *Monthly Digest of Statistics Supplement, Definitions and Explanatory Notes*, January 1950.

Central Statistical Office. *National Income and Expenditure* (H.M.S.O. annual).

Central Statistical Office. *National Income Statistics: Sources and Methods* (H.M.S.O. 1956).

Central Statistical Office. *Statistical Digest of the War*, History of the Second World War, United Kingdom Civil Series (H.M.S.O. and Longmans Green, 1951).

H.M. Customs and Excise. *Annual Statement of the Trade of the United Kingdom with Commonwealth Countries and Foreign Countries . . .* (H.M.S.O.).

H.M. Customs and Excise. *Tariff . . . on* [various dates] published by H.M.S.O.

Ministry of Fuel and Power. *Statistical Digest, 1955* (H.M.S.O. 1956).

Home Office. *Annual Review and Determination of Guarantees, 1958*, Cmnd. 390 (H.M.S.O. 1958).

House of Commons Debates, 30 April 1957, cols. 33–53.

Monopolies and Restrictive Practices Commission. *Report on the Supply of Electric Lamps* (H.M.S.O. 1951).

Board of Trade. *Accounts relating to Trade and Navigation of the United Kingdom* (H.M.S.O. monthly).

Board of Trade Journal, passim.

Board of Trade. *Final Report on the Fourth Census of Production (1930)*, Parts I–V (H.M.S.O. 1933–1935).

Board of Trade. *Report on the Import Duties Act Inquiry (1933)*, Parts I and II (H.M.S.O. 1935, 1936).

Board of Trade. *Report on the Import Duties Act Inquiry (1934)*, Parts I and II (H.M.S.O. 1936, 1937).

Board of Trade. *Final Report on the Fifth Census of Production and the Import Duties Act Inquiry 1935*, Parts I–III (H.M.S.O. 1938–1940), Part IV (1944) and *Final Summary Tables* [Part V, 1944].

Board of Trade. *Final Report on the Census of Production for 1948.* Vol. 6, Trade B, *Cotton Weaving*; Trade C, *Woollen and Worsted*; Trade D, *Rayon, Nylon, etc. and Silk* (H.M.S.O. 1952).

Board of Trade. *Final Report on the Census of Production for 1948.* Vol. 10, Trade F, *Paper and Board* (H.M.S.O. 1952).

Board of Trade. *Final Report on the Census of Production for 1948.* Vol. 12, Trade A, *Building and Contracting* (H.M.S.O. 1952).

Board of Trade. *Imports and Exports at Prices of 1900, 1900–9, 1900–11, 1900–12, 1900–13.* Cd. 5160, 6314, 6782, 7432 (H.M.S.O. 1910, 1912, 1913, 1914).

Board of Trade. *Statistical Abstract for the United Kingdom* (H.M.S.O.), issues for pre-1914 years.

H.M. Treasury. *United Kingdom Balance of Payments 1946–1957* (H.M.S.O. 1959).

H.M. Treasury. *United Kingdom Balance of Payments 1956 to 1959*, Cmnd. 861 (H.M.S.O. 1959).

(2) UNITED STATES OF AMERICA

Department of Agriculture. *Agricultural Statistics: 1955* (Washington, U.S. Government Printing Office, 1956).

Department of Commerce, Bureau of the Census. *Historical Statistics of the United States, 1789–1945* (Washington, U.S. Government Printing Office, 1949).

Department of Commerce, Bureau of the Census. *Raw Materials in the United States Economy, 1900–1952*, Working Paper no. 1 Preliminary (Washington, U.S. Government Printing Office, 1954).

(3) INTERNATIONAL

League of Nations. *Industrialization and Foreign Trade* (Geneva, League of Nations, 1945).

League of Nations. *Statistical Year-book, 1940–41* (Geneva, 1941).

United Nations, Department of Economic and Social Affairs. *World Economic Survey, 1955* (New York, 1956).

Economic Commission for Europe. *Economic Survey of Europe in 1949* (Geneva, 1950).

Organisation for European Economic Co-operation. *Industrial Statistics 1900–1955* (Paris, 1955).

GENERAL INDEX

INDEX OF NAMES

n. = *footnote*

PUBLICATIONS OF THE
NATIONAL INSTITUTE OF ECONOMIC
AND SOCIAL RESEARCH

published by

THE CAMBRIDGE UNIVERSITY PRESS

None of the Institute's books is sold directly by the Institute. They are available through the ordinary booksellers, and inquiry can be made of the Cambridge University Press, Bentley House, 200 Euston Road, London, N.W. 1.

ECONOMIC & SOCIAL STUDIES

* At present out of print.

OCCASIONAL PAPERS

* At present out of print.

XIX *Post-war Investment, Location and Size of Plant*
   By P. SARGANT FLORENCE. 1962. pp. 51. 12s. 6d. net.
 XX *Investment and Growth Policies in British Industrial Firms*
   By TIBOR BARNA. 1962. pp. 71. 12s. 6d. net.

STUDIES IN THE NATIONAL INCOME AND EXPENDITURE OF THE UNITED KINGDOM

Published under the joint auspices of the National Institute and the Department of Applied Economics, Cambridge.

 1 *The Measurement of Consumers' Expenditure and Behaviour in the United Kingdom, 1920–1938*, vol. I
   By RICHARD STONE, assisted by D. A. ROWE and by W. J. CORLETT, RENÉE HURSTFIELD, MURIEL POTTER. 1954. pp. 448. £6. 6s. net.
 3 *Consumers' Expenditure in the United Kingdom, 1900–1919*
   By A. R. PREST, assisted by A. A. ADAMS. 1954. pp. 196. 50s. net.
 5 *Wages and Salaries in the United Kingdom, 1920–1938*
   By AGATHA CHAPMAN, assisted by ROSE KNIGHT. 1953. pp. 254. 65s. net.

The National Institute Economic Review

This may be ordered directly from National Institute Economic Review, 2 Dean Trench Street, Smith Square, London, S.W.1. Annual subscription £2; single issues 12s. 6d. each.

Information about the Institute's Reprint Series and other pamphlets may also be obtained direct from the Institute.